"*Possibilities* is an unforgettable and powerful account of the untiring strength of love and beauty in life's most challenging circumstances. This book is wonderfully written, inspiring and tremendously moving. It is heartening to know that tangible breakthroughs in pediatric cancer research, like trials funded by the Simkins Family's Press On Fund, are making a difference because of this real-life story."

—WM. PAUL YOUNG, bestselling author of *The Shack, Crossroads* and *Eve*

"Never before has such a compelling story been told about a child's battle against cancer. Mr. Simkins's marvelously insightful story about his son Brennan's will and determination to conquer childhood acute myeloid leukemia weaves a fabric from the frequently segregated threads of science and religion, medicine and war, perseverance and desperation. Yet it is about much more than overcoming cancer; it is about a child's courage, a family's fierceness, and a hospital's will to push the boundaries of contemporary treatment.

During my decade as CEO of St. Jude, I stressed the importance of our culture of compassion, collaboration, innovation, and quality in all we do. Indeed, the enormous progress in curing childhood leukemia has been enabled by the courage of thousands of children and the willingness of their parents to participate in clinical trials of previously untested treatments. But occasionally there are moments when the forefront of science and medicine is moved forward by a single child who leads the charge and pushes the battlefront to more favorable ground. Brennan and his Band of Brothers show us the courage that is required and the potential rewards that await a successful battle at the forefront of science and medicine."

—WILLIAM E. EVANS, CEO, St. Jude Children's Research Hospital, 2004–2014

"The long ordeal that Brennan Simkins and his family have faced down is off-the-charts extraordinary, yet it is also one of universal resonance. Luckily, Brennan's father was there to lovingly document every moment. Turner Simkins' candid, raw account from the medical trenches will sadden and gladden your heart. But mostly it will inspire. In these immensely moving and sometimes soul-wrenching pages, we're reminded anew of the power of family—and of the miraculous things that can happen when a brave patient embraces life in all its fragile beauty."

—HAMPTON SIDES, bestselling author of *Ghost Soldiers* and *In the Kingdom of Ice*

"Two things transform us: great love and great suffering. *Possibilities* tells the story of how the Simkins family is confronted by great suffering, feeling into it with great love, which brought about true healing. That this healing coincides with physical restoration is a truly joyous gift, but I trust that these pages will speak to you wherever you're at, in the midst of gain and loss. Stories like this make us proud to be human beings, and assure us of the presence of a good God."

—RICHARD ROHR, OFM, founder, The Center for Action and Contemplation; author, *The Divine Dance: The Trinity and Your Transformation*

"I was inspired by this boy when he was fighting for his life. And I am inspired by him now, as he has proven that anything is possible if you believe in it."

—PEYTON MANNING, American football star, founder of Peyback Foundation, and member of the Red Cross Celebrity Cabinet

"*Possibilities* is a personal, poignant, emotional, and heartwarming story about courage, hope, strength, and faith!! When you are told that the dearest thing you hold in your heart—your child—has cancer, the world is suddenly upside down. Through Brennan's 'ups and downs' with cancer, his little spirit—as his dad, Turner, is quoted as saying—'has taught us that a miracle is not necessarily an unbelievable event, but rather how we respond to what is placed before us every day.' You will laugh and cry as you share the emotions that Mom and Dad (Turner and Tara), and brothers, Nat, Christopher, and Brennan, have shared with all of us. Life is *so* precious!"

—JACK AND BARBARA NICKLAUS, founders of the Nicklaus Children's Health Care Foundation

"A gut-wrenching journey of the eternal grit of the blessed Trinity inside a lad's irrepressible soul, surrounded by a thousand hearts and hands and minds joined as one in relentless love to defeat death—again, and again, and again, and again. Life cannot die. Everyone on earth should read this book."

—C. BAXTER KRUGER, author of the international best seller, *The Shack Revisited* and *Patmos*

"Real, insightful, inspiring, informative. Read this book and plan to never look at life, whether extremely difficult or unusually easy, in the same way. And expect to forever see those battling cancer and other life-threatening diseases with fresh eyes. Don't just read *Possibilities*, give it to others. You will have done them a great favor."

—RANDY POPE, Pastor, Perimeter Church in Johns Creek, Georgia

"This harrowing, moving, and ultimately uplifting book is more than a dramatic account of one family's war with leukemia. It's also a thoughtful meditation on the priceless rewards and sometimes unbearable weight of parenthood. Novelistic in its narrative momentum and profound in its unflinching confrontation with death, *Possibilities* is an unforgettable reading experience."

—MARSHALL BOSWELL, author of *Trouble with Girls* and *Alternative Atlanta* and English Department Chair at Rhodes College

"This is a beautiful, warm, sensitive, and anguishing portrayal of what the author's family experienced, and what any family who has a child stricken with cancer will experience. If you don't cry at certain parts of this story or laugh at others, then you need to get your heart checked. But at the book's conclusion, you should have a feeling of hope that miracles can and do happen when all the medical and spiritual elements are in line. *Possibilities* is not only about the power of faith, it is a very detailed and powerful documentation of how such a negative experience can be turned into something wonderful. To this generation, Turner Simkins's book is a celebration of a child given a second chance at becoming an adult. It is a must-read for any parent, whether their child is seriously ill or amazingly healthy—simple as that."

—DON RHODES, author of *Ty Cobb: Safe at Home*

"Simkins, who spent time as a newspaper reporter and now runs an advertising firm, offers an intensely honest account of the horrors and hope that face a parent whose child has cancer. His narrative is a testament to the importance of seeking out additional medical opinions while harnessing the power of family and prayer. Simkins admits in his foreword that his account may be too downbeat and overly detailed, but his memoir is nevertheless an absorbing, suspenseful read, complete with a heartbreaking dramatic crescendo as Brennan recovers but others do not. *Possibilities* is a harrowing, ultimately inspiring cancer journal."

—KIRKUS REVIEW

POSSIBILITIES

PERSEVERANCE, GRACE AND THE STORY OF ONE FAMILY'S LIFE WITH LEUKEMIA

N. TURNER SIMKINS

POSSIBILITIES

PERSEVERANCE, GRACE AND THE STORY OF
ONE FAMILY'S LIFE WITH LEUKEMIA

Published by

NewType Publishing
Get Your Words Out
NewTypePublishing.com

Author is dedicating 10% of his royalties to the Press On Fund, all of which will fund research grants at St. Jude Children's Research Hospital at a minimum of $10,000. The author, through the Press On Fund, has given more than $1 million to St. Jude to date. For more information visit: www.PressOnFund.org and www.StJude.org.

ISBN: 978-1-942306-72-6

Cover design & interior layout | Yvonne Parks | www.PearCreative.ca

Printed in the USA

DEDICATION

Dedicated in memory of George Bryan Simkins, Jr. and to my loving bride, Tara, the Band of Brothers and all the kids we've lost, and will lose, along the way.

Once upon a time there was a man who as a child had heard that beautiful story of how God tempted Abraham and of how Abraham withstood the temptation, kept the faith, and, contrary to expectation, got a son a second time.

SØREN KIERKEGAARD

FOREWORD

At the risk of sounding kind of sappy to my prospective reader who glances through the dust cover and foreword, please know that this book is not about "love" per se. But it is defined by this common thread, woven by decisions that, while neither right nor wrong, were made with faith, decisions made both for and by the love of a little boy who has dared to defy the impossible.

What follows is, on one level, a simple chronology of that young boy (Brennan Simkins), his diagnosis with acute myeloid leukemia (AML), his family's search for a cure, and the unyielding commitment of a support community.

This chronicle contains a lot of detail, some of it excruciating. To those who've fought or who live with cancer, this detail will be familiar. To those beginning this frightening journey, it will hopefully serve as somewhat of a guide in illustrating the types of things to expect along this path. But to others, it may provide insight into a real-life journey of defiance, faith, and love.

Reading through all of this and selecting what to include in this book revealed a story that cannot be recited in pure chapter-by-chapter form. And while purely chronological by nature, it discloses a layering of trials and issues that could not have been digested all at once. Rather, each entry deposits a new stratum on top of the old, each one representing a thicker layer of skin that allowed this band of "brothers" to survive.

Throughout this story, I found it difficult to avoid the "war" analogy, particularly that of the book and film *Band of Brothers*. (Of course, this story is very much about brothers, their devotion to and love for one another in the most demanding and hellish of circumstances.) Just as the D-day soldier believed, in June of 1944, that the war would be over by Christmas, I doubt they could have accomplished what they did had the crystal ball revealed the much more protracted and costly fight through the next year. Had our family been told that our middle child would be subject to three years of hospitalization and four bone marrow transplants with four donors—with the reality of death becoming more likely after each battle—I do not know that we could have braced for it, much less written about it. With that mountain ahead of me, it would have been too overwhelming for me to write anything.

What began as informational Care Pages posts from Brennan's aunt, when the verdict was first passed that our son had cancer, evolved into more descriptive narratives of the day-to-day fight by both his mother and father, and ultimately transformed into a descriptive outpouring of prayer and naked expression. All of this has been cut and pasted and revised to a hopefully intelligible degree. The entries that "made the cut" are preserved here because they all share a common source, having been inspired from a very sacred and vulnerable space. I believe that this common thread represents how this writing has affected many others who were kind enough to follow the story as it was happening.

The over-three years of blog entries that chronicle that struggle (effectively, a diary) can be an arduous read. But readers of our blog as it was posted were able to digest the story in small—yet often thick—doses. And just as those readers were offered portents of hope as they followed our story, battle-by-battle, so were we.

Throughout our lives, we take note of things worth remembering. My drawers and closets are full of photographs, letters, memorabilia, etc., things that at one time I had tagged as worth saving. The blog that evolved from my family's experience with pediatric cancer serves as my written photo album. Editing through all eight-hundred-plus pages of what was effectively three years' worth of writing, I found some things worth nothing more than snapshots: some whimsical, others simple journal entries not worth much to anyone but me, but others have been profoundly worth rereading. Indeed, I found some entries so powerfully emotional that I had actually forgotten the moment as documented. Like the details forgotten in the trauma of a car accident, these details were almost victim to amnesia, of sorts. Salvaging these links to my life's chain, I am grateful to have reached backward.

I have received comments from friends that this story is too dark, that I focus more on the difficulties than the positive lessons learned. I disagree, in that my most poignant lessons have been learned through pain. (Are not most?)

When one finds oneself (more than once) face-to-face with the ultimate sacrifice, that of a beloved child, one can find oneself pulled into one of two directions. The most immediate pull leads toward a path of anger. The other is faith, or as Kierkegaard says, "a passion for the impossible." Or—as I interpret faith—a belief in the possible.

Many of these words were written from that place. The air is very thin there. When there is anger and confusion, there are no words to describe anything else. But where there is faith there is clarity. And where there is clarity, the words come easy.

When put face-to-face with the impossible, the possible begins to erode. In the fight for my son Brennan's life, we faced numerous experts who told us, "There is nothing else to do," or "You have done enough." I have felt "the impossible's" cruel and relentless tug. My kids have seen too many other kids die.

But fortunately, I have also experienced the reflexive pull in the other direction—which, in this case, is defined by my love for my little boy. This book is one small and rare example of what is possible when all seems lost.

INTRODUCTION

I used to stay up pretty late. Of course there were the college years of late and sometimes rowdy camaraderie, but as married life began to take shape, the number of restless nights were primarily spent alone. Watching late movies with a beer or playing my guitar through the arms of Morpheus (to be awakened by the whiplash of my head jerking me back awake), I used to be quite capable of milking the clock well past a rational bedtime. And occasionally, whenever a like-minded neighbor or friend was within grasp, I could eagerly solicit company. I used to relish the late-night conversation, the "deep discussions" about Lord knows what, and powerful yet forgetful philosophical pining over profound, often absurdly abstract notions and issues. Looking back, most of those nights are a blur, and with good reason.

There is one, however, that stuck with me.

Tara was asleep, pregnant with our youngest son, Christopher. The oldest—Nat, who was not quite two at the time—had just migrated from crib to bed, making room for the next one in line. In the dim yellow light of a solitary lamp, my dear friend Frank Troutman quietly gazed at a photograph of his one-year-old godson, Brennan. He studied it carefully—his dark profile slightly kindled by the lamp, like the rust-hued ice inside his glass—seemingly mesmerized by the angelic face he held. I was noodling with my guitar when Frank said, "You know—there is a really weird feeling I get, but there is something special about this kid."

It stuck with me because I had always felt the same way, ever since the moment Brennan was born. Of course, being my child, it sounded gloatingly boastful for me to make such a comment, so I never really expressed it to anyone but Tara. But Frank's comment that night hit me as a powerful affirmation of sorts. It made me hopeful, but it also made me scared.

• • •

As the years went by, the late nights still came every now and then. But as the boys started coming into their own, developing their own totally cool and unique identity, my coolness was reflected more through shades of these boys than my own self. As I like to think most dads would say, "My kids are awesome."

Nat—the sports kid, responsible, studious, the perfect "big brother"—was the firstborn. He had always been smart, good-looking, and just plain good.

Christopher, the "baby," was a natural-born entertainer and sharp as a brand-new razor blade. His first word was profound ("Daddy"), and his devotion to his brothers represented something uniquely both precious and powerful.

Brennan—intensely sweet, thoughtful, child golfing prodigy, nature enthusiast—has served as the structural cornerstone for not only his brothers, but his larger family and community of friends. Indeed, his golfing prowess was inspiring as a two-year-old. I began to latch onto this: maybe this was his destiny, per his godfather's prophecy?

With regard to all three, Tara and I had been nothing but lucky.

1

SURPRISE ATTACK

FALL 2008 TO SPRING 2009

"Daddy, my leg hurts." Not exactly something unusual to hear a first grader complain about. Brennan's older brother, Nat, had leg pains at times. And as Brennan's became more and more frequent, and we took more and more notice, our comfort was slightly bolstered with reassurance from other parents that their kids had the same issue.

But Brennan was never a complainer. If anything, he was the tough one, always wanting to try new things. He had the capacity to take on grown-up sized chores as a little guy. Even as a pre-K'er, he would work on his golf at the driving range and the putting green productively until he could not stand any more. He would sometimes be asleep in the car before we could arrive home (which was just a few blocks away). He would watch the older kids and study their moves. He was strong.

So when fatigue started to layer itself on top of the pains, our parental concern produced an appointment with a highly regarded pediatric orthopedist. His prognosis was that Brennan appeared normal, but that in very rare cases, leg pain could be symptomatic of blood disease. He told us not to panic, but that Brennan should have a blood test in the not too distant future. This was December.

I honestly don't recall the pain becoming more severe, but Brennan started to get tired a lot, sleeping in more. The pain persisted. We scheduled the blood test just after the new year in 2009, at the finale of the Simkins birthday season. This started in November with me and Nat, who had just turned nine, and concluded with Brennan on January 21. We had all planned a great winter birthday retreat to the North Carolina mountains, and with snow in the forecast for the weekend of January 17, we all gathered with Tara's family for the big winter celebration, complete with snowmen, winter campfires, s'mores, cakes, movies, and a cabin full of cousins.

We awoke on our first mountain morning to the fulfillment of the weatherman's prophecy—a healthy foot of snow. Our beloved little Blue Ridge retreat was blanketed with a whiteness rarely seen by little boys in central Georgia, and like Christmas, the kids were up early, tugging our sheets, begging for sleds, snowman parts, shovels, and much parental assistance.

All but Brennan. He slept. And he slept.

By noon, the sun was out, and despite the accumulation, we knew that even in these parts winter is fleeting; so we felt he needed a little reminder. Leaning into his bunk, Tara stroked his light dirty-blond hair and told him, "Brenny, all of the kids are waiting for you to make a snowman. Why don't we get dressed and join in the fun outside?"

"I'm tired, Mommy. I just want to sleep," he said, groggily reaching his hands up to her for a hug. Then he smiled and looked over to me, reaching his hands out for more hugs. Since he had been a baby, he had yearned to be held. With his extraordinary tenderness and affection for others, it always had seemed an appropriate way for him to start his days. As his godfather said, "There is something special about that kid."

I wrapped him in a blanket and carried him from the bunkhouse to the main house through a path in the snow, made firm by the other children. The shady places were still lush, with spruce and hemlock limbs still weighted with heavy fronds of unwilted snow. We placed Brennan on the sofa to watch a DVD while the rest of the kids played outside, and then we both looked at each other with a powerful new concern.

As lunchtime arrived, the other children emerged indoors, tromping rubber boots on the worn wood floors and shedding wet clothing much to the counter-direction of parents. Tara's mom, "Mimi," began to make hotdogs as the little ones—which included Tara's sister Susie's two children Emma and Pierce in addition to Nat and Christopher—all piled on the sofa to snuggle with Brennan for a timely airing of *Snow Buddies*. Tara, Susie, and I decided we would take the lunchtime for a break ourselves and go for a walk down the snowy forest road outside of the cabin.

The sun was bright by this time. The light filtering through the massive trees revealed little rainbows showering to the ground as drops of melted snow. There was enough shade along the Whiteside Cove Road to have preserved a good solid compaction beneath our feet as we crunched our way along to talk away from everyone else.

"I don't want to sound like I'm overstepping my bounds," Susie offered, "but Brennan concerns me." Tara and I, having spoken in silence up to that point, through looks or concerned expressions, agreed.

When we returned, Brennan was up and getting dressed. The heavy clouds had returned, enveloping the mountains in blue-gray mist. The temperature was dropping, and blustery flurries returned as we compacted snowballs into larger snowballs, rolling them into the larger anatomical features of snow people. Little green tracks revealed the mossy earth beneath. The snowmen took shape, somewhat dirty looking and sad, but the kids revered their new acquaintances with pride. Before we could apply the finishing button nose to the first man, Brennan looked up to me with an ashen complexion and huge circles under his eyes.

"I want to go to bed, Daddy," he told me.

His mother took him in for a nap that lasted through the night, as we continued to put on our best face for the others. The sense of foreboding was suffocating.

• • •

The next Monday was semi–back to normal. All home. Familiar environs. Brennan made it up for school at St. Mary on the Hill to start his first winter semester of first grade. Christopher was across the hall in kindergarten, and Nat had moved up the food chain to the "big boy" building for second graders and older. I knew that Tara was taking Brennan to the pediatrician later in the day.

Arriving at work, I expressed the heaviness of the weekend to our bookkeeper, Rhonda, whose office is next to mine. But the day went on, as workdays usually do, with lots of phone calls and more than enough busy work to distract me from more central matters. Then the phone rang around four o'clock.

"Turner, Dr. Jones called and says we need to take Brennan to the children's hospital for more tests," she said calmly. "It may be a long night. We need to go talk to the boys."

I closed my computer, poked my head into Rhonda's office, and said, "Looks like it is something after all. Hope I see you tomorrow."

Her eyes revealed everything that mine were hiding. She got up and gave me a hug. I did not return to work for over a week.   —NTS

War on the Home Front
Posted Jan 29, 2009

I try to remind myself that gnawing feelings are just feelings, and that I need to be in control of my internal behavior. It is when the gnawing feelings bear out that the spiral begins.

For me, this validation occurred around 6 p.m. as we walked onto the Hem-Onc floor at the Children's Medical Center at the Medical College of Georgia (CMC). Taking the elevator to the fifth floor, with Tara at my side and Brennan in my arms, I was holding on to him in an effort to believe that I would be taking him back down soon.

"We are taking Brennan to the hospital for a couple of tests," we had told the Brothers as they sat attentively on our little back stoop, still in their little blue and white school uniforms from the day. A struggling poinsettia withered in its green tinfoil planter from the Christmas holiday. Brennan's birthday was tomorrow, and we assured the boys that the party was still on. Then, dropping the Brothers off at their grandparents' house, we headed for the hospital with as much of a positive face and cheerfulness as we could muster.

But stepping off the elevator onto the fifth floor, the first kid to greet us was a little boy, slightly older than Brennan, working alone at a computer play station, bald head, tethered to an IV tree overladen with fluids, pumps, and a bag of blood.

"Here we go," I said to Tara, holding her hand and walking into the rest of our lives.

That night is forever branded onto my soul, partly because of the fear and hostility Brennan demonstrated. I was forced to hold him down in his little hospital bed as the nurses delicately and caringly attempted to install his first IV. There was an army of nurses, doctors, and attendants, all prepared to generate sufficient blood work in order to quickly delve into a diagnosis, but also in order to harvest his blood before they could begin transfusing him. It was chaotic. It was loud. And Brennan was afraid.

Tara and I were clearly not aware of this, but at that time Brennan's cancer was so progressed that he was within a week or so of losing all of his red blood cells to leukemia. He was effectively bleeding to death from the inside out, in front of our eyes over the previous weekend, and we'd had no clue.

As the blood began to drip into his arms, his color began to return. A sweet nurse wrapped his hands in warming blankets to make him comfortable. "Hold his hand," she told me as I reached over to grasp his tiny blue hand while we tearfully looked away at a cartoon. They were freezing.

Brennan began to rest, and Tara and I walked out of the room to confer with Dr. Afshin Ameri, who was on call that particular night. He told us that Brennan's anemia was symptomatic of either aplastic anemia (a terminal blood disease) or leukemia (a terminal blood cancer). He outlined the survival rates for ALL (acute lymphoblastic leukemia), which are now over

90 percent. With that, Tara and I found a handhold, something with which to stop the emotional spiral. OK, this is big, but we can do this.

We called the grandparents and told them not to tell the Brothers yet, as we wanted to do this with Brennan, but we gave them the list of suspected problems. With the commotion seemingly under control for the time being, Tara and I made a trip to the McDonald's at the hospital first floor, got a Happy Meal for Brennan, and we settled into his room on the eve of his birthday. Before midnight, he took three units of blood. Happy Birthday.

The actual birthday the following day was amazing, considering what was happening. Although confined to his hospital floor and told he would not be home for a month, Brennan exuded everything pure and good about humanity that afternoon. Strapped to what was to become the ubiquitous IV pole, his friends gathered 'round him with laughter, cheer, and no real sense of awkwardness. Just kids being kids.

Brennan took the news well, as did his brothers, although one could read a higher degree of anxiety with Nat, who had recently lost a favorite teacher to cancer and understood its consequences. But we explained to them that Brennan was not a sick child, but a kid with a challenge, and while our temporary family home would be a hospital, nothing else had changed.

But Tara and I knew that a lot was changing. I have to admit that despite the gravity of the situation, the thing that kept crossing my mind was: And I may never get to see his potential as a golfer. Of all things.

· · ·

We were informed that Brennan had a rare subtype of AML, which was typically an adult cancer. His subtype, 7q deletion, required three cycles of chemotherapy, all in hospital over the next three months, after which a bone marrow transplant would be necessary as an insurance policy to help ensure that he was capable of achieving remission and holding on to it. Within a few weeks, his brother Nat was identified as a perfect bone marrow match.

But the transplant seemed an eternity away. Our first battle would be remission. Given all of the things we were to brace for—sickness, infection, loss of hair, susceptibility to infection, major lifestyle changes—Tara and I quietly, almost instinctively, made a pact that we would focus our energy on the task at hand. Only in that capacity could we be with this child, who so desperately needed support, as well as his brothers, who so desperately needed their brother. No second guessing, just forge ahead.   —NTS

Message from Tara and Turner
Posted Jan 31, 2009 12:24am

The wonderful energy created by you all was manifest in Brennan all day, from his beautiful smile, which greeted us in the morning, to a lively afternoon with his brothers, who are both thrilled to be out of school and spending the weekend with Brenny. Throughout, the doctors maintained guarded enthusiasm as they monitored an infection that has been developing on his left arm, presumably from the original IV that was installed last week prior to the installation of his port-o-cath. It bothered Brennan throughout and had been scratched and fidgeted with, as we are all prone to do, which presumably introduced fungal matter into his system. As a precaution, they are planning a small surgical procedure in the morning to drain the infection in an effort to keep it contained and away from the all-important "port" that delivers the chemotherapy to his bloodstream. He received a blood transfusion today and will receive platelets in the morning prior to surgery.

While the prayer books have not had time to gather dust, please keep them handy and in good working order. We continue to pray for the wonderful friends and family who make every day a thanksgiving.   —NTS

Update on Brennan's Infection
Posted Feb 2, 2009 10:13pm

We are just getting underway on Brennan's path to recovery. Tara suggested to me that perhaps we should replace the term "path" with "maze," given the complexities associated with its navigation.

Just as we assumed we had resolved the matter associated with the staph infection in Brennan's arm, today the infectious disease specialists determined that we are indeed treating a fungus, which is a much more virulent type of

23

infection. The good news is that it remains contained in the one location in the arm and is being treated with some hard-core medicine. We are monitoring his reaction to this new drug every fifteen minutes while it is administered through the evening and are expecting a thorough review of its status first thing in the morning to determine if more aggressive measures should be taken. Of course, my previous night's research into AML-related fungal infections left me struggling to maintain my own composure. Perhaps it was the frequent use of the word "catastrophic" that left my wits frayed. I have no choice but to latch firmly onto the love from the day before.

Yet for every way into the maze, there is a way out. Your prayers continue to give us much comfort and direction.   —NTS

A Tale of Two Worlds
Posted Feb 9, 2009 12:05am

When we arrived this morning, Brennan's chief surgeon attending the infection situation, Dr. Walt Pipken, was present, seemingly dressed for church. The previous night he had stayed late. Dr. Pipken was strongly concerned that he may have to take more radical action to excise the fungal area in order to ensure that it wasn't spreading. Before we had even showered, two attending physicians and Dr. Pipken had altered their schedules, and at 10 a.m. they were preparing Brennan for surgery to excise the affected area. Today was special because these dedicated people made Brennan's condition their priority and effectively rallied the troops for this one procedure.

Dr. Pipken emerged from the surgery suite with positive news. The tissue appeared good, and they are hopeful that the infection is contained and may not require additional surgery. Pathology will give us the full verdict on this in a day or two.

With Brennan back in his room emerging from the fog of anesthesia, Tara's mom, Susan, and I went to Mass at the Church of the Most Holy Trinity and were greeted with a serendipitous selection of Scripture readings from the book of Job referencing suffering as a conditional part of human existence, and from Corinthians, regarding the capacity of Christ to heal those in need.

The visiting priest who offered the homily is from a remote area in Africa. He led the sermon by saying that when he first arrived in America, he was baffled when he first noticed an animal hospital. He was astounded that there could be such a thing, coming from a nation that offered few even moderately equipped facilities for tens of thousands of people in need. He had lost his six-year-old brother to a snake bite because the hospital was over 30 miles away and the only automobile in his village was gone for the day. His father attempted to push the boy the 30 miles by handcart, but lost him on the way.

It is easy to take for granted the truly amazing opportunities we have in this country that are unthinkable in most places in the world. Not only is our son in a world-class facility located only minutes from his home, but we are under the care of dedicated people who are totally committed to healing children. From this perspective, every prayer we have offered, or can offer, has already been answered. I take faith that, regardless of the degree of suffering endured because of lack of human technology, God's love is consistent everywhere people are in need. Hopefully our prayers can extend to those who yearn for this same love in every circumstance.   —NTS

The Sum of the Parts Is Greater...
Posted Feb 11, 2009 3:00pm

When I arrived in Brennan's room Monday after dropping the boys at school, I was shocked to find him covered in a deep red rash that looked like the chicken pox. He was tired and unsettled and greeted me with an embrace that drew me to his bed for at least a half an hour while we just sat there quietly.

A new attending physician was on board whom we had not yet met. We had dermatologists, nephrologists, surgeons, oncologists, residents, and nurses in and out all day. And we still had no word on the fungus culture from the day before. Things were a bit tense.

When Brennan finally came around from the surgery that had removed the infected spot on his arm, he emerged a bit angry. We had previously told him he would not be having any operations anytime soon, and he felt very much let down by Mommy and Daddy. He stayed under the covers for a long while.

It was our opinion that Nat and Christopher would be the best medicine to bring him around, so we dispatched my parents (Pops and Nonnie) for the two brothers after church. They arrived with two happy boys, but to a room afflicted by a very unpleasant smell. In an effort to uplift Brennan and to get us out of the room for cleaning, we established a mini street-hockey game in the hallway.

The hockey proved a hit, and it looked as if the boys were back in their usual competitive form, though Brennan was limited to the goalie position because of the limited range of motion imposed by the IV tree. But as Brennan started to get tired, he got sad. He had had surgery that morning, he had not eaten for a while, and there were the rashes, among other things. We called the game and tried to retire to our room, only to find that the pungency of the cleaned room was even stronger than before. So we moved.

Moving is always unsettling, even across the hall, but the new room was a cozier place where Brennan could get some rest, the boys could say goodnight, and we could briefly gather our wits for the obligations ahead in the week (and other anxieties typically produced on Sunday evenings).

The next morning, Tara called me to come back from work to meet with the doctors about the situation. I arrived to find Brennan watching *Space Buddies* but feeling nauseous. I held him with a throw-up bowl for several minutes while he projectile vomited his breakfast and then began dry heaving. My heart was sinking when, wiping his mouth, he looked up at me and asked: "Daddy, do people really live in outer space?"

With the words of a boy, the clutter from the day was gone, and I began looking at the good things around me. He was grateful to me. And once he started coming around a bit, the Brothers showed up from school and we tried another hockey game in the hallway, with me, Tara, and the grandparents cheering in the audience. Brennan was still goalie, but he was performing well, knocking the tar out of the little puck.

As I got to bed, I started checking the blog comments online. In the photo section, I found a brand-new posting of the Aquinas High School freshman soccer team, all of whom had shaved their heads in honor of Brennan. Having been in my little cocoon for the past forty-eight hours, this one picture delivered a poignant message that the scales truly are tipped to the side of goodness. There are more angels than demons out there, and we just have to let them do their thing and keep the demons where they need to be.

The fungus culture came back negative today.   —NTS

The "New Normal"
Posted Feb 16, 2009 1:08am

Brennan's hair has begun to fall out at an astounding rate. This bothers him, both by the simple fact that he will soon be bald and by the discomfort associated with constantly having hair down his back and in his face. Amid the annoyance, he asked Tara if she thought his new look would make him swim faster (thank God for the perspective of children).

We purchased one of those little lint-roller things to harvest what we can from his pillow while he is sleeping, which is comparable to keeping gnats from bothering you with a funeral parlor hand-fan. He is well aware of the events and birthday parties that he is missing. Basically, every day he is here, the sense of being different is one of the biggest battles we assist him in fighting—outside of supporting the doctors with the war itself.

During our orientation as parents of a child with leukemia, a single point was repeatedly communicated in myriad fashion: Our lives will be different from this point forward. It is something that we needed (and need) to understand as we attempt to look ahead in a positive fashion.

Beth Fisher, who is on staff here at the CMC, expressed this in a way that has been very helpful to me and Tara. As we adjust to all of this new and often uncomfortable information, we simply have to understand that this is our "new normal." It is not necessarily the "normal" we would have chosen, but it is the hand we are holding and will hold for the rest of our lives.

Brennan continues to adjust with the strength and good humor one would expect in the strongest of men. I know childhood innocence has a lot to do with it, but I am quite proud of our little hero.

This week, we have a new infectious disease doctor on the floor who has ordered a CT scan for Monday morning to ensure that no microscopic bits of this nasty stuff are in Brennan's lungs. Concurrently, they will be taking blood samples to be sent to the National Institutes of Health for more detailed analysis, as well as to another laboratory in Indiana to better refine the medication protocol for the fungus part of the deal. Tara aptly describes this as the "storm tracker" in reference to the device used at the national hurricane center by the people who predict and anticipate events from way out for the purpose of being prepared if the need does indeed arrive.

All the while, the new normal is taking shape. Time in the room continues to be spent with the Beatles, art projects, games, and videos. We are all continually amused to eavesdrop on arguments between Nat and his grandfather, Pat Pat, regarding Paul McCartney's status among the entertainment elite. We attended Mass again with Nat on Saturday night while the boys' former nanny Laura and her husband, Josh, looked after Brennan and Christopher. The gospel reading was from Mark regarding Jesus' healing of a leper.

During the homily, Father Jerry made reference to our obligation, as humans, to embrace people who are stigmatized, or in some fashion outcast from society. It reminded me of an awkward time soon after I graduated from college regarding an advisor who had contracted AIDS. The disease took a quick toll on him. And, while I considered him a dear friend, I could not bring myself to visit or call him near the end, which is something I will always regret.

This regret has become more pronounced lately as so many people have gone out of their way for Brennan. Regardless of people's perception or understanding, they continue to reach out in so many wonderful ways. From simple greeting cards, to regular prayer vigils, to organized head shavings, to gift-card contributions for other kids on the hall, our community of friends is greasing the skids as we adjust to our new normalcy.   —NTS

One Down

Posted Feb 23, 2009 11:19pm

As with all good weekends, Sunday night offered its standard fare of anxiety and silence. Tara stayed with Brennan for his last night "inpatient." Over the past week, Brennan's blood counts continued to improve exponentially, and it is safe to say that everyone's spirits grew at an equal pace. Late in the week, the doctors gave us a fairly firm prediction that he would be discharged.

The next day, I retrieved the other two boys from school early. It was one of those nights where the mind bounced a continual volley between "what just happened" to "how far do we still have to go?"

The weekend atmosphere was celebratory from the get-go. Friday evening began with a buoyantly theatrical talent show in the nurses' break room. The crescendo came Sunday, when we were officially told that Brennan would be discharged the next day for a full week. To celebrate, he was offered the ultimate cast party, with permission to celebrate downstairs at the CMC McDonald's. This was the first time since his birthday, and the last until he returned for Act II in a week.

It was his first foray into public in a month. Anyone who looked at Brennan could not miss the smile beaming from every fiber of his body. It was the only time in years when I actually sat patiently and savored my food at a McDonald's restaurant, in no hurry to go anywhere.

It was a beautifully brisk day. Tara, Brennan, Nat, Christopher, and I all walked outside together for the first time in way too long. The boys wanted to explore the fountain and gardens between the children's hospital and the adjacent campus academic building. As they began to climb and play, I admitted to Tara a feeling of apprehension. "I hate to say it, Tara, but it feels like the day we took Nat outside as an infant for the first time."

"I know," she said, holding my hand.

Somewhat presumptively, we began packing a fairly large collection of clothes, memorabilia, games, food, books, cards, art supplies, plastic bugs (not bags), and other things for the trip home.

We packed letters, cards, and email from old friends that had delivered entirely uplifting messages to us both. In just a month, there now are some powerful new people in our lives who will always remain in the forefront of our prayers and thoughts. Many are the doctors, nurses, staff, and families at the CMC. Others are simply people who have stepped up with a helping hand. For example, our freezer at home boasts what is likely Richmond County's finest collection of casseroles, desserts, and breads. (It is worth noting that a third full-sized freezer was donated by friends who not only forecasted our need for extra storage, but who even delivered the unit.)

We also have a new stack of inspirational books and devotionals, which are used (and when appropriate, passed on). Personally, I have my buzz cut and my decorated-warrior's allotment of Lance Armstrong–style bracelets. The ones on my left arm read: "Faith," "Courage," "Strength," and "Hope." Tara is now covered with the bumper sticker equivalent of seven bracelets: "Peace," "Make love not war," "Pray," "Nukes—No, Chemo—Yes," "Brennan," "Nat," and "Christopher."

On the morning of expected discharge, I rushed the Brothers to school early in order to talk with their teachers about a non-school sanctioned family vacation, and rushed to the hospital, where Dr. Pipken had just expedited Brennan's bone marrow biopsy so we could hit the road. Brennan was already emerging from the anesthesia like a champ, and at 3 p.m. we loaded the last of the collectibles, with Brennan in the backseat. Before I could peel off, Dr. Colleen McDonough ran out, waving us to a stop. Tara opened the door to find her beaming. They embraced and held hands like two young girls talking wedding plans, and Dr. McDonough looked up to me and offered a thumbs-up. "No leukemia cells!" she shouted. They had achieved remission in the first cycle.

We have completed the first quarter of play in the game. The coaches have been tough at times, but right on with every play. The fans, well . . . they have made the difference in the fighting spirit. And the players . . . I cannot express how fortunate we feel in this regard, and pray wholeheartedly that this same spirit of solidarity will remain in all aspects of our lives forever.

I started my car, and we all headed for home. The same bands on my left wrist read "Courage," "Hope," "Strength," and "Faith." But on my right was a new one, "Brennan." In front of us is an overdue and well-earned week together.   —NTS

2

NEW NORMAL

SPRING AND SUMMER 2009

There is a scene in *Band of Brothers* when the Easy Company guys are back in England for the first time since D-day. While back in familiar, comfortable surroundings, the snugness of their little English village home feels different. Physically, those who are still alive look pretty much the same. Yet the native villagers and new "replacement" recruits look at them differently. They are different. They have seen death. The lens through which they see the world, and life, is of a different configuration.

The first real alteration in my perspective occurred just as we were preparing to vacate the CMC for Brennan's first "leave," which consisted of one week off between the first and second chemotherapy cycles. Granted, our interpretation of the world had changed on day one, turned upside down on day two, and was hurled to-and-fro from that point forward. But as the soldier must gather his wits in the midst of chaos, the landmarks and goals we set prevented a potential spiral into despair. But there are countless lifestyle adjustments associated with immune system deficiency. Each, considered independently, appears relatively benign. Collectively, they take their toll.

For instance, one would assume that many parents would pay for an excuse to avoid fast food restaurants. But as an indefinite restriction on a seven-year-old, this is hard to digest. Now we have little bottles of hand sanitizer literally everywhere. There are no more chips, Goldfish crackers, or any other snack that is served from a communal bag (as he cannot eat anything that has been touched by someone else). And there is the ubiquitous face mask.

As we venture out into the real world again, I admit to genuine distress. How could I enforce these vital details while allowing him to enjoy the freedom that he so clearly deserves? I would literally stay up at night, worried that grandparents, who have such a fun and loving pattern of bending the rules, would not grasp the weight of the consequences.

But the weight of all this seemed almost incidental when I inquired about another kid on our floor, the same bald-headed little boy who'd greeted us when we first arrived. As we were packing our bags for Brennan's first leave, I noticed that he was at the same computer working station with the same telltale IV pole, holding yet another bag of blood. I asked the nurse if he had been home yet, curious as to how he seemed to nonchalantly go through each day as if it were the normal thing to do. I also asked as to the whereabouts of his parents, whom I had not recalled meeting. At the time, the nurses weren't authorized to give me such information about another patient. But I started to wonder about it, and subsequently I learned that this boy had a single mom who was unemployed and struggling to make ends meet for a number of siblings. He too had AML and needed a bone marrow transplant. But unlike Brennan, he had no sibling matches, and as an African American it had been more challenging for the medical team to identify a match safe enough for him (there are simply fewer minorities in the donor registry). His immune system, affected by more than one infection gone awry, was effectively gone. This was his home now.

In between several trips back and forth from Brennan's room to the car that day, I finally stopped to ask the little boy how he was doing. He smiled and replied, "My brother is coming to see me this weekend. I'm really happy to have a friend in my hospital room for a change."

He was grateful. There was no lifestyle change in his universe worth mourning. There was only that day, and he was living it. He had a computer at his disposal, which he did not have at home. He had nurses caring for him. He had meals every day. He had a brother who looked forward to seeing him.

Tara and I have three boys, one of whom is fighting for his life. And he is not complaining. How can we complain about the changes in our routine?

Our little band of Brothers is fortunate enough to have both a mom and dad. And they can depend on us. It is therefore imperative that we embrace the changes and tasks before us, allowing them to know that we are in this together.   —NTS

Respite
Posted Feb 28, 2009 10:40am

Late breakfast-early lunch, and just quietly hanging out seemed to be the unspoken consensus for activity until Christopher showed up downstairs in cleats, batting helmet, and last year's Yankees' tee-ball uniform looking for a game. Competition suddenly filled the house. Within a few minutes, Brennan was out of his pajamas and into full Braves gear.

Despite the chill, it was a beautiful day to wake up, all together, at 2103 Gardner St. Following Christopher's spirit, Nat called everyone to the backyard. It was not the ideal place for a baseball game, with only trees serving as bases, and given that our players had a tendency to slide, Tara and I decided to avert the risk and packed up a box of snacks and a little cooler to finish the game and enjoy the afternoon at Redcliffe State Park in Beech Island, South Carolina.

Redcliffe had represented a special place for my family for many generations. The beautiful terraced front lawn was perfect for the baseball game, and the boys delineated an awkward but workable trapezoidal baseline.

It was Nat and Brennan versus me and Christopher, and we simply played ball while Tara rested on the soft grass and assembled a little picnic with our snacks. The wind whispered through the live oak behind me in the outfield, and I felt a powerful déjà vu moment. The wonderful image of everyone playing happily among the long wintertime shadows, the magnificent magnolia trees, and the beautiful house on the hillside in the background all seemed to have been replaying from memory.

As the day wound down I noticed that the old house, now a museum and typically closed on weekdays, was unlocked. The park director surprised me as I peeked in the door, but she allowed us to wander through what had been a family home of ours many generations ago. Its vast interior is furnished with dozens of portraits and busts of ancestors, many of whose names we share and who currently reside in the little family cemetery located next door. Holding the boys' hands as we walked, our footsteps creaked across the vast pine floors, and we engaged the faces of these people long-past gone to whom I often pray for hope and guidance.

Thus began a week long overdue for the three Brothers. For the past five weeks, everyone has been focused on the adjustment Brennan has endured, but outside of having a brother with a potentially terminal disease, life for the other two guys has been nothing but ordinary. Their relationship as a unit, their friendship, has been unaffected. They're like a group of old men playing chess in the park, day in and day out, for years. It rains. It snows. Someone's wife passes away. Someone else's child gets a divorce. But there they are: every day, the same table, the same game, the same friends, unchanged.

It is difficult to articulate the appreciation we feel for all of the attention directed to our family since January 20. I guess anyone who has been affected similarly can attest to the non-celebratory type of celebrity that is part and parcel of one's association with serious disease. I can only imagine the thoughts of a kindergartner who becomes suddenly known and recognized by every student in the school because something has happened to his brother.

We've shaved our heads. There are newspaper and TV stories about Brennan. We have bundles of letters and more gift packages than Santa Claus ever thought of delivering. We do our homework in the hospital after school. We now deliver McDonald's gift certificates to strangers. We wash our hands constantly. Things are different now.

Driving home toward a beautifully sharp and distinct sunset triggered the first of many conversations between me and Tara about our deep-seated intention to keep these boys together at all costs. We had taken the boys out of school for over a week for this trip. Sure, we said, too many such breaks may risk the boys' compliance with state school attendance policies. So what? What's a year of school? At least the Brothers know that they will be around to repeat a year of school. We made the conscious intention to consider the opportunity to keep the family together as a blessing.

We awoke relatively early the next morning for a family trip to Atlanta that would revolve around Brennan's first bone marrow transplant consultation at Emory. It was Ash Wednesday, so we first attended the St Mary's School Mass celebration. The congregation clapped with the priest's announcement that Brennan was present in the church. He stood, warmly accepting the greeting with a smile and a slight Queen Elizabeth-style wave of the hand. After the ceremony of the ashes, we began the hymn "One Bread, One Body," which the boys all knew from school and sang together strongly. Singing from the same hymnal, Tara and I traded tearful smiles at the moment. Maybe it was so powerful because our senses were all heightened to hyper-alert status. Or maybe we were finally just looking at things the way we are supposed to.

Afterward, we packed our gear, made a picnic for the road, and loaded up the car for Atlanta. As part of our new routine, the doctors had discouraged us from taking Brennan to restaurants and crowded public places; therefore, we used interstate picnic areas to take a break from the road and eat somewhere besides the backseat. Tara and I have become somewhat proud of this novel feature of our travel planning, like we've uncovered some nostalgic means of enjoying the day.

We arrived at Tara's sister Susie's house to a warm reception of loving family and friends in Atlanta. But we awoke the next morning to a slightly different energy. It was one of those wet, bleak winter days in the south. No sun, and therefore, the sensation of no shade. We barely gave ourselves twenty minutes to get across town to our 9 a.m. appointment at Emory, and I missed the exit, triggering a mild argument between me and Tara about directions. The boys were silent in the backseat, making me aware of my contribution to the collective mood. It was going to be a heavy day, and I realized my impatience was not helping anything.

While a bit late, we were greeted at the bone marrow treatment facility at Children's Healthcare of Atlanta (Emory) by a very nice nurse named Liz, who immediately let us know that she was familiar with Brennan's situation. Our examination room was small, and the ratio of square footage to human beings accentuated this. While the boys distracted themselves with wastebasket basketball and cartoons, Liz informed us that they needed blood from Brennan's arm. Despite all that he has endured over the past many weeks, he still hates having his arm poked, to the extent of needing physical restraint of every limb. Liz made good on her promise of a painless experience with her "magic spray," but unfortunately she couldn't prove this point without the experience itself. When it was finally all over, Brennan wiped the tears from his face and told us all firmly, "I do not want this cancer thing ever again."

After Nat's turn to give blood as the donor (handled without incident at the outpatient clinic), Susie took all of the children away with her while the transplant physician briefed Tara and me about the many issues involved with transplantation and recovery.

This was a heavy briefing. Neither one of us was emotionally prepared for what we were told lay ahead for Brennan. Whether through naiveté or optimism, we were both of the mindset that the process would be simpler and easier on him. Indeed, had we not found a sibling match in Nat, the fact of the matter is that a long and complicated process would have been longer and more complicated. But even with the match, the transplant portion of the treatment protocol would be very long and trigger a new series of lifestyle changes for Brennan and the family. Patients who receive allogenic bone marrow transplants are literally (physically) taken to the brink, their immune system totally replaced with that of their donor's. These transplants are dangerous and deliver threatening and often times debilitating and permanent side effects. One in ten allogenic transplants is terminal. At the end of the briefing, the staff diverted us from the heaviness of it all with a tour of the transplant recovery area. The briefing and tour together represent all of the information one can reasonably handle in a day. The saturation point has clearly been calculated by the transplant center through years of experience. As we got in the car to leave, Tara told me of her identical feeling to mine: had we stayed for another minute, she would have started crying.   —NTS

The More Things Change
Posted Mar 1, 2009 5:23pm

This visit to Emory underscored the heavy reality of what we were dealing with and the extraordinary procedures that Brennan must endure to beat his illness. After the tour, Aunt Susie graciously took the kids home with her while Tara and I took some necessary time to gather our emotions. After a late lunch, we found ourselves driving through the same old neighborhood where we had lived as newlyweds. We were quietly hoping that the drive back to Susie's house would offer a brief dose of nostalgic comfort. Indeed, while it had become cloudy with rain threatening, the drive through the neighborhood was beautiful. But something underneath seemed different. A significant number of garish new homes had sprung up in place of the smaller homes and traditional styles from when we lived there. Somehow, our therapeutic little detour began to feel soured by these surprising alterations to this place that used to feel so perfect. This meaningful place represents a body much older than Brennan's, yet it demonstrated how well intended powerful new cells can effectuate unexpected detrimental change.

Without a proper crystal ball, we cannot be prepared for every potential life-changing circumstance. One simply must understand that life changes quickly and, sometimes, severely. Change itself is ironically consistent and by nature neutral, but how do we find neutrality in our response to it? We have had several weeks to deal with Brennan's illness and its collateral effects on our family; but we also recognized that the road we were on was taking us somewhere far different than what we had dreamed. The visit to Emory frankly scared us in a very cold and sudden manner, so it was good that we were able to gather our emotions before reuniting with the kids. Later that day, on the ride home to Augusta, we intentionally kept our game faces strong. Fortunately—or unfortunately—our game faces were overshadowed by the stress of hitting the road at peak rush hour, which certainly kept the conversation away from bone marrow transplants but did little to soothe the already anxious afternoon.

As we barely snaked our way onto I-20, there were ardent pleas from the backseat for both restrooms and food. I held out for as long as I could, but eventually the urgency of the bathroom request could no longer be ignored. We spotted a Checkers, conspicuous because it has picnic tables outside and, while the views of the divided highway and an abandoned shopping center were less appealing than our bucolic rest areas, it seemed like a practical choice.

We were tired and hungry so we decided to make a one-time only exemption to the fast-food prohibition. Once we parked, I assumed a place in the drive-through line on foot. I felt more than a bit awkward as the cars stacked up behind me. Knocking on the window, I was mentally prepared for a standoff with an inflexible fast-food attendant. Instead, I was greeted with the bright smile of a very nice teenage boy who politely directed me to the walk-up window that I clearly did not know existed. The timing of his simple good nature and kindness was providential, and the fears and anxiety of the day were suspended. With our food at the plastic picnic table, Tara and I found relief in the silly prodding among the boys as they threw french fries at one another, blew bubbles into their soft drinks, and giggled uncontrollably. For a moment, I took pride in being mistakable for a normal family.

From that point forward, the drive was fun and ordinary. While Tara was forced to mediate a few disputes between brothers over "I want the DS!" or "Change the song!" there was no preoccupation of the day's experiences. Between songs and comical remarks among the three in the backseat, the ride was talkative and fun. Our love of being together has not been shaken.

I woke early the next morning in Christopher's bed, where he always has me read before he falls asleep, with Brennan taking my place to be with Mommy while Nat fell asleep on the couch in our bedroom. Leaving Christopher to dream a little longer, I started back to our room to dress for work. As I walked through, I could not resist an opportunity to slide back in the bed with Tara and Brennan for a little quiet time before starting the day. They were both sound asleep, so I just lay there, with Brennan between us, staring out of the window as the sun slowly came up through the trees in our side yard. An intense orange light reflected off the hackberry tree out back, which just moments earlier had been defined as a gray, craggy silhouette. The Lenten rose given to us by Tara's mom several years ago was in full white bloom in the corner of our small garden. The cat jumped on the bed and curled at our feet. Brennan's head was on my shoulder. It was going to be a beautiful day, same as it ever was.   —NTS

Apollo 13
Posted Mar 10, 2009 12:04am

All the way back to the CMC for round II, Brennan was quiet and withdrawn. I can still see him leaning his little forehead to the side of the car door as we made the solemn drive away from his leave. He appeared to be simply looking up to the trees and buildings passing by. One month ago, he had arrived at the hospital in blissful ignorance of what lay ahead. Today, he knew he did not want to be there.

Compared to the initial admission in January, Brennan was a new person. He felt better than he had in months (when he'd arrived in January, he was a very sick child). His blood counts were strong in response to the last round of treatments. He understandably did not comprehend the purpose in going back to the hospital when he felt fine. Further, he was NPO (an acronym for a Latin phrase meaning "nothing by mouth") for admission—having had nothing to eat since dinner the night before—and he was hungry and grumpy. So the closer we got to the hospital, the angrier he got.

An intrathecal chemotherapy injection was first on the list once we arrived, which is done under anesthesia in order to inject chemotherapy directly into the spinal cord fluid. Afterward, the doctor called to let us know that everything had gone well. But this time around, it took a bit longer after that call for us to be asked back to the recovery area. When we finally were allowed in, we found Brennan wrapped in a warm hospital blanket, breathing heavy, quiet breaths. But he kept on sleeping, eerily still. I opened one of his eyelids in an attempt to wake him, but I was disturbed by finding his pinpoint-sized pupils fixed at nothing. I was clearly becoming nervous, so Tara requested that the attending nurse attempt to revive him so that he could return to his room. With a wet washcloth, she was able to garner a sufficient complaint, and we took him upstairs. He slept all day and into the early evening.

His brothers came to see him after school. Worried that they would not have a chance to see him before they headed out to their grandparents' house for the night, Tara woke him up.

And wake up he did. Suddenly awoken from a deep sleep, he found himself back in the hospital room, hooked up to the ever familiar chemo-IV pole. The dream of our past week together was over, and he was flat-out mad. He was screaming like Linda Blair and demanding that everyone leave the room. Then he tried to get out of bed, only to be jerked back by the port in his chest, which was attached to the IV pole full of chemo fluids. I tried to place him back in bed, but he fought me to the extent of yanking the IV tube from his port connection. Chemo juice was flung in every direction, spraying on us, around the bed, and on the floor.

At this point, the nurses had to be called in to restrain him and get the chemo mess cleaned up ASAP. The stuff is poison—if it's bad enough to kill a cancer cell, it can kill a regular cell—and will burn your skin in a matter of minutes. If it gets in your eyes, you can be blinded. With the rage and the mess under control, I sat in the hallway outside, dangling my feet over the desk of an unused nurse's station. My thoughts swung to and fro with my feet as I looked down, discouraged, praying that it was just the anesthesia talking and that his beautiful disposition had not been affected by our putting him back in this position. He was clearly angry at us, and had every right to be. I could hear his muffled shouts at the nurses through the closed door.

"He is feeling burned up on reentry, but will get over it," Tara said to me when she came over to my time-out area. She spoke calmly, in the way that she manages to do in difficult moments. It made me think of the Apollo 13 astronauts who, while careening back to earth in a crippled ship, had every right to expect to be vaporized reentering the Earth's atmosphere. But with a lot of help from some really smart people, and a lot of faith, they made it through.

41

We walked back into the room to find Brennan still glaring at us. As we sat on the bed trying to regain our reputation as loving parents, Christopher came back upstairs with his grandmother, entering Brennan's confined room with his Stormtrooper helmet on, which we had packed among the necessary gear. Looking up from his bed at his three-foot-tall brother in a one-foot-tall white plastic mask, I could see Brennan experience his first sense of normalcy since he'd arrived back at this sterile, serious place. He instantly started to talk with his brothers the way they had for the last week, and when his Grandfather Pat Pat burst into the room, loudly teasing and making fun of each boy as if he had walked into our back door at home, the ice began to melt.

So, here we are: finding our hospital groove again. The balance we were discussing at lunch yesterday may be a little further off than we hoped, but we feel it near. The chemo drips on, and Brennan wakes up with a smile every day, regardless of how he feels.

His first weekend back is the second Sunday of Lent.   —NTS

Happy Easter
Posted Apr 12, 2009 8:54pm

After a relatively familiar and uneventful month-long chemo cycle, Brennan's bone marrow continues to deliver wonderful news. He is still in remission and presumably on an even stronger path. Throughout the past two weeks, and indeed throughout Brennan's journey, we have experienced the gift of the Easter season virtually every step along the way. Every gesture, every offer, every gift of kindness and compassion, every hug, every helping hand, every bit of laughter, which helps lighten the load and brighten the day, can be seen as nothing less than God's love shining through each and every one of us.

On Brennan's second week off, he enjoyed golf, his first turkey hunt, two memorable days meeting his golf heroes at the Masters golf tournament, and an extraordinarily thoughtful gift of healing from Ireland as our friend Brendan Cooling personally delivered a sacred relic from St. Therese of Lisieux, which now remains at Brennan's side. Brennan recognizes and acknowledges how lucky he is. He truly takes nothing for granted, with or without cancer. It was amazing to witness a kid savor so many unique life experiences with such a sincere sense of gratitude. This week provided him the opportunity to make some new friends who offer him a greater sense of normalcy as he works to "get this leukemia thing over with." This included Patrick Chance, a stage 4 neuroblastoma survivor, who came by Brennan's room yesterday with his sister and father. Patrick showed Brennan where his port used to be and served as a great reminder that Brennan, too, will be able to help other kids one of these days.

As I write this brief update, we are back at the CMC. Brennan is completing a day of treatment for the third and last cycle here. We have faith and confidence that his predisposition for a strong response will prove his mettle again.   —NTS

Hello in There
Posted Apr 21, 2009 2:19pm

Since we began documenting Brennan's progress, a great number of people have commented that these updates provide snapshots into our lives and experiences in this family journey. While all of the attention is certainly due to Brennan and his demanding and sometimes grueling protocol, I hope people understand that everything communicated is generated from the perspective of a hyper-emotional and often confused parent. After all, we cannot expect a seven-year-old to dictate his feelings and concerns about all of this. Indeed, we try very hard to protect him from excess concern about anything, much less the cold realities of his disease and its potential dark consequences.

The role of the child in this crazy game is to stay focused in the present and not to worry about the future. That means living with as much immediate happiness and love as can be generated amid the bombardment of fevers, drugs, infections, and nausea. The role of the grown-up in these situations is that of coach, cheerleader, and trainer, all in one. We are the ones who should be worrying about the big picture while staying strong and keeping our player motivated throughout the game.

The difficulties, at least from my perspective, stem from the fact that while we feel totally drawn and obligated to Brennan's situation, the outside world still turns. Two other boys need to be loved equally as much. We have to work—not just to find the time, but to find the capacity to focus on anything but the medical situation. We have to take care of ourselves, take care of the house, pay the bills, and find time for a date every now and again. We have a cat, fish, and two frogs, all of whom need some form of love and care (at least the cat needs some, I think).

Over the past few weeks leading up to a long overdue trip to the beach this past weekend for our sixteenth wedding anniversary (with the help of an army of friends), tension had grown between me and Tara. A lot of this was simply a product of not being able to talk much to each other, but also due to the fact that we had both been afraid of stepping on one another's feelings. This timely weekend afforded us the time to reconcile a lot of stray feelings that were starting to get the best of both of us, particularly regarding the upcoming transplant that has us both quietly terrified. We were both relieved to recognize that a lot of our emotions and reactions to certain situations had been identical.

We talked about the challenge of ordinary conversations with friends and acquaintances, how we struggled to listen to whatever it was people had to say with clearness of mind and without the clutter of thoughts that were pretty much bouncing around us all of the time. We both admitted to even feeling unsure of how to respond to the many kind offers extended by family and friends over the coming months, as we genuinely have been unable to work through the labyrinth of our own needs.

I thought about a recent comment from one of the attending physicians. In the recovery room, staring at Brennan as he slept off his anesthesia from a spinal fluid aspiration, I was clearly preoccupied, thinking about potential orthopedic issues and long-term side effects for pediatric bone marrow transplant patients. After turning to express these concerns to the doctor, he simply looked at me, puzzled, and asked, "Why are you thinking about that now?"

He was exactly right. All we can control is what is happening to us right now. If remaining in the present is Brennan's best medicine, why is it not also ours?

The natural tendency of the parent (in our case) is to dedicate our full attention in crisis or panic situations. But, when everything is calm and peaceful, we typically find ourselves distracted by the world of career and social pressures. The old normal still lingers.

This afternoon I felt a shift. I left work to briefly attend Nat's baseball practice before heading to the hospital to spend the night with Brenny. It was an absolutely perfect spring day. The sun was low, there was a cool breeze, and the fields were filled with boys playing ball. When I arrived, Tara was attentively watching Nat from the bleachers, sitting somewhat apart from the other moms. Christopher was bouncing a baseball off the back of an adjacent dugout, playing catch alone. Everyone was peacefully doing their thing when my Blackberry vibrated in my pocket. I suddenly found myself typing out an email and getting agitated about, of all things, a meeting scheduled in Atlanta. A slight tug to my shirt made me come to. I looked down to find Christopher standing there, his little baseball glove in one hand and a bat in the other, politely asking if I would help him in the batting cage.

I turned off the Blackberry, grabbed Christopher by his little hand, and we walked to a vacant batting cage. He was really good. I realized that with all of my attention on Brennan for the last three-plus months, Christopher's life was evolving beyond my periphery. The moment started to sink in. I looked behind me to see Nat making a play at first base. It was a perfect snapshot and a beautiful moment. I just had to make the time to look at it.   —NTS

Trust the Guide
Posted May 20, 2009 4:35pm

It was three-thirty in the afternoon on Tuesday and quite windy when the five of us loaded onto our quiet, well-tanned guide JR's small creek boat and set out toward Capers Island to catch a fish. The third and final chemo cycle had come and gone, so this was our last big chance to create a "summer vacation" before the transplant, and probably our only chance at any semblance of a family outing this summer.

As we bounced into the rough waterway, bundled against the cold salt spray from the little fishing boat, I was not feeling optimistic about things. A ten-minute attempt to hook a redfish at a spot close to the marina turned up goose eggs, so I did my best to keep the crew optimistic and happy.

Because of the risky exposure to bacteria, fishing had been officially off-limits during Brennan's breaks from the hospital. But it is one of his favorite things to do, and this would be his last vacation for—who knows?

Of the three boys, Brennan has always demonstrated the best disposition for fishing. Patience, combined with an inherent interest in nature, is a strength that's served him well since he was a small child. Nat has never experienced the same charge from the outdoors. His preoccupation with glamorous things—scoring the winning basket with time running out, catching the "Hail Mary" for a goal-line barrel roll—creates, for him, the impression that fishing is boring. But he knows that Brennan will be off to Atlanta soon and that this trip is more for him than the rest of us.

JR seemed to intuitively understand the uniqueness of this particular excursion. Gently moving Brennan to a softer seat in his little flat-bottomed boat, he did his best. Christopher and I sat on a cooler while Brennan, Nat, and Mommy wrapped themselves in a large beach towel, forming an expressionless cluster of arms and heads on the boat's only seat.

Finally finding a tranquil spot behind an island, JR poled the boat to a shallow grassy area where he believed some redfish to be feeding. He anchored the boat and threw out three lines. The usually black and reflective water was churned up and muddy because of the weather.

Our patience was tested. Boredom was setting in, and Nat began to grumble about alternative activities we could be pursuing. Through tears, Christopher mouthed to me, "I want to go home."

Tara reminded the boys that we were doing the right thing and that they needed to hang in there. "Trust the guide," she said.

The fishing trip seemed a quietly yet profoundly relevant rite immediately following a quick, one-day flight back and forth from Charleston, SC, to Emory in Atlanta. Brennan's physical being, we think, is exactly where it is supposed to be at this stage. But as we proceed into this next phase, we must place even more emphasis on the emotional and spiritual side. To date, keeping him happy has been made immensely easier with so many wonderful helping hands on all fronts. In between cycles, Tara and I have tried very hard to make sure that he is able to enjoy the tastes of home and to feed from the encouraging energy of friends and family. He never feels alone.

Still, the gravity of Brennan's pending procedure seemed to be underscored by every element of our back-and-forth visits to Emory, which included an assessment of both Brennan and Nat (as donor) during the same week as our fishing trip vacation. The hospital campus, accented with massive Italianate buildings, nature parks, and buzzing plazas, has a powerful rhythm, from the traffic outside to the low constant hum of the doctors, patients, and staff people everywhere. But unlike our first arrival at the CMC—as ignorant parents and a scared child wondering what they could possibly be doing in this place—each visit to Emory has been prefaced with a firm awareness that Brennan's life, and hence all of ours, will change here. This was not the surprise battle of Pearl Harbor, but rather the long and grueling preparation for the last major battle of a grueling tour of duty, its unknown horizons and clearness of necessity.

For this latest visit, Nat and Brennan had been scheduled for a variety of evaluation procedures, a process that was helpful in getting Nat used to what still remains a relatively foreign concept. And for the second time, Tara and I were thoroughly briefed about the BMT process itself.

This had been a heavy conversation, and does not exactly leave a parent feeling warm and fuzzy. A successful transplant will offer Brennan an added 10 percent to his overall capacity to stay in remission and recover. The short-term side effects to the transplant are many and will make life pretty tough for the first one hundred days following the transplant itself (also known as "Day Zero".) Long-term side effects to the transplant, however, include heart and lung problems, cataracts, infertility, cognitive problems, and acute myeloid leukemia (the very problem that we are in here for to begin with).

After this part of the orientation, our sentiment tilted toward "Why are we risking this?"

So here we are, just before game time, beginning to have doubts about the conditions and the playbook, on our way back to the beach. We decided to express our concerns to Dr. McDonough at the CMC. The blunt bottom line is this: while Brennan is currently in remission, given the type of leukemia that he has and the advanced stage during which time he was diagnosed, he has a better chance of relapse without the transplant than he does with it. The transplant risks are very real, but the odds of surviving AML after relapse are not favorable.

"What happens if he relapses?" we asked.

Dr. McDonough seriously replies, "That is something we do not want to consider."

• • •

"Trust the guide," Tara said. At that instant, Brennan looked up at his mom. "I am going to catch a fish now."

In a seemingly scripted response, JR asked Brennan, "Well, if you really want to catch a fish, why don't you reel this guy in?"

He smilingly handed a rod to Brennan. It bowed in response to the fish on the other end. Within a second, Brennan was grinning ear to ear while struggling to manage the reel. Christopher and Nat shed their misgivings, stood by their brother, and cheered him on as Brennan landed the first redfish of his life. It was plenty big.

Through the remainder of the afternoon, Brennan brought in four redfish and fought a bonnethead shark for a few minutes. Nat caught two, Christopher caught three, and Daddy got the consolation of another bonnethead, which, when brought into the boat, mesmerized the boys with the humble respect due a creature that they have read about and feared since they were "little."

While we continued to reconcile our concerns, the rest of our time off was fabulous. The love that we share, and that has been shared with Brennan and our family over the past many weeks, feeds us. While it may have taken one of life's sharpest slaps in the face to feel it, the love that is built into each and every one of us is completed when we share it with others. As Brennan begins this process, we are grateful for the opportunity to nourish ourselves in this way. Despite the cold harshness of it all, I am grateful to have been reacquainted with the love of these people who share my life.

Trust Yourself
Posted May 22, 2009 11:59pm

The time had come. Tara and I dropped off Nat and Christopher at school and said goodbye to them for a while. My car was loaded full of Brennan's gear, as well as enough clothes and work stuff for me and Tara to get ourselves through while our little soldier was readying to "hit the beach" in Atlanta. The trip was pretty quiet, with Brennan playing the DS in the backseat, Tara listening to an audiobook, and me in the driver's seat. As we passed the "Perimeter" and entered into Atlanta, a truck passed us with a rear window decal reading, "God will find a way . . . somehow."

It was a crisp, cloudless day. As we passed through Druid Hills and got close to Emory, I felt like we should roll down the windows. With the cool wind blowing our hair, Brennan looked outside as we gently maneuvered through the beautiful old neighborhoods. I started thinking things like, *My God, this is the last time Brennan will smell the outdoors for a long time.*

We weaved our way into the parking garage and up to the third floor transplant unit, where we entered the little room slated to be his bone marrow transplant home away from home for the next thirty-odd days. Brennan immediately began his final round of "conditioning" chemotherapy, designed to wipe clean the last of his stem cells to make room for his brother's. The view looks west toward the setting sun, the same as his room at the CMC. The Emory University campus spans the horizon from his single window.

Day Zero is May 28. Nat and Christopher will arrive on the 27th. But even Nat, the donor, will not be allowed to see his brother.

Christopher graduates from kindergarten on Friday. The rest of the world is turning. Trust the Guide.   —NTS

Learning to Pray
May 27, 2009

Despite a relatively conventional Christian upbringing—church most weeks as a child, Sunday school, church youth groups in middle school, religion classes and chapel in high school, religion and philosophy classes (lots of them) in college, and converting to Catholicism at forty-three years of age, which involved making first confession and learning a new liturgical framework and prayers—I do not recall ever truly learning to pray. Certainly I learned Now I Lay Me Down to Sleep, the conventional prayers before meals, the Lord's Prayer, etc. But I have no recollection of having a material conversation with anyone, really, about focused prayer. I always thought of prayer as a deeply personal exercise: something that could be discussed, but not necessarily something I could be taught.

But when you are told that your child has a disease with basically a 50/50 survival rate, I don't care what your background is. You may be the most devout atheist on the planet, but if your child starts to die in front of you, I truly cannot believe that you won't beg for intercession from something greater than yourself. In that moment, one's love for that child eclipses all; just to hold one's child and truly feel their love, that sublime and sometimes overwhelming feeling of both joy and helplessness, is vastly more powerful than a conscious decision to believe or not to believe. That is a form of communication greater than thought. It is prayer.

There is one particular church that has been very special to me—Tara and I happened to be married there—located in downtown Augusta, close to the CMC. There are noonday Masses there. Representing the oldest Catholic church in our city, it is blessed with a beautiful Romanesque sanctuary, illuminated with towering stained-glass windows that commemorate parishioners long gone and create a sacrosanct context for silent thought. Its downtown congregation is also much more diverse than our neighborhood. Whenever time allows, the daytime services become a place of sanctuary for me.

But in the face of so many fears, so many things unknown, more often than not the readings and liturgy go only partially heard. But even the occasional message can trigger focus and can channel all my emotion toward a single purpose.

And despite the constant gnawing of uncertainty and doubt, through persistence and repetition I began to stumble into a combination of method and place that offered me at least occasional respite from my fear.

In truly allowing the love of others to direct both my conscience and my voice, I have found respite, strength, and a tangible sense of faith. But as a chronicler of this experience with pediatric cancer, I am sensitive to the nakedness of my own faith, and I recognize that some readers may accept my words with judgment, others perhaps with skepticism, others hopefully with understanding.

But as Brennan's situation began to deepen, saints, Jesus Christ, God—all of these constantly began to run through my mind as participants in my conversations and pleas for mercy. We carry crosses in our pockets. A relic of St. Therese of Lisieux sits at Brennan's bedside, a material reminder of a life devoted to prayer. As we enter the transplant phase, the meaning of each day takes on more and more significance. This begins with the language of bone marrow transplant: Day Zero represents the day itself, with each conditioning day represented with a minus and each day post-transplant as a plus. The odds of survival after an allogenic bone marrow transplant are linked to time, theoretically improving each day as the new immune system takes root, matures, and fully accepts its new host as home. Until then, however, the human body is precariously subject to disease. Viral, bacterial, and fungal infections—all commonplace ailments that an ordinary person can manage with a healthy immune system—become suddenly deadly.

If a transplanted immune system is triggered by a contagion of some sort, it can throw itself into such a hyper-responsive state that it attacks all parts of its new host. Organs, skin, and muscles are regarded as foreign and thereby attacked, as would be a virus or infection. This response of the new immune system, graft-versus-host disease (GVHD), is the number one killer of transplant patients outside of relapse, and it can only be managed and secured with time (and some hard-core drugs).

Immersing oneself into the high-alert environment of a bone marrow transplant center is the emotional equivalent of preparing for and placing oneself into battle. Fear is ever-present: your senses heighten, and your thoughts move through narrow channels. The outside world passes by in whispers; pedestrians five floors down glide to and fro. Traffic heading one direction signals morning, the other direction the afternoon. Shadows moving through window shades are the only changes to your environment. You pray for news of positive change. Prepare for problems. Anticipate every outcome.

The walls of the pediatric BMT unit at Emory are graced with portraits of "heroes," one of which is of our friend Patrick Chance. His is a particularly inspiring portrait of hope to us. But there are also portraits in remembrance of children. I recall discussing the little plaques commemorating the nonsurvivors with Tara: While paying tribute to fallen warriors is a more than commendable tradition, the choice to do so in the corridors where other children still question their immediate mortality seems risky. We want our soldier focused on living. But this is sometimes difficult to achieve. Many new acquaintances on the floor struggle. Some kids never leave.

Writing becomes daily therapy for both me and Tara. Days of the week click along, and our fingers type away concerns while Brennan builds a new Lego set or watches TV.

> Tara writes: Through a new lens, I am now seeing the BMT unit in a different light. Instead of a containment cell, I see a cocoon, a nurturing environment in which we are literally surrounded by Portraits of Hope—a beautiful project consisting of portraits of childhood cancer patients and encouraging words hanging along the hall, both in memorial and honor.
>
> This is the place where Brennan will receive the gift of life from his brother. The butterfly will emerge from the cocoon in due time. Until then, Brennan is safe in this quiet, enveloping place where hope grows. We add to our "Trust the Guide," "Surrender," and

"Celebrate" mantras the Cure Childhood Cancer slogan, "Believe," and we reinstitute our practice of daily gratitudes.

Her practice at prayer and meditation becomes much more methodical than mine. She finds her rituals everywhere: watching Brennan work at his games, listening to my guitar playlists, or celebrating the visit of a grandparent. She seeks goodness every day, and she feeds from Brennan. I feed from them both. Brennan feeds from someplace else.

Day Zero, Plus Eternity
Posted Jun 30, 2009 2:55pm

We have all been feeding from a place we have yet to experience in our lives. Even in Nat's short nine years of life, he visibly exhibited a grasp of his role and its magnitude. On Day Zero, he was quiet and clearly nervous, despite our attempts to distract him with discussions of his golf game and attempted jokes about Christopher's silliness. While he had been gradually briefed about this role for almost three months now, his questions had become more frequent and our answers more detailed. Despite his obvious apprehension, he would let go when we focused on helping his brother.

He came through the procedure with flying colors and, despite a little soreness in his lower back, a great deal of pride. He remained groggy for most of the day from the anesthesia (and to think that just a decade ago, this was performed without it!). At 11:52 a.m., Brennan began to receive living cells from his brother. Now, at this moment, Nat's bone marrow is being absorbed intravenously by Brennan, who is sleeping quietly. As foreign as the concept sounds, Tara and I literally watched Nat's immune system replace Brennan's. As we sat there, it slowly dripped into Brennan and, hopefully, established a better chance for him to live a normal life. The entire process seemed so simple and peaceful and totally different than anything I had imagined. When he awoke, Tara and I held hands in silence as the nurses supervised his vitals and Brennan watched Disney Channel. Each rhythmic drip fell in time . . . drip, drip, as a quiet incantation. The candle was lit.

On Day Plus One, Tara began a little game, from Brennan's perspective, where we all chose our own individual gratitude "Word of the Day." These were posted by each of us on the nurse's little board with magic markers. The first day we all predictably agreed upon: "Thankful." Brennan expressed his gratitudes as: (1) "Nat's blood," (2) "Seeing my brothers," and (3) "Grandparents in the room." Our gratitude as parents has been impossible to articulate completely, but we are mostly grateful for the normality that we were beginning to experience with this major rite of passage behind us.

Things had been expected to get rough for Brennan once the bone marrow engraftment process began, as the transplant team had prepared us. Nausea, pain, diarrhea, etc., were all predicted as an oddly hopeful sign that things were going according to plan. Indeed, after week one we ended up in a somewhat serious debate with the nutritionist on staff, who insisted on installing an NG (nasal gastric) feeding tube into Brennan for nutrition, given the predicted loss of appetite. But we dug in, knowing that the appearance and discomfort of having this apparatus hanging from his nose could potentially affect his fighting spirit. We eventually negotiated a deferment until such time that Brennan demonstrated material signs of nausea and weight loss. Neither occurred. In fact, he gained weight!

But as Tara and I developed relationships with other parents in the BMT unit, in the parent TV room and walking the halls, we realized how different Brennan's case really seemed in comparison. Indeed, the little bald-headed boy who greeted us walking onto the CMC floor back in January was on this transplant floor finally. We met his mom, who, while not present back in Augusta, had volunteered to be with this charming ten-year-old during his transplant. While he had no sibling or other truly preferable match, he finally made it to transplant. However, the transplant was failing.

Next door to this boy, we met a beautiful man whose son has been on the floor for over two months. His first transplant failed. His second had too. This boy, presumably still, is effectively trapped in his room with no immune system, not producing red blood cells, living on blood transfusions and waiting on the hope that yet another match can be found. In the TV lounge, we talked as his father made himself a sandwich, rhythmically pasting condiments onto two pieces of white bread. I observed his focus on the mundanity of this simple daily ritual as he described his son's situation to me. He had also lost a daughter to this same disease several years ago, his only other child. Like a field leader reporting the grim reality of his battlefront, his delivery was very straightforward, with no anger.

But Brennan never took a turn for the worse. He never even became lethargic. He never got sick. Despite the predicted side effects, he effectively sailed through the month in the blink of an eye, while we were prepared to have a lethargic and mostly sick and distressed child on our hands for a long time. According to one of the transplant physicians, Brennan experienced enough conditioning chemotherapy to literally (physically) kill an adult; but he just cruised along. We were buckled in for a war and ended up watching a sparkler show. With Brennan's new immune system having taken root, with no side effects to speak of and no signs of GVHD symptoms, we accepted it all as a miracle. But deep inside, we also felt as if the war had missed Brennan. Sometimes, we worried, things just felt a little too right.

On the broader front, we felt like we had no choice but to count our blessings. We learned just before discharge from BMT that our close friend Patrick Chance, just one year younger than Brennan, had relapsed. Little seedling neuroblastoma tumors had appeared on his scans on both his brain and spinal cord. Patrick's mother and father were close friends of mine and Tara, and the two of us had been taking turns staying in the Chances' garage apartment while in Atlanta. The news cast a heavy pall over our freedom.

The day that Patrick arrived at CHOA for his scans, I happened to pass him and his mother in the hallway on my way out for exercise that morning. With Patrick's signature ear-to-ear grin greeting me on his way in, Erin took a deep breath and rolled her eyes heavenward. "I hope you guys have a great day," I said somewhat dispassionately, not having grasped the real meaning of their presence that day.

"The 'scanxiety' is killing me," she sighed. "Talk to me back at the house tonight when I have a glass of wine in one hand and a good report in the other, and I will feel better."

That night never came. As Patrick's dad Stephen reminded me, "You know, we've been doing this for two years already and know what's in the cards for Patrick. We are going to keep him alive and enjoy him for as long as we possibly can. But no one has ever survived relapsed neuroblastoma."

So our prayer list grew in divergent proportion to the win list. And with an odd mix of guilt, alleviation, and trepidation, on June 20 we packed up our collection of completed Lego sets and get-well cards, as well as our laundry list of preventative and immune suppressant medications, and Brennan was discharged to the Ronald McDonald House one week ahead of schedule for a period of closely monitored independent living.

This summer, there would be no more beach trips for Brennan. No trips to the mountains. No trips to the movie theatre or McDonald's, as his new immune system was not to be tested beyond our immediate living area, and an occasional trip outdoors with thorough sunscreening and a soon-to-be-ubiquitous blue HEPA filter face mask. But now, out of the hospital, he is gratefuly reunited with his brothers.

We have begun biweekly trips to the hospital for checkups, but with his brother's immune system so seemingly happy inside Brennan's body, he has never needed one of the many projected blood or platelet transfusions. He sleeps, a lot. We stay with him in the bed, relishing the touch of his hand and the new nubs of hair on his head as they silently grow back.

He likes to go for drives. We drive around Atlanta, watching the world pass by with the pure and joyful interest of a little boy seeing a new city for the first time. On weekends, we slowly cruise through the little village of Virginia/Highland, watching boys and girls holding hands along the sidewalk and young couples with young children in strollers standing in line for ice cream while a large group of college kids cheer and toast their glasses of beer. Brennan marvels at his world through a car window and a blue mask.

At our home away from home, Legos are still the major activity, along with games of pool and lots of movies on television. And as the Disney collection has become worn, the war movies have started to flourish. It began the week preceding July 4 with the more benign "all American" John Wayne WWI flicks and segued into the slightly more serious *Kelly's Heroes* and *Where Eagles Dare*. Brennan started becoming fascinated with the WWII story. Despite the profanity and graphic nature in which the war scenes were presented in these movies, there was a story of strength through commitment to a cause and to one another. But there were also stories of perseverance.

There had been kids dying down the hall from Brennan. Tara decided that if these kids could handle this subject matter in real life, they could handle it in a movie.

As the list of kid-friendly war movies depleted through simple attrition, we began letting our guard down and allowing them to watch more serious stuff. *The Longest Day* led to *Saving Private Ryan*, which in turn led to *Band of Brothers*.

"A lot of brave people have fought hard for us," Tara said to the boys as the credits rolled through the dramatic soundtrack on the eve of July 4, 2009.

Curled up next to his mother in his little Independence Day flag T-shirt, Brennan looked up to her and said confidently, "I think I understand." — NTS

Independence Day
Posted Jul 11, 2009 8:03pm

Everything was panning out to be a picture perfect July 4th summer day. The weatherman brought us some temperatures from the low 90s, and some thunderstorms cooled it down even more. Knowing that we needed special arrangements in order to see fireworks, a close family friend offered our family the balcony of their midtown condominium, which overlooked the Centennial Park where the main City of Atlanta celebration was to take place.

This would be the first major holiday that we would all celebrate this year without hospital limitations, so when Tara and I were given the general timeframe for transplant and dismissal, we both quietly earmarked Independence Day as an important time for our little family.

Our new temporary neighbors in Atlanta had invited us to join their family and friends for the neighborhood parade, which was scheduled just prior to the fireworks celebration and would lead us to the larger city fireworks show at the loaner condo around the corner. Yards were donned with red-white-and-blue bunting, and dozens of little American flags had been placed cemetery style up and down throughout the front lawns.

While these types of gatherings are generally off-limits for Brennan, he was eager to see the commotion, and we were willing to facilitate, albeit from a safe distance. Donning his protective face mask, he rode on my shoulders just long enough to see everyone marching by, dressed in all varieties and forms of red, white, and blue. Kids on bicycles with colorful paper streamers weaved in and out of families and dogs, walking in time with a pickup truck blaring "Stars and Stripes Forever." The main float pulled a hayride with kids waving from the rails and a female mannequin hastily made up as Uncle Sam as an oddly patriotic centerpiece. Our new neighbor and friend Eric brought up the rear on his unicycle, barking orders to his springer spaniel to get back in line with the rest of the marchers.

Brennan remains on a very restricted regimen, generally having to remain indoors and away from other people. But the doctor visits continue to go extremely well. He has shown virtually no signs of graft-versus-host disease, and his blood counts continue to grow at an aggressive rate. Last week, Dr. K.Y. Chiang indicated that should Brennan's progress continue at this rate, he may be given clearance to move to Augusta earlier than expected.

Brennan is a listener. Comments stick to him like flypaper. As a little guy, you have to be careful about mentioning both the fun stuff along with the scary stuff, as he has always had a hard time letting go of both. But he has changed since all this started. The negative stuff tends to roll off his back, while comments like Dr. Chiang's about going home can make him focused. Like the soldier reaching the end of a long and tough tour of duty, getting himself free from this confinement motivates him like nothing else.

On Wednesday, Brennan was scheduled for a bone marrow biopsy for the purpose of confirming that he currently has no leukemia in his system. But equally important in our minds was that Wednesday represented exactly two weeks since his last blood test to establish the origin of the stem cells that were reproducing in his body. Through a complicated genetic fingerprinting test, known as a chimerism test, the Emory researchers can determine whether these cells are Nat's or Brennan's. I was somewhat surprised about this test when we were first told about it two weeks back. Maybe I did not read the fine print, but I thought the whole point of the transplant exercise was to kill off Brennan's bad cells and to replace them with Nat's good ones, and the notion that there was even a chance for this not to be the case has had me feeling a bit touchy. He has done so well through each phase, but the worrywart-parent side would occasionally kick in with unhealthy negative thoughts and scenarios playing in my brain on a fairly regular basis. Maybe the reason he has not shown any side effects is because his cells are the ones that have been there all along and we are going to have to do this again . . . Things are too good . . . There was another kid on the floor in trouble and looking to do this twice . . .

Well, these demons were kicked in the pants Thursday when Tara got a call from the physician's assistant telling us that although the results from the blood test are preliminary, all indications are that the cells are 100 percent donor cells, and that we should find a cork to pop. To make things even better, the preliminary biopsy report indicates no leukemia cells in his body!

With one simple phone call, we have effectively been told that all the frightening procedural hurdles are over and done with. Brennan is now inspired with the possibility that he may see his own house, his cat, and his fish sooner than he expected. However, whatever his allowance of freedom, he will remain subject to the conditions associated with being a recent transplant recipient. The cyclosporine medicines he is taking will keep his immune system severely suppressed for several months. Until he's weaned off of them, his capacity for handling infections and viruses will be compromised, hence, the seemingly hyper-restrictive visiting rules, etc. The central venous line will remain in his chest for the full one-hundred-day period.

When you talk to Brennan, you cannot help but be encouraged by his positive nature. At the same time, we know that these circumstances and restrictions on him will dictate some major changes in the way he continues to live, and we pray for the guidance to keep him in the same emotional and spiritual path that has brought him this far.

On the morning of July 5, Tara and my sister Martha took Nat and Christopher to Piedmont Park for a chance to run around a bit and play outside, while Brennan and I stayed home under the blanket to watch the

1970s movie *The Bridge at Remagen*. The pre-movie credits listed a cast of characters whom Brennan did not recognize, so he asked me, "Who is in this movie, anyway?" I told him that it was mostly a bunch of actors from when I was a kid. Brennan replied, "I think the best actor from when you were a kid is Don Knotts." I told him he was right on.

As the movie went on, I was getting hungry. "Do you know what I want right now more than anything?" I asked Brennan. He didn't respond, so I volunteered, "I would really love a smoothie right now."

Brennan then asked me, "You know what I want right now more than anything?"

"What?" I answered.

He paused for a moment. "I want to go home."   —NTS

Strike the Tent
Posted Sept 20, 2009

I find it interesting that as Brennan reaches the end of his long and arduous treatment protocol, he has taken up such a strong interest in serious World War II movies and stories of heroism and survival. My personal favorite, and now Brennan's, is *Band of Brothers*. What became particularly interesting to Brennan were the real testimonials from the surviving members of Easy Company shown at the beginning of each series. The common thread in these prologues is how, for the right reason, ordinary people can handle extraordinary hardship.

In watching these elderly men speak to the surreal nature of their experience and how they struggled to balance those memories with life back home, I couldn't help but think about how we'll all soon begin to reacclimatize ourselves to our ordinary world. Only equipped with the realism of twenty-first century cinematography and my imagination can I come close to experiencing what these guys experienced. Nonetheless, you still wonder how weird it must have been for these soldiers to step back into their old shoes after the war was over. As in all wars, some were successful with this, while others struggled, and some were never able to find themselves again. It always seemed as if Brennan's homecoming would be accompanied with a greater feeling of finality and celebration. He endured his war in heroic fashion, and in our strong opinion, he deserved a hero's welcome. But the reality was much different. There has been no sense of finality to which one should adjust. Maybe it is related to the fact that the protocol was measured with such clearly defined benchmarks along the way: By definition, once the protocol is complete, it should all be over. But the awful taste of it all still lingers.

As we assimilate Brennan back into his role as a normal seven-year-old boy, we are adjusting to the fact that it will take years for us to know that he has truly recovered. So we celebrate to the extent that his recovery has been right on the money thus far, and with the knowledge that this is one tough kid. There is also a new understanding of the importance of faith as we assimilate this experience and prepare for the road ahead. We have certainly learned that, like most things in life, faith must be used if it is to remain strong. As, rusty as it may have been, we could not have endured this year without it.

Brennan has now been home for a solid month, and every single day appears better than the one before it. But I think all of the Brothers—and certainly Tara and I—will tell you that our nerves and senses have been heightened to an unusual degree as we get back on the horse. I guess part of it stems from the fact that getting back on a horse presupposes that you got thrown off of the thing in the first place.

For the foreseeable future, the "what ifs" will gradually taper off. Brennan's positive attitude will continue to lead him from milestone to milestone and, we pray, to full recovery. We enjoy the new freedom and accept any inconveniences as a small price for such a fortunate situation. We all try to make the best out of our family quarantines, which are pretty tough at this stage when you find yourself this close to a bunch of boys who want to do nothing but play and have fun together. It makes for a few tears when they are separated, but, when you think about it, the fact that they are such close friends is one of our biggest blessings and one of their biggest assets.

So, Brennan not being able to visit with his friends and neighbors when he returned home did not trigger too much disappointment. Playing war with Christopher and indoor football with Nat offered up some pretty solid entertainment, and with Ms. Hoffman coming from school three times a week for studies, access to grandparents and the many temptations at their respective homes, DVDs and Wii games, he has been pretty well occupied. We thought being next door to our friends the Berrys would be awkward for him, but with the occasional newsflash of information about the new Nerf machine gun or the real Nazi helmet that Brennan's godfather Frank dropped by, the Simkins and Berry boys seemed content to stand in opposite yards and shout at one another, just as people do when they have something to say face-to-face.

For Brennan, the most inconvenient factor has been the central venous line, which has been dangling from the center of his chest since it was installed by Dr. Pipken in May. The line has always been a source of concern, primarily because it predisposes the patient to infection. I cannot even count the number of patients we have met along the way who offered stories of emergency line removal as a result of infection. But Day One Hundred was on the horizon: September 5. If all systems checked out, this day signaled the end of the line and Brennan's final deliverance from his treatment protocol.

This past Wednesday, my mother ("Nonnie") accompanied me and Brennan to his one-month follow-up appointment at Emory's BMT clinic. On the way, Brennan reminded us that if the doctors gave him permission to eat food from a restaurant, he wanted a hot dog and a milkshake from The Varsity. The appointment went well; his blood counts reflected those of any healthy kid.

With high-fives all around, we left the hospital for The Varsity. We parked for curb service at the rear of the restaurant, with the welcome greeting from the attendant of "What'll ya have, what'll ya have?" Eating on paper plates in the car, Brennan said, "This is the best hot dog I have had in my entire life." I got out of my seat, opened his door, and gave him a hug. He was eating his hot dog and fries while slurping his shake, resulting in a chocolate mustache that dribbled into a full goatee. His eyes were beaming as bright as I had seen in I do not know how long. And that smile . . .

Shortly after the removal of the awkward central line, a house full of neighborhood boys and school friends all gathered at the next-door neighbors' for Brennan's first real homecoming party. These kids had been quarantined from their little friend for half a year (or the equivalent of almost 10 percent of their lives to date), and the event had the atmosphere of a lively birthday celebration.

Needless to say, because Brennan's disease caught us so off guard, our larger world was borderline chaos. Work had been on hold, with countless projects piling up and countless clients and colleagues testing their patience. The house was littered with boxes and suitcases, some unpacked for months. Like getting swept up in a large ocean wave that tosses you like a rag doll upside down and around, everything had happened so quickly that our heads were spinning. As soon as we'd gotten our arms around Brennan's problem and his chances, we had to adjust to the treatment strategy, all while constantly praying that all of this would have a happy ending. But as an ocean wave arrives in a crash, its boiling white water gradually simmers into quiet foam that glides onto the beach, depositing its contents, and receding back to its source. So here we are on the wet beach, the safety of inland dwellings in our reach, praying that we've washed up far enough to just sit for a while and figure out what happened and where we are to go from here. We've just spent almost an entire year totally focusing on our children and the things in our life that provide meaning. Isn't that the ultimate goal anyway?

Rather than with an exclamation point, we conclude this journey with an ellipsis. —NTS

Just When You Think . . .
Posted Oct 15, 2009 12:39am

There are plenty of stories about the D-day guys. Over 150,000 Allied troops in various roles prepared for battle, all pondering uncertain fates, but with the understanding that they could pull off the impossible. Certainly not all of those 150,000 could have claimed the intense experience of Omaha Beach, Pointe du Hoc, or Pegasus Bridge; there were some beaches where the troops effectively walked on shore unopposed. And even after the bitter fighting or the greater Normandy campaign, once our guys walked into Paris, the enemy seemed to just melt away for a while. Replacement soldiers who hadn't yet been acclimated to real war arrived having heard all of the horror stories, only to be greeted by affectionate mademoiselles, heartfelt cheers, waving American flags, and toasts of champagne (or whatever they could find). To these guys, it must have seemed like their timing was pretty lucky.

That was in the late summer of 1944. The war lasted another year.

While we have been home now for about two months, we still live among the unpacked boxes and bags. People would greet us with cheers and congratulations at work or out and about with the family. "Way to go," they say. "He did it!" But as much as we fervently prayed that he had, something inside told us that unpacking was not the right thing to do.

We were damn close to it, though. Tara was getting back to the law firm, and I had been sticking as many irons in the fire as I could conjure, grabbing at business opportunities wherever I could find them. But fate once again began to take its own course.

Since September 20, Brennan has broken his arm not once, but twice. To both of us, this represented a little red flag.

Then, late last week after an ordinary scheduled trip to the clinic for blood work, Dr. McDonough notified Tara that Brennan's platelet counts were unusually low. Hoping that this was simply an error, they requested we bring him back in for another work-up. Unfortunately, this second work-up confirmed that Brennan's platelet counts were down from 200,000 a month ago to less than 50,000 as of last Friday.

I left early that day for a family weekend/golf tournament event in Atlanta with our friends and hosts, Tom and Laura Pearce. I was looking forward to our reunion in the very house that had served as our post-transplant home, but as a guest. Tom and I drove to the house after golf to meet the girls for dinner. Tara had already arrived with the boys and immediately pulled me aside to apprise me about what was happening. The doctors believed that Brennan could have either a virus, somehow affecting his platelets, or that the original leukemia was still there, having survived the chemo treatments and the transplant in some quiet, latent form. A bone marrow aspirate was scheduled for Monday morning.

The boys, thankfully, were oblivious to the situation. For us, their fun was a much-needed distraction from an otherwise frightening weekend. Every night I woke up around 3 a.m. crying and praying to God to please not allow this situation to turn in this direction. With him sleeping in the bed next to me, I wrapped my arms around his bony little body, stroking his new hair, feeling the smoothness of his youthfulness, trying everything within my power to empower his spirit and his resolve from the outside in.

But while we agonized inside, we managed to keep the news quiet from almost everyone. What was the point in freaking out our family and friends? After all, it could be a false alarm. On the way home, we stopped in Covington to see our Turner cousins at the old family cabin of which Brennan has grown so fond, and Brennan introduced the Brothers to Uncle Frank Turner's sweet Welsh corgi, Maude, who became so special to him in July. They climbed on the big rock with their cousins Ivy and Julia, played Poohsticks in the creek, and threw footballs in the yard.

The coolness of that beautiful fall afternoon unknotted my thoughts. In the shade of the tall pines, Brennan and I lay in the hammock, looking at the clouds, talking about what it was like when I was a kid at that same special place. We rocked back and forth. Brennan hugged me and said, "Daddy, we love the same things, don't we?"

"Yes, we do," I said.

On Monday morning, I dropped the boys off at school. It was rainy, and they were very quiet in the backseat. Christopher stayed in the car to give me an extra long hug before saying, "I love you, Daddy" and standing on the curb to watch as I drove off. He must have felt our body language, as he typically never waits.

When I got home, Brenny was still asleep and did not want go to the hospital. For several weeks, he has had the night terrors, crying and screaming at unseen demons that have been following him somewhere between sleep and consciousness. Bloodcurdling screams of fear from his room would wake me, and bolting in, I would hold him tightly and rock him gently until it subsided. I carried him into the clinic asleep, where we turned on *Air Bud* in the clinic examination room while we waited for an open OR. Waking up to the movie and the sweet CMC nurses to whom he had grown so close made him smile.

The biopsy and recovery went smoothly. He was simply amazing, sweet and beautiful, and when I dropped him off at the house, I was feeling positive. There had been a lot of viruses going around, and we were just coming out of quarantine. He probably just had my bug. We floated on the waves somewhere between home and denial until Tuesday, when Dr. McDonough called and thoughtfully asked to speak to "both of us." Putting her on speaker, she hesitated. "It is rare that I tell my patients that I wish for a virus. In this case it is true, but unfortunately the problem is not that simple."

Tara and I were silent. "Are you still there?" she continued, to our stuttering reply of "Yes."

"Unfortunately," she continued, "we are facing the very situation that we have all been praying to avoid. I am sorry."

Brennan has relapsed. Brennan's AML arises out of unique irregularities with the number 7 blood chromosome, and falls within the MDS (myelo displacia syndrome) group of AML. For the non-leukemia geeks out there: This is a very nasty bugger.

The first thing to know is that while he has relapsed, we can feel some comfort in knowing that the transplant was not fully for nothing. Nat's immune system is now giving Brennan's white cells and hemoglobin a boost that would otherwise most likely result in a faster decline. It is why Brennan currently feels as strong as he looks. Other than his strange dreams, there are certainly no outward symptoms, as there had been initially.

Clearly the chemo and transplant have not been able to eradicate the cancer in Brennan's blood. Additionally, we now have a related chromosomal irregularity that did not present itself eight months ago. In Dr. McDonough's much understated words, "This is not where we wanted to be four and a half months post-transplant."

Tara and I left the next morning for Emory to meet with Brennan's BMT doctor, Dr. Chiang, in order to discuss the situation and to learn of any and all options to consider. The drive to Atlanta was solemn, to say the least. Listening to the CD player transmit the beautiful guitar solo of "Si dolce è'l tormento," I recalled this same song playing as Tara and I drove Brennan in for what could have been his last biopsy two days ago. As light rain speckled the car windows, Brennan's head rested against the glass, watching the droplets slither downward like little blood cells to this slow and haunting rhythm. Would there be another such moment without death knocking at our door? Would we ever experience love without torment?

The meeting at Emory was short. Dr. Chiang, while compassionate, was not capable of much conversation, primarily due to the limited options.

"Unfortunately, your son has relapsed so soon after his transplant that a second one is out of the question," Dr. Chiang told us.

Tara's mouth was agape. "Are you telling me there are no options?" I asked.

He began to elaborate on a treatment called DLI, which would involve injecting more of Nat's stem cells as a means of boosting Brennan's immune system. "It may buy a few months," he said. "We can offer nothing curative."

Tara asked if there were any other new or alternative treatments that we could consider as options. His response was, "There is a convention being held in Washington, DC, at the National Institutes of Health specifically related to relapse leukemia. It is being held in November. Perhaps you could travel there and meet someone. I wish I could offer you something more. If you want to proceed with the DLI, we will need to know fairly soon. I am truly sorry."

I felt we had been sucker punched two days earlier when we first heard that Brennan's platelets had dropped, but I honestly did not expect this. The brevity of the entire conversation was such that neither of us could believe that this was indeed the final word. It truly knocked the wind out of us both; we were numb, both with the news and by the matter-of-factness with which it was presented. I'm not being critical of the BMT team, as how can one express that someone else is going to die without being direct? But there was no sugar on that coat whatsoever.

Shortly after our meeting with Dr. Chiang, a twenty-something Childlife specialist approached us with a professionally choreographed yet saccharine recommendation that she sit down with us and the three Brothers to explain about death. We can certainly understand the role that this person plays in an institution that large, with who knows how many kids dying each year and who knows how many parents that must endure "the talk." But regardless of how professional she may be, there is not a specialist anywhere on this planet who is going to talk to our children about anything but living.

Walking onto the elevator, I looked at Tara, disoriented, and asked her, "So this is it? This is all they have to say? The whole thing took less than ten minutes." She embraced me, strong and long, and whispered, "What else can they do? This is obviously something we have to figure out ourselves."

I cannot begin to describe the feeling that our son had effectively been given a death sentence. It started to rain. Driving out of town, we both started making calls independently from our respective cell phones to tell the close members of the family what was happening. The four-lane interstate suddenly narrowed to a halt, and as I looked up at a traffic light, I realized that I wasn't even on the right highway, and had no idea where I was. I turned left, arbitrarily, until I saw signs for Stone Mountain and Lawrenceville. For the first time in my life, I was lost in Georgia.

We stopped for a minute and just sat there together. We were quiet. We held hands. We cried. We hugged with our eyes. And we told each other that we were not going to allow this—"three months, best case"—to be the last word.

About halfway between Augusta and Atlanta, it started to rain fairly hard. I called Stephen Chance to let him and Erin know. After all, we were right there when they got the word about Patrick, and they needed to be on the front end of this. Tara and I walked through every detail about our conversation with Dr. Chiang with Stephen, indeed probably with more detail than with anyone else that day, considering his cold familiarity with the world of pediatric cancer.

Not being totally familiar with Brennan's disease, he could not offer anything specific for us to lean on. But in response to Dr. Chiang's comments about NIH, he said, "Screw that. Screw that." Hell, yes. That was exactly what I needed to be told. What did they see us doing? Standing on the curb in front of an oncology convention with a sign that reads, "Save My Child"? No, the medical cards have not played out. It is not the job of the medical team to affect our decision to either press on or to quit.

So, the cards as of right now? The only curative option we can think of is to find any other institution willing to give a second bone marrow transplant a shot. The reasoning behind Emory's reluctance here is twofold:

(1) Brennan's body cannot tolerate the big-gun chemo again. The standard of care is that the human body requires one year to recover from a transplant, and we obviously do not have that much time.

(2) The chemo did not work the last time anyway, so more big-gun chemo would presumably do nothing more than offer unnecessary risk.

Brennan's cancer has effectively thumbed its nose at chemotherapy, so a more aggressive bone marrow transplant effort—one that delivers him an immune system that recognizes his cancer as foreign—seems to be the only path. (To think that we thought sailing through his bone marrow transplant was somehow a sign of good things to come! The doctors did tell us that they preferred to see some friction, à la graft-versus-host disease, which of course never manifested itself.)

We arrived home not defeated, but ready to fight. At that point we split up, with Tara taking a list of pediatric cancer institutions, me taking a list, and Dr. McDonough taking a list. Independently, we began calling other institutions to seek opinions and to find someone willing to do a second transplant in such a short time frame. If we were to get another shot at this thing, we decided we would have to mix it up this time. Whereas the protocol before was clearly defined, what was required now was a little vision and more than a little willingness to accomplish something that had been deemed undoable.

Whether we find another transplant option or try the DLI, we need to make a decision soon. Dr. Chiang suggested a two-week window to weigh these options and to research other institutions that may have new protocols and therapies for Brennan's specific type of AML. Otherwise, according to him, we may lose the "quality of life" treatment options, such as DLI, moving forward.

Unfortunately, the responses we began to get indicated that Emory's diagnosis fell within the "acceptable standard of care." Tara and I found that, as parents, our passion was effective in generating fast and considerate responses, but the inquiries Drs. McDonough and Chiang were placing personally were not giving us favorable responses. We were hearing that a second transplant remained the only real hope, but we were not finding anyone willing to do it.

So here is the bottom line now. We just got sacked, but there is time on the clock and—despite what we are hearing from some of the experts—there may be a play in the book. We have the best possible fans cheering on the team and the best damn player running the ball. This player needs to feel and believe that he is winning through our hope and encouragement, as do his two key teammates, his brothers in arms. We cannot take our eye off the ball nor can we afford to see anyone in the stands looking dejected and talking about the odds. In the between, we are going to have some fun. We are going to the North Georgia mountains this weekend to the old family home of some dear friends. While we need to figure out how to deal with blood transfusions between jaunts, we hope to do some fishing, hunting, and catch some football games. We are praying that Brennan's arm heals within the next month, as we have been planning a family day of golf on Thanksgiving. Before we dive back in, we are going to smell a rose or two. And we are going to do it as a team.

Last night, Christopher and I were debating which book to read for bedtime. We have dog-eared every book in his room, and I was not in much of a mood to read the library book he recently checked out about tanks and armored vehicles. But as I rummaged through the bookshelves, I snagged *The Three Questions*, a retelling of a Leo Tolstoy story by Jon Muth, which was given to Tara and me from Mimi and Pat on Valentine's Day, 2004. The last paragraph of the book goes like this:

> Remember then that there is only one important time, and that time is now. The most important one is always the one you are with. And the most important thing is to do good for the one who is standing at your side. For these, my dear boy, are the answers to what is most important in this world. This is why we are here.   —NTS

3

ESCALATION

FALL 2009

D-day represented the end of a beginning and the beginning of an end, a transition from one war to another. Up to that point, millions of people had already fallen victim to the awfulness of world war. Millions more were yet to fall. To the world at this point, D-day became a representation of hope. While progress had been made against a seemingly formidable Axis power, the Allies were not taking an eventual victory for granted. If anything, the vicious tenacity of the enemy had become more clearly defined, and therefore more frightening. To counter that, conventional thought processes and methods had to be scrapped. Innovation and a renewed commitment to win against the worst possible odds had to be adopted and embraced.

Just a handful of years prior, young and green men from all around the world had received notice—whether through draft cards, direct recruitment, or simply through the commitment of friends—to be part of something larger than life. And seemingly overnight, many accepted a role that, in aggregate with countless others, was to contribute to a much grander purpose. The goal for which these men and women pressed on was nothing less than the security of a free world and the elimination of evil: in effect, a cure.

As each and every one of these young soldiers and participants signed up for the cause, one must assume that all involved experienced the uncertainty of survival. It was clear from the outset that many would die. I envision the first volunteers sitting on the table during their physicals, scanning the room, wondering who was going to make it and who wasn't.

One's perspective of time almost disappears when one is coerced to focus, intently, on the present. It's funny to think now that almost every task, every goal, every assignment is assumed with a general anticipation that something will change, that the future will be painted differently than that experienced in the present. A college degree, a state championship, a larger paycheck (a paycheck), a new model airplane: anything we set out to do, we set out to do with an intent to be, feel, or experience something not currently there.

But death? When the immediate goal is to defy the ultimate enemy, our instinct triggers a suspension of time. Soldiers effectively have only two things to think about: winning and dying. The other stuff just happens.

Death represents for most an unthinkable truth, a fact that sidesteps consideration because of its contrariness to the things we can understand and embrace. Yet its inevitability and permanence trigger appreciation for the present. This is particularly the case when it looms in close proximity.

As a kid, with the Vietnam War woven into the fabric of daily sound bites and popular culture, I remember watching the war on TV and wondering how those guys could function without being scared. The draft was still in place, and I assumed that the war would just go on forever and that I would be in it one day.

Living next door to me was a Mrs. Dross, a reclusive, seemingly lonely lady whom I rarely saw. As I recall, her unkempt backyard was a wasteland owned only by her loud dogs and landscaped primarily by residual shrubbery and sandspurs. Invisible across the fence, their growls and barking made them seem mean. Indeed, we owned a kitten that never made it home from "across the fence."

While I was playing in my army outfit one day, Mrs. Dross saw me from her driveway and asked me to come over to her porch. Thinking she had overheard me bad-mouthing her dogs, I walked up the stoop reluctantly.

She asked me to "wait here." I smelled good cooking from her kitchen as I peered into the dark, drapery-shrouded living room. She returned with a model battleship.

"I want you to have this," she told me, informing me that it had been made by her son who had been killed in the war. She thought I would like to have it, and she hugged me for a long time before I mumbled something that I pray was gracious.

But I still have it. It's just a gray, plastic model, residing in my old room at my parents' house. But every time I see it or think of it, I think of that sweet, caring lady and how time changed on the day her son left for war.

I cannot speak for other families whose children have been given a terminal sentence, but when Brennan's diagnosis was rendered, "death" always retained its status as the conspicuously silent given. We never outwardly made reference to death or to its collateral traits, like suffering and fear. But it was always there. As parents in particular, there was the foreboding of our child suffering and a sense of his being alone. Will my child be afraid? Will he be in pain? Will he die with regret? Will he miss me?

We never really had the courage to talk to the boys about death before, even given the obvious implications of Brennan's diagnosis. After all, death lurks around everyone's corner. We all have an inherent sense that the curve of life is gradual and manageable, so what is the point in clouding our enjoyment of the moment with foreboding? But suddenly, as with a path along a cliff's edge, the unthinkable comes into view, way out in the open and hard to avoid.

Nat, being the oldest, was clearly the most equipped of the three boys to handle such concepts. He had been very attached to his art teacher in kindergarten and primary school who had eventually surrendered to cancer, and while he occasionally would make reference to Mrs. Amy, we never truly discussed these same consequences as inevitable for Brennan. Christopher was too young to burden with such weighty topics. And Brennan, the primary soldier in this particular situation, could not, in Tara's and my judgment, risk his self-esteem and confidence being tainted with discussions of defeat.

Because of this, the war movies became valuable metaphors for the larger issues on the table. He could comfortably talk to us about how those men made it through the day wondering whether they were going to die, or how important it was for people to depend on others to make it from one day to the next.

The New Normal presented to us in January of 2009 appears, in retrospect, to have been a concept almost rudimentary when compared to the verdict given upon Brennan's relapse. Before, everything we managed with regard to Brennan's disease was accepted as temporary, a rough but passable detour. While effectively living either in the hospital with Brennan or at his side in the post-transplant "bubble," everything regarding our attitude and demeanor toward our family, friends, and work relationships took on an aura of resilience. *It's a tough hand of cards to play,* we thought, *but by golly, we are going to play it and get back to living our lives the way we want to.*

Regardless of how much time I was spending on my knees or how conspicuous my change in habits (going to church more, writing about my faith, asking people to pray for Brennan), I felt, in 2009, that I was simply being afforded a second chance of sorts, an opportunity to reevaluate my personal and spiritual priorities. But one of these priorities was not to concede my material needs. There were certain luxuries and lifestyle features that I wanted to keep and that I superficially could not see myself living without.

I guess it was OK for me to sit back on my couch with the boys, eating ice cream and watching Hollywood representations of life-as-you-know-it literally burning up for the poor souls who resided in Carentan. But despite how much I focused my intentions on the goal of all three of my boys growing up together, I felt it almost incumbent upon me to view all of these changes as temporary.

Sure, we were making some major adjustments to lifestyle. Sure, we were tap dancing around some pretty weighty subjects with our kids. But we were managing it all at a pace commensurate with our endurance at that time. We didn't know it, but we were taking baby steps toward the real battle. With each one, we were building up more and more endurance for the much larger fight to come.

Ultimately, we had to learn to deal with the "verdict" both on a rudimentary and a spiritual level. The first layer is where we mostly reside. It is the most tangible to our limited understanding of time, the only layer accessible to us while we walk and breathe and commune with one another. It is also the layer that we have one shot at experiencing. Whether we appreciate it or not, it goes black with the termination of life.

The other layer, however, is experienced both within and apart from the other. It appears three dimensionally, and becomes intensely revealed upon the realization that life as we know it may expire at any moment. Here, motivation is ruled not by ambition or cravings, but by something that seems to extend well beyond the boundaries of the other. Once on this layer, linear time does not so much slow down as continue outside, like writing a book in a storm cellar with no perception of the weather outside or the time of day. Tara likens it to life in a submarine. Mindfulness thrives there. It is unlocked through intense and sincere love for another. It is also unlocked with the instinct to survive.

On the day of the verdict, our time became split. On one level, we managed (although in retrospect, I'm not sure how) the day-to-day stuff that we have to do in life.

In the other dimension, we just had to focus more and love one another harder. The spiritual exercise we experienced during the first campaign was proving to have been invaluable as we anticipated what lay ahead. The clock was not in Brennan's favor—soon, our plan would have to be determined either "a go" or infeasible—and it was certain that we could be called into action at any moment.

We learned a lot between January and November 2009. In retrospect, I never would have placed myself in the position of becoming a hastily contrived specialist in pediatric AML and bone marrow transplantation. Neither Tara nor I saw ourselves becoming bloggers, or people who were tapped with the mission and privilege of opening our lives up for others to both understand and experience. And while Tara has always demonstrated the attributes of a genuine caregiver, I never saw myself as having the constitution for managing hands-on physical illness and all of its nasty and grimy manifestations. Endless episodes of vomit, rashes, sheets of withered hair, blood . . . lots of blood.

It was disorderly, confusing, and intense. But each of our experiences opened a small crack in the conduit of time. Hugs were felt. Clocks ticked. Suns rose. Moons evolved. Microseconds of life that flash by at light speed, raising their hands to say, "Hey—don't forget us!" But for the blog entries, many of these details would have vanished in the shuffle.

All the while, we loved each other harder, but the rest of our world would never feel the same.

Battle Plan
Posted Oct 18, 2009 11:58pm

It was a weekend mission in the town of Helen, GA (Zermatt of the south), to buy implements for the construction of a "funnelator," which consisted of about 20 feet of surgical tubing, a heavy duty commercial funnel, and about one hundred water balloons. Saturday college football was followed up with a planned attack on some of our host's college-aged cousins, who were camping out in a pasture with about fifty of their best friends for the weekend.

The fireworks started around ten or eleven that night. The enemy was tightly congregated around their campfire, located in a small pasture across the creek. They appeared festive as our primary school soldiers crept up to a secure position under the cover of our targeted prey's loud music. The first volley of bottle rockets established sufficient confusion and disorder for our little guys to begin the full-scale water balloon barrage. Four funnels launched four balloons each. One appeared to land in the campfire, scattering bright cinders and a hiss of steam. Most of the balloons were broken up in the tree limbs, but they provided enough drama and confusion to allow us to fall back and relocate before the college kids could regroup. But as we quickly gathered our gear and loaded into the pickup truck, Brennan grabbed me by the shirt and asked if he could take "just one shot," having tasted the thrill from the bigger boys and grownups in the first wave.

Uncle Will and I held the tubes high, and Brennan held back the funnel. It launched his single balloon several hundred feet across the creek and made a direct hit on the back of a co-ed who, it was reported, had been preparing to launch eggs back in our direction. She squealed in surprise, and Brennan literally leapt into the air with a grin bright enough to reveal our location. The boys were cheering and slapping him on the back as we peeled away in the truck. They rolled in laughter, high-fiving, singing the "Airborne" fight song. When we arrived safely back at the cabin, each kid claimed this to have been the "best thing we have ever done."

These kids were truly living, and for an hour or so, I was too. It had been so hard getting through a single minute of the day without getting sucked back into the confusion and fear of what we are dealing with. I cannot even tell you the number of times that I have broken down, literally on my knees begging God to take care of this sweet boy and to please give us some comfort that His plan is something from which we can ultimately derive hope and understanding. Little events like the balloon barrage show us that the spirit is alive and well, if we can simply allow it to live among all of this craziness.

• • •

Next morning, Tara and I began the day with a conference call with the leading pediatric oncologist and transplant doctor at CHOP (Children's Hospital of Philadelphia, University of Pennsylvania). We will also be talking with experts in similar positions at St. Jude's, Dana Farber, Duke, Texas Children's, and Memorial Sloan Kettering. The bottom line is that we will find the person with the right kind of winning attitude who can inspire us and inspire Brennan before we make our decision.

We will not be swayed by the cold realism that can drag us backward. We will not work with any institution or expert who cannot feed Brennan's ego and self-esteem in this fashion. Statistics at this stage consume oxygen, create fear, and suffocate the spirit. So, screw that. Somebody has to be the first statistic. Brennan has proven it before. And, while we understand the realities and dangers ahead, we believe that he will do it again.

Brennan knows something is up. He does not feel great. He gets tired. We tend to baby him because of a recent broken arm, and consequently, he does not really feel part of the group. This bothers him to no end, and we have begun to see some episodes where he breaks down more than usual. At one point over the weekend, I was posting new photos on the blog site from earlier in the day. We were kind of proud of the shots, and I was showing them to my friend Will Morris and the girls when Brennan looked over at my computer screen to see what I was doing. He locked down instantly and left the room. I followed him into the TV room, where he was sitting fetal style in a chair staring off at nothing in particular. I tried to get him to talk. Angrily, he finally said, "I wish people would just *stop* talking about me . . . I am sick of it!!"

And you know what? He was right. I should not have been doing what I was doing in front of him. It was a standard procedure in the hospital, but not on vacation, and certainly not around friends. (Lesson learned and big note to self.)

Before we packed everything up from our weekend respite, we assembled our group into several cars for a side trip to Aunt Shell's family home at Nacoochee (the Big House). This beautifully preserved Italianate farmhouse had been constructed in the mid-1800s adjacent to a pronounced pyramidal Indian mound, the top of which has been embellished with a gazebo of the same architecture. Two tranquil spring-fed brooks flow through the property, one of which runs adjacent to the main house and through a beautiful white brick springhouse where the residents kept the butter and milk fresh back in the day. Despite a little chill in the air, some of the boys had removed their shoes to search the brook for salamanders and treasures. Brennan was determined to find a rock that would be special to him, inspired by his mother, who still keeps on her bedside table a very special rock she found when staying at this place as a little girl his age.

I was taking pictures of the boys in the barn, walking through fields, etc., and suddenly started feeling a little melancholy about the beautiful day with my family and their friends. I could not help but feel that this may be the last time we would ever visit this place as a family.

As we walked from the barn back to the house, Brennan wanted to go into the creek bed to find his rock. He fished out of the water a smooth, flat rock that was broken into three distinct pieces. He noticed that it could be put back together, almost as a little jigsaw puzzle. He said, "Look, Daddy—it was one rock, and now it's three, and I can put it back together."

Everything seems fractured now, but we are putting it back together. Tara and I thank God that we have in our midst a little man with the insight and the delicate temperament to do just that. He is doing it.

Tomorrow, Tara and I will tell the boys what has happened, and we will do so with the determination and positive team spirit that allowed Brennan to handle the first part of this ordeal in such a strong fashion. We will provide him the environment in which to put things back together, along with the encouragement and love necessary to keep moving. We are going to fight like hell and are counting on everyone to be right there with him and these other boys as we do everything we can to sustain this spirit, which is the most powerful tool in the bag.   —NTS

Decisions, Decisions
Posted Nov 4, 2009 3:05am

When Christopher and I returned to our campsite in full camo, we were greeted by Brennan leaping up into my arms, shouting, "Daddy!!! I shot a deer!"

He had shot the deer all by himself, and from just under 200 yards away. Uncle Morris, his guide, said he was nervous as a cat, but Brennan told us, "Not me. I knew I was going to hit my target." The entire scene was surreal. I simply could not believe that he had done this—he was the youngest kid in our clan ever to shoot a deer. The boost to his self-esteem was beyond anything Tara or I could have ever done for him on our own.

There is absolutely no way to look at Brennan and feel that anything could be wrong inside of this amazing, loving person. He is so good, so beautiful, and so generous, the source of which can be nothing less or more than divine. He oozes love and life with every fiber of his body and soul. As we enjoy these moments and prepare for the tough road ahead, we have to believe that he can do it, that he will do it, and that he will continue to share this love with many more people along the way.

79

As of one week ago, we had nearly settled on Children's Hospital of Pennsylvania as our best hope for a cure. Right after we returned from a visit to the hospital in Philadelphia, we felt a great sense of relief in knowing that we had found a great hospital, in a great city, with great family members nearby. Yes, there was a place for us out there; yes, our exhaustive search had not been in vain. But although we finally had some hopeful news, Tara and I had made the commitment to our son to open every door and use every connection available to us (or even conceivable to us), as well as to be thorough and balanced before making any decision that could define his fate. Thus we owed it to Brennan to complete discussions with the doctor in Seattle, the guy at Fairview in Minnesota, and revisiting discussions with the people at St. Jude. At that point, we could determine whether our choice was worthy, and we could look our son in the eye and say, "We have done all that we can."

The day after we returned from Philly, our family friend Dr. Bob Waller called me to ask if we were considering St. Jude. I told him that we had been in touch but that our physician advisors at home had a lukewarm feeling about what we had discovered so far. According to those doctors, St. Jude concurred that the Emory diagnosis met the standard of care. I talked with Dr. Bob for a long while about the outstanding reputation of CHOP as well as the other hospitals still in the running, but he kept coming back to St. Jude, offering a passionate and convincing argument that it would be very much worth our while to look again. "Maybe you can ask the question differently than the way Brennan's doctor asked it," said Dr. Bob. "Sometimes it is different coming from a parent."

With less than two weeks remaining before we had to check into CHOP to seek a pre-transplant remission, I almost reluctantly told Dr. Waller I was willing to have another conversation with St. Jude. Within a few hours of the call, I received a call from Dr. Bill Evans, CEO of St. Jude. He had served on a university board with Dr. Waller and heard all of the details about our situation. Presumably prompted by Dr. Waller, he interrupted a panel discussion in Hawaii to call me and reinforce that perhaps we had not been given the whole picture about the hospital. He told me he was confident that St. Jude had familiarity with this type of transplant and encouraged me to consider a face-to-face.

So, there I was, standing on my front porch holding my cell phone as a school bus full of kids made its way up Gardner St. As it made its way slowly up the hill, I noticed the sweet face of a single boy looking at me through the rear window, alone and pensive despite the horseplay and laughter around him. I walked inside and told Tara about the call. She hugged me, looked me in the eye, and said we should accept the invitation from St. Jude.

I called the doctor in Philadelphia and told him we would have a decision in less than a week, and then proceeded to make travel plans to Memphis for the next Monday, including all five of us and Aunt Susie.

Like Emory and CHOP, St. Jude's was flat-out impressive. Tara and I knew it would be, and to be honest, we began this consultation expecting to be "wowed" with a very polished and professional presentation. Although significantly more suburban in scale (a characteristic that did not initially appeal to me for a variety of reasons), the campus atmosphere is much softer and less intimidating for the arriving kids. We arrived around 10:30 a.m. to find *The Today Show* crew camped out on the front lawn, loaded in for a full week of pre-Halloween coverage for this facility. But despite the TV glitz, within minutes of walking in the door, we were introduced to a genuine feeling of hospitality and care.

Our consultation with the medical team was frank and to the point. We both liked that the leukemia specialist, Dr. Jeff Rubnitz, and the transplant specialist, Dr. Wing Leung, were physically in the room together, talking with us about their collaborative approach to Brennan's problem. They each commented that Brennan's general healthy nature and his track record of having handled the previous transplant with little detriment to his organ functions gave them a sense that he could indeed be a candidate for a second myeloablative transplant. The risks associated with a second transplant by this point were clear to us, and so far only CHOP had been willing to even try it. But these guys spoke with such confidence in their abilities to coordinate the chemotherapy preparation, the donor-matching process, and the transplant itself. It was all outlined efficiently yet flexibly, and they remained open to potential new alternatives in the event that the second transplant did not work. They were the only institution to even suggest this.

However, both men indicated that they would need to proceed with the next step of Brennan's pre-treatment work-up at St. Jude.

The second part of their proposed treatment protocol was something we had yet to encounter: an active family role with both parents and siblings as a critical component of the treatment process. The very notion that Brennan could see his brothers during both treatment and transplant was more than compelling, and offered the greatest sense of relief I had felt in weeks. Again, this was the only institution that even suggested this.

As the visit wound down and we started to say our goodbyes to our tour guides, I found myself standing in front of the main entrance waiting on a cab to a last-minute tour of Graceland while Tara rounded up Susie and the Brothers, when I noticed myself feeling unfrightened for the first time in three weeks. When Tara made it back to the car with the rest of the gang, I sensed in her demeanor the same feeling of relief. "Let's all pile in and go see Elvis," she said.

While pressed for time before boarding our flight home, we did our best to soak up the quirky coolness of Graceland. The boys were truly captivated by all of the Elvis stuff, and as I envisioned the good old days, with so much creativity and perseverance coming from this unique man, I felt the King's spirit everywhere. Finding a quiet spot just away from the Presley family gravesite, I felt compelled to step away from the crowd and call Dr. Rubnitz. We spoke while I sat on a bench, watching a large family of eastern European tourists placing flowers on Elvis Presley's grave. Dr. Rubnitz confirmed that Brennan did have options at St. Jude but that we were running out of time and needed to make a decision.

"Remember," he said, "families move here from all over the world all of the time. We would welcome your family."

I felt like I had made up my mind before we started the meeting and calls the next morning. I was uncertain as to Tara's feelings about St. Jude vs. CHOP, as she had not had an opportunity to say either. I was afraid she was leaning toward CHOP, as her first cousins live near Philadelphia and we would have family nearby. After talking with Dr. Aplenc from CHOP and Dr. McDonough's office in Augusta the next day, it was clear to us that we would get outstanding care at either facility. But the ability to keep our family together through this difficult experience at St. Jude pushed us, particularly Tara, overwhelmingly in that direction. By this point we had heard many stories of couples who disagreed about critical treatment options, so I found amazing relief in her affirmation.

Later that evening, I emailed Dr. Rubnitz that we would like to begin the pre-treatment baseline evaluation. We set up an appointment this past Monday (November 2) in Memphis to begin this process. The results of all of the tests there would give us the data needed to determine exactly which chemo regimen we would begin with in order to help get Brennan into remission prior to transplant.

Within a single week, we were able to look Brennan and all of the boys in their collective eyes and tell them that we were confident and that we had a plan that included everyone. And thus we were on the road again for Memphis to coordinate our housing situation and to prepare, once again, for war.

First thing upon Brennan's check-in Wednesday, a new central line was successfully installed. Brennan woke up from this procedure in significantly more pain than usual in his back, as in addition to a bone marrow aspiration, they performed a bone marrow biopsy and a spinal tap, as well as administered intrathecal chemotherapy into his spine. The recovery nurse dosed him pretty hard with morphine and a couple of other things, so he was slow in coming to. Thus Tara and I handed our recovery vigil over to the grandmothers, who we invited to accompany us, and somewhat nervously walked over to the clinic.

Once in the little meeting room, one of the leukemia nurses presented a New York City-phone-book-sized binder for new patients. The saccharine décor of the room, embellished with stereotypical landscapes and peaceful watercolors, brought back memories of the consultation room at Emory where we were given the bad news and made me feel unnerved. But when Dr. Rubnitz entered the room, he addressed us like friends.

While anyone with the credentials of a Dr. Rubnitz would be presumed to be bright, I can say that his light shines far beyond the boundaries of intellect. Having studied the nuances of Brennan's case, he now demonstrated a keen interest in the more personal aspects of our family: who we were, what we liked to do. He wanted to know what sports the boys enjoyed, the places we liked to visit, even to the point of sharing insight into the idiosyncrasies of his own family, thereby revealing an awareness of passion that is equally imperative for both the doctor and the patient's will to persevere.

Hefting the large binder into his lap, Dr. Rubnitz scanned a page or two; but before having time to digest anything, he placed the thing aside, looked up, and matter-of-factly told us that while the detailed analysis of the biopsy would not be complete for a day or so, he'd had a chance to look at the samples in the microscope and confirmed that the disease was indeed spreading.

"Cancer cells proliferate much faster than normal cells," he reminded us. "As in nature, the predator is inherently more perfect than its prey. We do not need to begin treatment immediately, but you should plan on arriving at St. Jude as early as next week. The goal is to get him in remission as soon as possible so that we can begin the transplant process as soon as possible."

On the transplant front, the donor pool has been already narrowed down to seven perfect matches (the original pool included over 600 people), for which the science folks at St. Jude are doing their more detailed DNA matching to select the best one of the bunch. This process takes time but is being coordinated by the transplant team in tandem with the leukemia team to ensure that time works in Brennan's favor. A Christmas holiday at home before the transplant is a real possibility, and one on which we place much value.

Tara and I decided an overnight stay at the famous Peabody Hotel would be special, particularly considering the presence of both grandmothers. After getting Brennan's feet back on the ground, we experienced one of those magical evenings that offered both Tara and me a nostalgic glimpse into our own childhoods when, as children, we visited special places with our grandparents. We checked in too late to see the legendary Peabody Ducks walk from the grand interior fountain to the elevator, but we found our way to the roof to see them sleeping contentedly in their duck penthouse. Thus inspired, Brennan purchased a simple little push toy that consisted of a small duck-shaped wooden block and a dowel-style handle. Each of the wheels, constructed with a rubber flipper, created an adorable lifelike waddle as

Brennan blissfully pushed it up and down the halls and the restaurants and lobby.

We concluded a great dinner with a carriage ride through downtown. Brennan was particularly drawn to a colorful carriage constructed generally in the shape of Cinderella's pumpkin coach but adorned with hundreds of lights and plastic angels from the Dollar Store. There was little sound other than the clomping of hooves along the quiet wet streets of downtown Memphis. Arriving at the Jefferson Davis Park, our colorful driver hopped the curb and told Brennan that he would secretly allow him to drive the carriage, which he did, allowing Brennan total control of the reins as he drove us around and around the statue of Jeff Davis and "deadman's curve," which Brennan made with the confidence of his 200-yard rifle shot. Having safely gotten us through, he handed the reins back to the coachman and moved to the back to snuggle in a soft blanket with the rest of us.

We circled the fountain at Court Square, allegedly given to Memphis from the citizens of Paris. The driver stopped the horse and handed us all a handful of miscellaneous coins. "Whoever has the biggest problem, use the quarter, and the rest of you take what you can and make a wish," he exclaimed. Brennan took the quarter and was the first one to throw. I did not ask him what he wished for, but I would be willing to bet that it was for a rapid-fire Nerf machine gun. Tara, Nonnie, Mimi, and I threw our coins in too. I did not ask them what they wished for either. But I think I could guess.

Defining the end of this quick round-trip to Memphis, we left for home the next morning to coordinate things with the boys, pack our gear, and drive back, yet again, to begin treatment. Christopher will leave school and join Brennan in Memphis as wingman, making him the first first-grade dropout in family history. We have talked with his teacher and will attempt to keep him up through a homeschool regimen with me as his instructor. (Brennan will keep up with his studies through the teachers at St. Jude, who will coordinate daily lessons with his teacher in Augusta.) Nat, being older and more ingrained in his class culture than the little guys, is to remain in Augusta with his grandparents until Christmas. Given that he is a bit more dependent upon his network of friends, and also the fact that we are in the thick of the college football season, staying at home and in familiar surroundings will be important to him. But we need him with Brennan prior to transplant.

With so much focus on Brennan and so much brainpower being directed toward both his game plan and his cure, getting things packed and organized is truly a blur. But with our departure scheduled for just after the school's First Friday Mass and having just come off of what could be our last Halloween celebration as a family, we somehow tightened up the loose ends, closed up the house, and made it to Mass on time for this last communal celebration with our full family until Thanksgiving.

As the service concluded, Tara and I caught one another's glance as both of our minds began rolling about the obvious decency that has and continues to pour out from so many people, a pure sense of goodness that obviously comes from the same source. Different folks from many different places, backgrounds, and means continue to do so many good things for Brennan. And the goodness and patience that flow from him? Well, I do not know what to say about it other than it represents an energy that inspires me more than I can ever understand.

I guess we all recognize portals into the sublime throughout our lives, but seeing so many from this perspective fills us with confidence despite the confusing circumstances. It fills us with what we must have in order to supplement our faith in what's possible. —NTS

Switching Gears
Posted Nov 19, 2009 8:19pm

Diving straight into the fray, our first Saturday as an official St. Jude family began with chemotherapy. Brennan was nauseous after lunch and sleeping things off in his room all afternoon. Tara stayed with him while I took Christopher out to see the town for a few hours. Prior to leaving Augusta, Brennan gave Christopher half of his fifty dollar piggy bank balance so that he could, in Brennan's words, "Buy himself some fun stuff for coming with me." Once the money landed in Christopher's pocket, it started conducting a fair amount of heat, so the opportunity to spend some of it offered relief to me and Tara, who were tiring from his frequent announcements about needing to buy a new army knife.

I took him down to A. Schwab's department store on Beale Street on a warm sunny afternoon. Brennan and I discovered this eclectic emporium during our previous trip with the grandmothers. Fortunately, it delivered two key items: a pair of airbrushed Elvis Presley pocket knives (one for him and one for Brennan) and a French policeman's hat, which Christopher was convinced was from a Japanese army officer. Donning his new hat, which made him look a bit more like a toy soldier or nutcracker than an army man, he proudly marched through town holding my hand and asking question after question about his new knife and the Peabody Hotel Ducks.

His Elvis dog tags, purchased during his last visit to town, hung on the outside of his shirt, demonstrating to people that he is both a member of Brennan's Brigade and a qualified Beale Street regular. The shopping spree consumed every penny he had; so, with a slight subsidy from Dad, he also acquired a little "adopt-a-pet" puppy dog for Brennan who has been dreaming of owning a real one of his own. Satisfied with our purchase, we headed to the Peabody Bar for a Shirley Temple and made it back to the hospital room before dark.

With his head high, Christopher walked into that hospital room bearing gifts from one soldier to another, ultimately delivering the best medicine all day to a kid who had been feeling pretty alone, sick, and scared. Before you knew it, we were all up late holding his toy puppy, watching movies, and talking about "the next hunt" and when the boys would be allowed to officially use their Elvis knives.

However many gears we have in the wheelhouse, they have all been grinding pretty hard these last number of weeks. The spiritual engine has been driving the boat more than anything lately, and Christopher—who has stayed in Brennan's hospital room throughout the entire reinduction process—has been key in keeping it well oiled.

During the first campaign, and being new to the world of leukemia, we were ironically comforted by the fact that treatment protocols for the different varieties of this disease are, for the most part, standardized within the civilized world. Brennan's case may have ridden the line a little bit close, but the treatment protocol prescribed by the COG (Children's Oncology Group) would not have varied were he to have been diagnosed at any COG facility, be it in Augusta, Philly, or anywhere in the Western world where the COG is the standard of care. I do not know what it was about the standardized care protocols that gave me comfort, other than that they offered evidence to us that there was enough experience with Brennan's situation that a cookie cutter had been developed. Although we were certainly scared and had to make some major life changes, we made each decision along the way during the first campaign with a certain sense of security. The odds of the standard protocol curing him were better than 50/50 with a successful transplant, and given how he sailed through the transplant this summer, we can say that it was successful. The coin just landed on the wrong side.

We now find ourselves switching gears. While the disease is the same, the reality of its ferocity is as clear as crystal. The standardized protocol has been deposited in the bin with last season's playbook, offering nothing but a record of how we thought we were going to win. We now have a new coaching staff who is versed in the art of the "hurry-up offense." The players are tired, and everyone's confidence has been shaken.

It is no secret that our contemplative faculties have been in overdrive with the St. Jude decision. So landing in Memphis was like finally diving into the deep end, having stood on the end of the board in fear of the jump. It also represented a major emotional change for me, Tara, and the boys, as we abruptly leapt from our dualistic world of medical care decisions and keeping the boys entertained and motivated into the daily routine of IV drips, port maintenance, nausea, dangerously low ANC counts (no immune system), calorie intake, and all of the routine crap that goes with intense cancer treatment.

The goal here is simple: Get Brennan into remission. Keep him in remission. Pursue a second stem cell transplant. Induce a manageable level of graft-versus-host disease in order to allow the new stem cells to kill the leukemia. Achieve a successful recovery. And . . . cure.

The differences between St. Jude and other places has served as a significant component of our decision to be here. Here in Memphis we can keep Brennan with his brothers to the greatest extent possible, and in a place that allows him to maintain the grace and dignity of being a seven-year-old brother. I don't care how great the doctors are; hospitals alone just can't do this, in our opinion. The "power of place" and family are two things Tara and I firmly believe in.

But once the treatment music started again, the key was no different than in our other hospitals. Brennan's movie collection is here; his stuffed animals are at his side. Even the relic of St. Therese is at his bedside again, having been returned to us by our friend in Ireland after we had returned in to him earlier in the summer (looks like maybe we should have kept it). The hospital is filled with staff who all provide equal amounts of enthusiasm for what they do and sensitivity for who they are there to serve. Refreshingly, siblings are treated no differently than patients from the perspective of engagement and attention.

But regardless of the many positive "differences" here relating to the inclusive family culture, life in any hospital room with your kid for chemotherapy is pretty lame. The hospital smells are the same. IV alarms sound regularly. The hourly vital sign checks are bothersome. The crappy little extend-a-couches that are provided for parents are all typical features of inpatient life and are the same regardless of the facility. And with every little alarm or interruption, it seemed that although I opened my eyes in Memphis, I was awakened back into the ubiquitous feeling of uncertainty that clouded our lives for the first nine months of the year.

But with Brennan's last dose of chemo completed on Monday afternoon, he has now been awarded outpatient status, which means a transfer of housing status. In just a few short days, we bounced from the hospital to interim housing at Grizzly Hous to the clinic to the long-term apartment housing at Target House. Blood and platelet transfusions are constant. The parent's role is that of a para-nurse. There is formal training for outpatient caregivers. In addition to ensuring that each kid gets to all of his or her appointments and procedures while overseeing their nutrition, etc., the parents are tasked with basic home nursing duties. There is much more freedom, but in tandem, there is much more responsibility.

In and out over a period of several days, we were visited and educated by pharmacists, line-nurses, immunologists, doctors, and RNs regarding

Brennan's daily nursing needs. He has seven pills to take every morning and afternoon (including three additional ones Monday through Wednesday) and an antibiotic via IV morning and evening. Each day we are to flush his lines. Three times per week we are to change his dressings and the leads on the central port line, which requires total sterilization in order to avoid life-threatening bacterial contamination. In Augusta and Emory this was always done by nurses in the hospital.

His temperature is to be checked during the day. Should a fever, rash, or anything unusual pop up, he is to be brought to the hospital. Three days per week he has regular appointments there, regardless, for blood work and vitals and a checkup with Dr. Rubnitz in the clinic, as well as school at a beautiful facility located in the hospital. And again, there are always blood and platelet transfusions, which are basically supplementing his entire blood system and keeping him alive until he achieves remission.

As we move along, he will have appointments for various organ function tests, etc., to establish a solid baseline before his pre-transplant conditioning. Now that the reinduction chemotherapy segment is behind him, this process will begin to pick up steam, and we will eventually transition his care from the leukemia group to the transplant group. Again, remission is required. We just have to pray that it all goes according to plan.

All of this represents a significant departure from our previous experience, both from a day-to-day care perspective and responsibility-wise. We have had little time to focus on anything else. We are constantly on the move. We also must care for Christopher, and in whatever downtime we can find, we try to contact Nat to let him know that he is missed and loved and that we are looking forward to seeing him as soon as we can.

Our stuff is moved into the long-term patient resident facility, Target House. Our drawers are full, grocery shopping has been done, laundry is underway, etc. Just having the physical move stuff behind us simplifies things considerably and allows us to try and find a groove somewhere.

But while we think we have it hard, we need nothing more or less than to talk to another family in the elevator to realize that we just represent another soldier in the war. The very fact that we find ourselves at an institution that, inspired by its namesake, is both willing and capable of taking on the "lost cause" prepared us to meet a lot of other families at various stages of their own desperate journey. Just the other night, Tara had to shelter Brennan and Christopher while they were sitting in the lobby area near a father who had apparently received the worst of news about his child's prognosis. Cursing out loud to no one in particular, he smashed his cell phone against the wall, slumped to the ground with his face in his hands, and lost it. This type of scene worries me. As in *Band of Brothers*, "fear is contagious," and you don't want your soldiers exposed to any more than they generate on their own. But the boys took it in stride, with Tara's graceful way of handling things, and they talked about the importance of respecting other people's differences in handling situations. Fortunately, they have met many, many other people who are handling things with dignity and a smile, demonstrating to them the importance of communicating love and care to others regardless of how we feel inside.

We are going to feel a lot better inside when Nat gets here for Thanksgiving. By the time Turkey Day rolls around, we will finally gear this thing down for a little while, sit back for a day or two, and be thankful for what we've got.   —NTS

Thanks in Thanksgiving
Posted Nov 30, 2009

Every now and again you look forward to something so eagerly that the sense of hollowness when you say goodbye to it is all-consuming. Thanksgiving represented our first huge milestone. More so than normal, everything this year has been broken down into broad, chunky increments of time: time that we would share with Brennan between treatments; time that Brennan would have between the commencement of reinducement therapy and transplant; the times between Nat's visits to the clan in Memphis, etc.

We knew Thanksgiving would be the first time that the entire group would be together.

When Mimi and Pat Pat delivered Nat this past Tuesday, it was clear that this meant everything to the boys, as evidenced by the almost immediate controversy about who would stay with Brennan and when. While Target

91

House is a fine place to live, the only downside is that by code, we have a maximum occupancy of four people per unit per evening. Consequently, every night that Nat was here, we had daily debate about who would stay at Target with Brennan and who would stay at the hotel with the grandparents. We realize that we must find resolution to this issue, as Nat will be living here with us full time by Christmas. Until then, we're proving that juggling rooms is something we can handle.

Needless to say, on Thanksgiving Day itself we probably hammered the whole "Thanksgiving/thankful" thing down to a redundant drone. The big meal and late afternoon football in Target House yard seemed like a pretty normal way to spend the day, however, with the only unconventional part being a scheduled platelet transfusion for Brennan at 6 p.m. Mimi and Pat Pat offered to take Brenny with the other two guys in order to offer me and Tara a chance to have our first two hours alone together in months.

Nat's participation in the transfusion experience was important. Christopher had been in the thick of the St. Jude experience since we arrived. But Nat, while certainly no rookie to hospitals, has been out of touch, so we thought it would be good for him to have a couple of hours in Brennan's shoes. But the "couple of hours" turned to six. With a smaller Thanksgiving Day staff working in the medicine room, the blood typing took much longer, and then the platelets took their sweet holiday time getting to the transfusion room, and then Brennan had an allergic reaction. Brennan managed it in stride, but when Nat arrived back at the little apartment, his hair was ruffled and he looked undone. Slipping into his bed after midnight, Nat told Tara, "Mommy, I am proud of Brennan. He's a tough kid. I don't know how he does it."

Brennan is sleeping late these days. Although he won't tell you, he gets tired. After keeping up with his brothers to the best of his abilities every day, he zonks hard and stays in the rack until almost noon. Rolling out of bed late on Thanksgiving Friday, we got off to a late start for a visit to Oxford, Mississippi, a first for all of us.

The day before, Nat was chomping at the bit to see the Ole Miss football stadium and to see if we could get permission to get on the field. When Nat gets an idea in his head, he is focused, almost obsessively. We used to call him "Rain Man," but given the time he has been away from all of us this past month, we were giving him a bit of a break with the redundant personal requests. Once we loaded the car for Oxford, and seeing his brother struggle to get out of the bed, he started to back off. The football field thing came up, but with much less frequency and certainly more sensitivity to the real purpose of our family outing. The conversation became less about what he wanted to do and more about what we were going to do as a group. As his natural inner selflessness began to emerge, he was rewarded with an unlocked Ole Miss football field, left wide open by a guardian angel (or a slack security guard). The boys ran and threw the ball freely on the turf, fulfilling all of their imaginary plays before heading home in the dark.

As the weekend came to its true close, we delivered both sets of grandparents and Nat to the airport. Nat was to stay home for the last of his semester before returning to Memphis for as long as necessary. As they prepared to board the plane for Augusta, the goodbyes were tough on everyone, particularly the boys. Nat became choked up about leaving his brothers again, much more so than when we first left Augusta for Memphis. I think seeing Brennan in this environment gave him a real understanding about the seriousness of it all.

As they proceeded down the terminal hallway toward their plane, Brennan grabbed Nat in a huge bear hug and said, "Please don't ever leave me again, Nat." Nat hugged him back firmly. "I won't, Brenny, I won't."

The love that these boys have for each other strengthens our entire family, allowing us a more focused perspective about what is truly important as we prepare ourselves for the road ahead and with the greatest sense of hope this Christmas season.   —NTS

Wave Goodbye, Say Hello
Posted Dec 2, 2009 5:41pm

In my adult life, the Sunday after Thanksgiving has been more of a depressing day than not, representing the end of the only real no-strings-attached holiday. Other than the big meal, Thanksgiving involves no special services and no gifts: just fellowship and a reminder of the many things we have to be thankful for.

The tenor of the day was set much earlier, when we attended church service next door in the little chapel belonging to the St. Peter's retirement community, located across the lawn on the same campus as Target House. Predictably, the makeup of the congregation spanned from a small number of Catholic St. Jude families to a wide assortment of retirement and nursing home residents.

The eclectic makeup of the congregation allowed me to relax and feel somewhat inconspicuous. During the recitals, Tara and I grinned at the innocence of one particular old gentleman whose deafness elicited a much higher volume than anyone else in the sanctuary while keeping him about a half step behind everyone else. His "amens" were always solo.

This was the first Sunday of Advent, the Christian season of preparation prior to Christmas, and the gospel reading was from Luke, when Jesus offers his disciples the apocalyptic message about judgment day, the end of this world as we know it, and the necessity to remain vigilant in preparation for the next:

> But when these signs begin to happen, stand erect and raise your heads because your redemption is at hand. (Luke 21:28)

I found this to be an interesting message for the conclusion of Thanksgiving and the first day of the Christmas season (particularly this one). Conventionally, this is thought of as a time of pure celebration, but in its essence it represents a time of preparing ourselves for the reason we celebrate. The passage can be considered as a warning, but on this particular Sunday, it rang as a reminder of hope and encouragement. It is a message to remain steadfast in our love for one another because, ultimately, we are not in charge. We are reminded that we must prepare ourselves daily, through our conduct and how we treat others, in order to prepare for what God has in store for us.

In an ironic way, we have been blessed this year with an exemption from the typical Christmas preparation items. But we are already grateful beneficiaries of much generosity and thoughtfulness, which is preparing us for a much more personal and tangible experience of advent.

Tara and I have had to make some serious adjustments in leaving home and finding out how to manage the other two children. The waiting game is a slow day-to-day process of vigilance. We shelter the fragility of our little family, and like the generals minding the weather prior to D-day, we are on constant watch for things that can make Brennan sick, watching his counts daily to see when his body will begin to produce its own blood cells, hopefully leukemia-free.

Being outpatient versus living through all this in the hospital, as we did back in Augusta, has made it difficult to sense what is happening inside of Brennan. Outside of his gaunt appearance and some bruises (because of the relatively low platelet levels) and lack of appetite, the only real sign that anything is happening is the recent loss of his hair.

While we knew it was once again inevitable, we avoided the hair talk with Brennan, not wanting to bring up anything that would upset him, but also knowing that time would tell us all when to bring it up. Of course, daily life in a children's hospital and apartment facility, occupied with mostly baldheaded kids, does not exactly shun implication, but we have learned not to drop things on Brennan too soon.

The right time occurred Sunday morning when he walked out of his bedroom to the kitchen area, grinning with a clump of hair in his hand. He acted as if he had just heard a joke and said, "Look, Daddy, my hair is falling out again!" He tried to rub it in my mouth and started a belly laugh.

I asked him if it bothered him. "Not really," he said, "but my bed is a mess." He giggled some more.

This physical transformation means that things are starting to happen, and the waiting game will soon be over. We are gearing up for the real deal. Since Monday, batteries of tests have been scheduled back-to-back every day. The transplant team is in full swing, fast tracking him in order to nip this thing while there is time. He must be in remission in order to undergo transplant, so at this point we just have to have faith that he will be there.

Otherwise, well . . . we are told there are "options," but we do not want to get sidetracked with those thoughts.

The top donor candidate has been identified. He or she is on standby, waiting for the green light. If Brennan has a good remission early next week, they will immediately begin the conditioning regimen for transplant. From that point forward, there will be nothing ordinary about a day in the life of Brennan Simkins. The nature of this transplant outlines a dangerous and painful path for him in the coming weeks and months. So in the season of preparation for the hopefulness that is offered the world, we find it no coincidence that this loving, beautiful boy prepares for yet another chance at life, and to share his love and goodness with the others he will meet along the way.   —NTS

Keeping Faith
Posted Dec 10, 2009 12:26pm

We woke early enough for Tara to make coffee, and the morning smell of fresh brew had put a slight spring in her demeanor. As I slugged down a large gulp of orange juice from the bottle, Tara shook her head at me, and with her signature bright smile, said perkily, "You know, I am feeling kinda good about remission."

It always seems like the days that are supposed to feel uneventful often bring the most surprises, and the "important days" more often surprise you with a sense of wasted stress. We finished our juice and toast, then wrapped the still-sleeping boys in their Air Force jackets; with a couple of extra blankets, we grabbed the boys and quietly walked them to the elevator.

En route to deliver Brennan for his biopsy, which would determine whether or not he had achieved remission, Tara and I were prepared to split up with the boys when we ran into our new friend Cameron (also an AML patient) and his father, Lonnie. Lonnie asked if Christopher wanted to go back to Target House with them to play games while we waited on recovery. This was a welcome gesture and one that Brennan welcomed too, asking if he could join them for Xbox and a game of pool after his surgery. "Save me a place," he said.

Three hours later, having shaken the anesthesia grog, he went straight from the hospital to the game room at Target House, still in his morning pajamas, to play with Cameron and Christopher. For what had started out seeming like a bleak, rough day, everything was going along in a very pleasant and comfortable fashion.

The boys digitally jousted from their beanbags, laughing and joking for a good hour. Looking up from my book, I saw Tara through the window. She was sitting on a bench and talking on her phone—clearly having a serious conversation with someone—when she looked up at me. Putting my book in my backpack, I stood to meet her. She put the phone in her pocket, walked inside, and pulled me to the side.

"Dr. Rubnitz called," she said, almost vacantly. "Bad news." Considering how calmly I reacted initially, I guess in the back of my mind I was more prepared for bad news than not. Tara explained to me that the pathology report was effectively identical to the one that had defined the initial relapse. In other words, a lot of time, a lot of toxic drugs, zero progress.

So much for redemption. But Brennan had been so strong and things had been going so well that I'd felt confident that getting him into remission was a given. He was right there before me, playing a game, laughing with his brother and his new friends. How could this be?

It was dark and time for dinner. I stepped outside to call Dr. Rubnitz myself, trying my best to fight the same sinking feeling I'd had when we talked with Dr. Chiang about Brennan's odds back in October. With each ring of the phone, the more I thought and the faster I dropped.

Jeff Rubnitz is a very nice and cordial person who maintains a seemingly aloof but keen sensitivity to our emotions. He repeated everything Tara told me, but he was careful to reiterate that "while we are in a worse position than we were in October, we may certainly have other chemo alternatives to help achieve remission prior to transplant."

As I walked back into Target House, where the kids were announcing that karaoke night was starting in the dining room, keeping my composure was as hard as anything I could ever muster. I wanted to run up to the apartment, slam a beer, and pound the floor.

Intuitively, it seemed like being around the other kids and families for dinner and karaoke would help, but conversation was strained, and to make it harder, Christopher and Brennan kept pushing me to sing a karaoke song, an exercise I was not prepared for under any stretch of the imagination. But with an empty plate, nothing to say to the folks at my table, and an empty heart, I grabbed the book for a song. I decided on "Baby, It's Cold Outside" by Ray Charles. Tara, seeing that I needed some ego stroking, held my hand and walked to the little stage as my duet partner. Christopher left the table and jumped in my arms. Brennan walked up to the stage and climbed into Tara's. We sang.

Looking out at everyone in the audience, I felt that every parent watching was fighting their own demons, keeping a lid on their own problems. Each had a child in danger. Some kids were in wheelchairs. Some had breathing and feeding tubes. All had no hair. It was "cold inside" for me that night, but it was just as cold for a lot of other folks.

And I may have been a nervous parent, but the children were still happy children. So we sang together, and then Tara and I left the party to snuggle with the boys in front of a movie in our little apartment until we drifted off.

Morning, December 9 . . . I was tired and worried from my dreams, which seemed to represent an endless string of Freud's Greatest Hits. Consequently, the ride to the hospital for our consultation/re-strategy session with Dr. Rubnitz was mostly quiet. I could not help but recall the dreadful conversation at Emory several weeks before, but I was holding onto the faith that we were dealing with a new team now.

Tara contacted the Childlife team to distract the boys for this open and frank conversation. The main issue at hand was how to reestablish remission. Our questions were: How many reasonable options do we have left? And what sort of risks do these impose on Brennan?

I had already asked Dr. Rubnitz the night before if they had ever proceeded with transplant without a patient being in full remission, to which he indicated that they had, but only in a last ditch effort when no other alternatives were available. Consequently, I knew we weren't going to get the bucket-list pitch again, but at the same time, I was praying that whatever the pitch, it offered something that we truly felt we could hang our hat on.

We entered the conference room and got the report. The leukemia was still there. The chemotherapy did not do its thing. The fifth leg of Brennan's original protocol remained, per the protocol, the only chemotherapy option for Brennan. However, Dr. Rubnitz suggested a custom protocol using three types of chemotherapy that in his team's mind had a better chance than the dated COG protocol. We had been warned about the significant toxicity of one particular drug to the liver, but our team believes this is only when used in combination with another drug that Brennan will not get. They also will be giving him Sorafenib, which has been used in trials with some success with adult AML patients at MD Anderson, but has not been proven in pediatric cases.

The only question remaining for us applied to the timing of everything. Since Brennan is currently strong and healthy, despite needing transfusions every week or so, it was suggested that we take some time to go home for a while. But taking into consideration the time necessary to complete this next cycle (twelve days) and our faith that he will get through this thing feeling "strong enough," we decided to roll the dice that the pre-transplant would be over relatively fast, allowing us to bring him home in time for Christmas.

While we still have weapons for remission—albeit ones that involve a bunch of dangerous drugs—Tara and I see ourselves at basically the same place we were a month ago. But now we have a chance to be with our family at Christmas, offering Brennan the greatest possible conditioning therapy before he has the opportunity for transplant.

As far as the donor goes . . . well, I have not asked, but I assume that they will remain on board while we prepare just a little bit harder for a chance at new life . . . a chance that, indeed, we are all offered at Christmas.

St. Therese of Lisieux, to whom we pray every day for intercession, remains on our mantel here. We are asking for a lot of help at this time from every corner of every dimension, and we thank God for every day that we are still in the game—and for this Band of Brothers.   —NTS

Let It Shine . . .
Posted Dec 16, 2009 12:28pm

Monday turned out to be another bleak, cloudy morning in Memphis. Tara slipped out to the gym here at Target House, so I took the opportunity to slip into the bed with Brennan and hold him for a while. I looked out the window at the building next door. My view is of another apartment building, one that houses seniors in need of some level of physical or medical assistance. Peering through the horizontal slits of the blinds and trying to focus through the limbs of a magnolia tree, which resides about halfway between the two buildings, I saw a person sitting in their chair adjacent to the window. They are there every morning. I can't make out whether they are watching TV, reading, or just sitting there, but on this morning I just sat there holding Brennan.

The irony of these two healthcare-related residences adjacent to one another struck me as I stared at this person who sits there daily, seemingly waiting, while I hang onto one of the dozens of children in this building. What seemed last week like a setback had no effect on Brennan's spirit at all. Anyone would agree with me that he has not changed a lick. If anything, he is just as strong and maybe even a bit more stubborn since hearing all of this talk about new chemo and transplant schedules.

Almost every waking moment outside of the apartment or the hospital is in search of some kind of game or activity that he can "win." He takes on every little thing that he does as a challenge. From the Legos, where he prides himself in being able to follow the instructions and assemble the models without assistance, to shooting (and making) baskets, to Nerf gun battles or games of pool. He is always looking for some kind of activity that he can win and thereby show people that he is more than fine. He even bets me on which elevator will arrive first.

While I may show cracks in my armor, Tara and I are inspired by Brennan's tenacity and are further encouraged by the promise of the custom protocol he has started, as well as by the strength and confidence of his team of doctors. The Sorafenib, which is the most experimental of the three medications, makes him possibly the first pediatric AML patient to use this drug. Despite its success with adult AML patients, its track record with kids is unknown. He began taking this on Friday in oral form, and thus far he has shown no side effects (although the potential rashes often associated with this drug come after at least a week of therapy).

The game plan is to keep the spirits strong and to remain as hopeful as possible. The first half of the week is relatively uneventful, although I am writing this from a recliner in the medicine room. Brennan has just received a platelet transfusion, but thanks to an allergic reaction, he is being held for another hour or so until the Benadryl does its thing. We seem to go through this same cycle on a routine basis, but once we get back to the house, his light always brightens.

Brennan and Christopher have been inspired by their friend Cameron. A spunky kid from Shreveport with two very cool and loving parents, Cameron has achieved remission and is just now headed home. He is a bundle of energy. During our brief time together, he challenged Brennan to show him that not only can Brennan hang, but he can do it better.

Tara and I had become as close with his parents as anyone thus far at St. Jude. Of course, we make friends here and there. Yet we got to know Cameron's parents a bit more, in part because of the sharing of disease and doctors but mostly because of the Brothers' attachment to Cameron. Cameron's parents are thrilled to be leaving, but they also admitted feeling somewhat hollow, leaving a place that has been so intense for so long. They've gotten to know a lot of families and kids here who were not offered the same means of exit, and consequently, they feel like they are stepping out into the unknown. But we are back in the saddle with evidence of victory from others and a decent sense of direction, and while I honestly believed we were going to hit remission on the last cycle, I feel more confident now. Clearly, we have been given more than our share of bad luck, but Brennan's light is so much brighter than any sense of defeat or helplessness.

And tomorrow morning, when I slip next to him and hold him for as long as I can before he wakes up, I will focus on Cameron and his parents, the many children and families we have met and will meet, the many doctors and caregivers who earnestly thrive on helping others, our many friends who continue to help us, our loving family, and the person who sits in the window across the way.   —NTS

Merry Christmas . . . in Memphis
Posted Dec 26, 2009 7:09pm

When the inpatient chemo started on Friday, December 18, Brennan had already been taking the Sorafenib orally for one week. That was also the day that we confirmed the promising news that since he had started the drug, the leukemia cells were indeed responding in a positive manner. Despite a little nausea, there was really no outward sign of side effects—with the exception of a mild rash, almost not worth mentioning, on his cheeks and across his forehead.

I was getting excited, and even joked about printing up some "Sorafenib, The Real Thing" T-shirts, hoping it may actually get us to transplant and get the boys a surprise trip home for the holidays, which the doctors said could be arranged. Nat was already scheduled to be here for Christmas and had arrived in town that same day, accompanied by Tara, who immediately returned home to get things ready for Christmas. Her mission was to make everything perfect for us at home, do another quick turnaround, get the A-OK re: Brennan's status, check him out for a week, and return full circle to Augusta with the entire family.

When Brennan first started this new drug, we had been warned of the potential for a painful rash that typically begins in the palms of the hands and the soles of the feet. We were instructed to keep Brennan's feet and hands well covered in Eucerin cream as a precaution and to notify the hospital immediately if the rash became severe so that they could stop the medication. We began lathering the cream with as much good humor as possible, telling the boys that we were going to massage their feet and hands every night but that they were going to have to return the favor. (I got some mileage out of this from Christopher for a couple of nights.)

Brennan made it a solid ten days and appeared to be on track. But Tuesday night, his legs started to hurt. While raising a few eyebrows, we brushed it off as nothing, particularly when he literally sprinted out of the car to play video games before the 10 p.m. Target House curfew.

He became giddy when we told him we were going home for Christmas the next morning. As the boys played their games in Memphis, friends from Augusta were setting up an artificial tree in our house for us and working to have everything decorated for our arrival. I felt like George Bailey at the end of *It's a Wonderful Life*. So many great people were coming together on Brennan's behalf and ours, putting their things aside, offering the finest possible example of Christmas spirit. It was shaping into the best homecoming ever.

That night I helped Brenny pack his little bag. He was excited about not packing too much because he wanted to wear the Christmas clothes he had back home. But then the pain started to kick in a bit more. We did our best to take his mind off of things and make him comfortable, to the extent of giving him Benadryl and, eventually, oral morphine. We got restful and watched a movie until the wee hours and tried to sleep in his single bed together, when he suggested that I would be more comfortable if he were to "sleep with Mommy in your room."

It was Mommy who poked me awake in my little single bed. "Brennan has a fever," she said. We were due at the hospital at nine o'clock for a transfusion prior to getting on the plane anyway, but Tara decided to go early to determine what was happening. Word quickly came down that Brennan would be admitted inpatient to manage both his fever and his pain, but primarily to make sure that he did not have a bug of any kind. I hung around in the apartment catching up on email for a while, hoping that we would get word of the possibility of resurrecting our trip home, but we only succeeded in establishing the one thing we were hoping against. I then got on the phone and effectively canceled Christmas in Augusta.

We have developed experience lately with regrouping. Within an hour or two, Mimi and Pat Pat switched their plans and made the journey to Memphis. We already had a little tree in our apartment with a number of gifts under it from our St. Jude family, and the army of good folks working to make our home ready for us in Augusta began to send gifts to Target House as well. After all, the trip home had been a long shot anyway and was not even in the cards a couple of weeks earlier. The problem was that we could smell the barn and got turned away. The disappointment still burned. And then it started to really burn.

Brennan probably handled the news better than anyone, but this was primarily because he was oblivious. His fever had painfully progressed (or digressed) to a head-to-toe rash. His internal temperature was about 100, but his skin temperature was closer to 102! Dr. Hiroto Inaba had stopped the Sorafenib the day before, switching to major pain management mode. The blood cultures to rule out infection would not come back for another day or so, and it was clear that he would be in the hospital at least through December 26. And he was miserable.

Nat was the one most affected. He was really looking forward to having everyone home, and he had been really hopeful for Brennan, knowing that grandfather Pops had secured a new golden retriever puppy for him for Christmas. Brennan had been dreaming of puppies since the beginning of treatment, surfing adopt-a-pet websites and bouncing around between different types of dogs, from border collies to Welsh corgis to Labs to goldens and back again. But the *Santa Buddies* movie put him over the top, and he finally locked in on the golden retriever. His only condition was that it had to be "the white kind," like in the movie.

Pops had dispatched his confederacy of dog lovers to find just what Brennan was looking for, and sure enough he found a six-week-old, very blonde golden around the corner in Aiken, SC. Nat was aware of this gift and knew it would make Brennan as happy as anything in the world. As much as Brennan longed for this dog, Nat was longing to see the smile on his brother's face on Christmas morning.

But with all the boys stuck in Memphis, Tara returned to relieve me at the hospital and suggested that Nat and I spend the afternoon shopping to ease his disappointment. We spent most of December 23 together driving through rainy Memphis and helping him find gifts for his brothers, but basically just spending some overdue time together to talk about how things were different this year and to reconcile our worries with the many good things we had that would never change. In short, I was trying desperately to conjure the Christmas spirit for this sweet kid whose dream of being in his own living room with his brothers had been dashed.

Arriving with a handful of Christmas videos and smiley faces, we delivered some overnight relief for Tara, but Brennan's situation was getting worse. The morphine injections were moved up from every four hours to every two, as the rash had turned to goiterous blisters that covered most of his body. He had taken off his pajama bottoms entirely, as the friction of the fabric against his skin was becoming unbearable, and Benadryl was thrown into the intravenous mix of pain management tools. He slept in the morning; and he slept, and slept, and slept. Nat, who is the early riser in the crowd, quietly moved from Brennan's room into the adjoining "parent suite" so that he could watch TV without bothering Brenny.

Nat's transformation since Thanksgiving is remarkable. While always conscientious of Brennan's situation, it seemed to him that time in a hospital room was considered time that could have been better spent doing things that he, or any nine year old, would have preferred. Now there is none of that. Indeed, his sense of his brother's situation has become quite sensitive and serious.

On the opposite side of the child maintenance equation, Christopher has maintained his beautiful spirit the entire time. In or out of the hospital, he is all smiles. And when his grandparents arrived in Memphis on Christmas Eve, he was unpacking the car with all the curiosity of any other kid this time of year looking in the backseat for presents and signs of Santa. His brothers were here, and the presents were too. No signs of regret or worry from this kid.

The only question was where Santa would deliver the gifts: in Target House, where Nat and Christopher were sleeping with Mimi and Pat Pat, or in the hospital were Tara and I were staying with Brennan. As the eldest, Nat felt certain that Santa would deliver his gifts to the hospital in the parent room adjacent to Brennan's. He even wrote a last-minute note for me to leave at Target House tree with full instructions for Santa. While not much room for maneuvering (the "parent suite" is exactly 6' x 12'), it offered enough to allow presents to be delivered unmanipulated by anyone but Santa Claus.

That night was challenging from the perspective of time management. But with Mimi and Pat Pat in town, each taking duty at Target House and the hospital, Tara and I slipped out for what was intended to be an evening dinner. We felt fortunate to find a late-night Chinese buffet just before they started to break things down for their own Christmas Eve curfew. Two middle-aged girlfriends represented the only other couple in the cavernous 1970s-era dining room. The freshly mopped linoleum was still sticky with pine-scented cleaner, hammering home the fact that closing time was nigh and that the buffet items we were eating more than likely had been sitting for a while, as evidenced by the density of the sweet and sour chicken chunks. But the pure comedy of the meal diluted what had become an unnecessary veil of tension weighing over us both for the past several hours, and we both laughed that it was really the perfect "last supper" before heading back to the parent room for our big late-night Christmas obligation. We were able to fall asleep early enough to awake precisely at 7 a.m. without protest, and had been counseled several times that Santa made the absolute last stop of his route at St. Jude in order to see all of the special kids in the hospital. We had to be there in time for that.

The Brothers awoke early, and we arrived about seven-thirty. Mimi and Tara were helping Brennan into a wheelchair (because the blisters on his feet made it too painful to walk) as we took everyone into the adjoining room for the consumption process. He was very tired and hurt tremendously, but with his vision of packed stockings and stacks of Santa gifts, he was focused on Christmas. My iPod serendipitously played "Wherever you are, Santa will find you."

No sooner had I switched the music on than Santa himself walked into our room with two pixieish-looking elves and three full sacks for each of the boys. For a few moments, it made no difference if we were in our living room by our tree or all crammed into a closet on top of each other. It was Christmas Day. We were together and all was good. Brennan managed to play with some things for a while but quickly needed to get back in bed for pain meds. He felt so bad that he was almost begging to get back in bed and to be left alone. The Christmas magic made it, but the reality of cancer's awfulness was pervasive.

With a child in danger, it is amazing how one's personal needs and wants are totally put aside at Christmas. But physical circumstances do not mitigate the intangible gravity of Christmas for children or the magic that they anticipate regardless of these other conditions that offer anything but magic. Once the stress associated with the material side of this day is over, and with everyone gathered under the canopy of the real reason we celebrate, thankfulness, appreciation, and love for one another can flow as freely under adverse circumstances as they can in the most propitious.

It is now Saturday morning, Boxing Day. Brennan's rash subsided dramatically overnight. After an evening mixed with anger for being in the hospital and the strained effort to enjoy some new toys and games, his smile returned and he began to bud. No pain meds since midday yesterday. The blisters on the feet have subsided. We are up and about walking for the first time since Tuesday and in the process of being discharged. A handful of presents are still under the tree in our little apartment, and we will gather again for one more small taste of the receiving side of things. It will be good for Brennan, whose memories of yesterday are cloudy at best. Later today, our little group of families is gathering again, this time for the sixth birthday of a sweet little boy who has become friends with ours. We will all be present this time, and we will celebrate again wrapped in the comfort of the season, which is far from over.

We do indeed feel like George Bailey this Christmas. We have been touched by many. Happy Boxing Day.   —NTS

The New Year
Posted Jan 6, 2010 11:47am

Last year, Tara suggested we all establish our individual word of the year, which would be used to bind our good intentions and therefore to weave them into the fabric of experiences ahead of us. My word was "prepare." Tara chose "trust."

Looking back, it is pretty amazing to see how the meaning of the words evolved to our reality. The economic and political forces outside of our immediate lives that most likely affected our choices at the time, while still very real and serious, now appear trifling and castrated by our focus on a cure for Brennan and happy, encouraging environs for all of the boys.

My word for this year is, not surprisingly, "live." Tara's is "believe." This year, the boys are on board with the new tradition. Nat has chosen "win." Christopher has exercised his right not to provide a word at this time, on the grounds that the demand for a word is too much like homework and that we will get it in due time. Brennan's word, with no prompting from us, is "shine."

For a while there I thought that we would be saying good riddance to 2009 with zero pangs of conscience. But looking forward to the year ahead, you realize that all of the hope and promise for this year has been established through the trials and lessons of last year. The tangible signs of hope that have been provided by St. Jude's willingness to step outside the box and take risks that other institutions cannot take were delivered at the tail end of 2009. This roller coaster of a year represented an aggregate mix of good, despite all the bad.

This past week, Brennan has been feeling great; therefore we were all fortunate and relieved to truly experience the New Year. Celebrating New Year's Eve among friends and in a refreshingly pedestrian fashion served up some simple pleasures that we have not had in a while. It tasted damned good.

One major change thus far this year is represented by a new school for the Brothers. Initially screaming in protest about being labeled "drop-ins" in the little Montessori school located near St. Jude at Mud Island, they soon changed their tune and were presenting themselves with a small glimmer of enthusiasm. The credit for this transformation goes to Nat. A vocal opponent to his move to Memphis at first, he became our lead delegate in converting Christopher, who has been reluctant to leave his favorite homeschool teacher (moi). Together, they have provided me and Tara a great gift, knowing that the first quarter of this year will be a critical one and that we will both need the extra time afforded with Brennan and to take care of running our little home away from home while at least keeping in touch with our careers.

We started the first week of the new year with this frame of mind. Nat and Christopher accompanied me to the little Catholic church adjacent to

Target House. We arrived in our own style, Nat serious and grown up in his button down and khakis, while Christopher appeased me with a button down yet maintained his unique flair for fashion with camouflage crocs and a pair of newly acquired Ole Miss sweatpants. Tara and Brennan spent the morning at the hospital getting a platelet transfusion in preparation for Brennan's upcoming bone marrow aspiration and biopsy. The weatherman was predicting snow Sunday night and a "for sure blizzard" on Wednesday and Thursday. The boys were giddy with these prospects ahead. Yet despite our positive attitude for the new year, we were admittedly nervous about the biopsy.

During the procedure, Tara took the Brothers upstairs for some pre–Montessori school work while I sat with Brennan in the procedure room. Until the anesthesia guided him to La La Land, he was his beautiful self. But he was also quiet, and seemed to sense something. He did not want to play games on my new phone but just held my hand quietly, squeezing me now and again with his sweet smile. When it was all over, we settled back into Target House and he became his old self, playing and laughing with the Brothers and talking about the blizzard.

That afternoon, I was still restless about the results, so I called Dr. Rubnitz. Pausing for a tense moment before responding, he told me that he had intended to wait to call until the more accurate computer-generated analysis was completed, but that he was "concerned" about what he saw under the microscope.

Nat and I were on our way to the grocery store. His honest opinion was delivered via my cell phone while I feigned focus on this task. As would be imagined, his words hung in my mind loudly, beginning to consume every aspect of my consciousness. Nat was sweet as we walked the aisles of the store, talking about the football games ahead this week, oblivious to this news and my dread. I walked along at his side almost blind, pretending to be interested in what he had to say. Totally consumed by the news, I thought of Charlie Brown's teacher—blaa blaa, blaa blaa blaa blaa—as my thoughts raced between reflections of hope and death. Nat was simply a happy kid, walking with his dad and expecting nothing more of me than to be present. I regret not being capable.

While Nat slipped into the restroom, I managed to call Tara, and when I got back to the apartment, she was already home. We contacted Dr. Rubnitz, who told us that the final analysis demonstrated that he indeed had reason to be concerned. The disease was still significantly present. However, while he was certainly disappointed with this news, he was able to reassure me that we were not out of the game. Indeed, while I was at Kroger with Nat, he had already spoken with Dr. Leung, who told him that he wanted to move the transplant schedule forward, stating that he'd had curative success with other AML children who had received transplants despite the disease being present.

More chemo does not make sense. It clearly does not work in Brennan's case, and it would put him more at risk for infection or compromised organ function that would disqualify him from transplant. The doctors are trying to contact the donor today. We are to meet later this afternoon to discuss details. Believe it or not, and assuming they can pull all of this together, we are hopeful that we may be afforded a window to come home for a few days before it all starts. Brennan is dreaming of his new puppy, Lucky, who has been waiting to meet him since Christmas. And the team believes such a trip could be vitally important for Brennan's spirits pre-transplant.

Back in the apartment, I wrote down my thoughts for a blog entry while Nat watched football and began helping with Orange Bowl snacks for the little guys. When we had the opening, Tara and I embraced for a long time. We simply smiled at each other and talked about how, since being here, we had received so much confidence from parents in worse situations.

As they came back from a movie last night, Brennan told Tara that he was changing his word for the year from "shine" to "believe." His light had gotten us all this far. His "belief" would carry us the rest of the way.

We are still giving Christopher a leave on his word, but spending so much time with him lately, I know it will be "love."

They say it's going to snow today.   —NTS

Crossroads

As Brennan disembarked the airplane in Augusta to meet his puppy, Lucky, one could not help but think of this trip as a first "hello" and last "goodbye." Had we accepted the offer to proceed with transplant at CHOP and not achieved remission, as our then current circumstances provided, this truly would have represented Brennan's last step onto the tarmac, his first and last greeting with his first and last puppy. But now, it was a leave before we were given, by grace, luck, and a tenacious little boy, one last hand in the game.

When everything in the world to which you place meaning begins to literally slip between your fingers, the sense of foreboding is suffocating, like a mountain of wet dirt towering above you, teetering at the angle of repose, pouring down in sheets as it envelops your being, one heavy layer at a time. The weight of panic and confusion prevails. It's only a residual glimpse of clear sky above the dark and cold peak that lets one summon a tether to the other side, despite the enveloping darkness.

Every single chip we retained in the gamble for Brennan's survival is placed on one color, one number. This soldier has his back against the wall and only one way out of the fight (alive). We have been told over and over again: "It is imperative that he achieve remission to qualify for transplant." We learned this in Philadelphia. It was reinforced by every single other pediatric oncology institution we encountered. St. Jude too had reinforced this premise, not only in words but through their painstaking efforts to obtain a second remission. Now, like a gambler anxiously shaking his dice while his mind races through plans and delusions about the future, we retained hope and fought skepticism, knowing that everything depended on this one roll.

To Brennan and the boys, the actuality of desperation was never really discussed. The realities of cancer and the fact that there were a lot of serious people having a lot of serious conversations around them clearly meant the stakes would be at least noticed, but the notion of finality was never to be broached. To them, we were simply going home to meet Lucky before another treatment.

And it truly was a homecoming, serving as a vital rest stop both for the boys and for us as parents. The furry little puppy delivered the greatest dose of needed energy as these hitherto unacquainted partners greeted one another on the tarmac outside of Brennan's Angel Flight. Running directly to the one she sensed to be in need, the loving warmth of this little puppy was literally reflected in his face. Her kisses and softness fed him the warmth of a happy and loving place back home. He saw his things. He lived in his own house for a few days. He visited friends.

He exhibited a powerful and serious spiritual demeanor in every activity during this short visit home, most profoundly as he received his (hastily scheduled) First Communion. Our parish priest, in coordination with his second-grade teacher, Ms. Ellen Hoffman, prepared his entire school for a special school Mass created so that Brennan could experience this sacramental rite among friends. To them, their hero walked in on his own two feet, proud and as tall as he could be, reflecting back to them their powerful collective energy. Other than his shining bald head, there was absolutely nothing about him that implied the proximity of death. Had we dived straight into transplant without the trip home, I am not sure how Tara and I would have managed what was to come. This trip allowed us to rest, to take a break from the hecticness of the hospital, and to recharge our batteries. It had to, as the weeks to come were a whirlwind of confusion and focus, pain and caring, hope, defeat, faith, and prayer.

Thus the two paths of time converged for a moment as we left the bubble to take a breath in the real world again. Off at the front, however, Dr. Leung and his team were marshaling and getting ready.

Our weekend pass had come to a close. And like the good soldier returning to war, we said our goodbyes and saddled back up. Brennan's second transplant was scheduled just ten days away on January 27. Everyone, even the boys, seemed prepared for something very different.

We arrived back in Memphis with barely twenty-four hours to spare. Brennan entered the unit for conditioning, which was scheduled to begin just before his eighth birthday, representing his second straight birthday spent in a hospital room. The afternoon before we checked him in, the boys reaffirmed their fraternal spirit with a game of Nerf war on Target House lawn, rolling in the crisp leaves that remained from the fall and playing as best friends with nothing else to do. The Band of Brothers arrived at the BMT still in uniform and fully armed from earlier in the day, savoring every last minute together as we checked in no sooner than "on time." The boys entered still in character, stalking their enemy through the empty corridors. Only when the elevator doors closed did I lose my composure. The echoes of the day were suddenly silent, and my mind wandered to a place that told me this may be the last time we all enter this door together.

With the breaking of a new day, the Brothers migrated to their new little school while Brennan got ready for transplant. His conditioning treatment had been customized for his unique situation, including the use of a drug called Plerixafor which was to mobilize his T cells to more actively enter his bloodstream prior to his receiving total body irradiation ("TBI," which occurred two times per day for a week).

Beginning with the irregular schedule of the TBI, where he required anesthesia both first thing in the morning and at night, his internal clock started to spiral. Able to visit him in his transplant room, the Brothers never knew if they were going to find him smiling and playing or groggy, nauseous, or sound asleep. And despite his usual tenacity in handling the medications like a champ, as we approached transplant, he too began to change.

The two temporal worlds were firmly diverged from their singular places, one with the Brothers, their school, and their attempt to be regular kids while their brother fought for his life, and the other in transplant, as we daily/hourly watched every sign that he was responding in a positive way. The relics were always nearby, and we graciously accepted the gifts of the biweekly Eucharistic minister who would visit Catholics in the hospital on Wednesdays and Sundays. We even began to plead for prayer in our blogs, requesting scheduled hours of focused prayer, or simply meditation from our non-Christian friends, believing firmly that the energy garnered collectively could be directed to a single intention.

The first such request was at the time of transplant on January 27. We gathered around his bed and held hands, and we could feel the energy from outside as thousands of people prayed around the world. Simultaneously the bag of red stem cells slowly dripped into his IV. It too represented yet another prayer from another human being with no knowledge of the boy whose life was being affected. Whether together or alone, I would regularly find myself pleading for this little boy and the others with whose legion we shared, every single child, each with his own family, his own friends, his own life, his own disease, his own soul.

But as things become more intense, the reality of the conscious mind takes firm hold of one's thoughts. It's like treading water alone far off in the ocean, waiting on the reality of the inevitable, but praying for a boat. You never stop swimming until one or the other takes final hold. But as the battle continues, the wavering between faith and hopelessness envelops the mind, like vines choking a tree, or like cancer itself.

The intensity truly began to take hold with regard to the uncertainty of the transplant. Ultimately, the capacity of the eventual new immune system from this kind, unknown donor must demonstrate some symptoms of graft-versus-host disease, seemingly the only remaining weapon to kill his leukemia and win the war. The drugs had failed. It all came down to the life cells of another unknown and unrelated human being and to the prayers of the world.

Every subsequent day became a confusing swirl of focus on both Brennan and his brothers. And in the midst of caring for kids in these two radically different worlds, we were obliged to maintain our own sanity, or at least appear like it. Everything just seemed to take so long. And when word came after the transplant that the hospital was to stop visitation of children under fourteen to the BMT due to an RSV virus outbreak, the disunion of our two realms of time and experience affected us like a nation by secession.

We got word of this major policy change from a nurse one evening with the Brothers gathered in Brennan's room. Like the innocent messenger telling the commander that his unit was being split up, this nurse left our presence with more sneers from our side than gratitude. But she was simply caught in the middle. Caught off guard in the room watching Disney Channel, the Brothers did not grasp the meaning of the news until they were leaving, being told that they would not see one another for what was basically sugarcoated as an indefinite period of time. Brennan, having felt lousy and nauseous anyway, had asked to turn off the TV before they left. This was met with an objection from Christopher and resulted in a short, sharp altercation between the two Irish twins, with Christopher calling Brennan names from the hall. Brennan replied by thrusting his back toward his little brother as he left. Shutting the door, Christopher stormed down the hall, fuming until we reached the car. It was then that it kicked in for us all. Driving to our Target House apartment in angered and frustrated sadness, we each peered through the drizzle of our assigned car window to watch the outside world click by through the light of our individual fears, governed by our individual minds.

Tucking the boys in that night, I knew we would be sending them home to Augusta soon. With Brennan's status questionable and his health literally in a tailspin, it seemed like the right thing to do. Why make them suffer through being in this cold, wet, strange environment to be with a brother whom they were not allowed to visit? And perhaps Tara and I should accept the opportunity to focus 100 percent on Brennan as a gift.

But the day that the boys were to leave for home, I felt in my gut that it was wrong.

My distracted subconscious told me over and over that the bond between these Brothers was the most precious thing in their lives. We had to keep them together at all costs. Nat underscored this imperative point of issue as his mother dropped him and Christopher at the airport to return home with their grandmother. Thoughtfully reading the inscription at the St. Jude plaque installed at the Memphis airport, "No child should die in the dawn of life," he asked his mother the first point-blank question of his experience thus far. "Kids die at St. Jude, Mommy. Do you think Brennan will?"

But we managed the transfer of the heartbroken Brothers. The ensuing weeks were a blur of confusion, anxiety, hope, frustration, prayer, and determination on the transplant front. Wavering between the helplessness associated with the post-conditioning/pre-engraftment health issues of constant nausea, pain, fevers, and diarrhea, our strength as nurses and caregivers was stretched to the limit. Many times neither of us could gather Brennan to the bedside potty in time to prevent the mess in his pajamas or get the vomit trough under his chin in time. We would often change sheets five times per day. There was another major fungal infection scare, manifest with daily fevers over 103. Delirious midnight bathing episodes to wash his paper thin little body of our failures would generate spontaneous declarations of love and forgiveness. "That's all right, Daddy," he would say in his kind tenor. "Just being with you and Mommy makes me feel better."

And our lives somehow kept going. The ensuing weeks were held together primarily through prayer and the continual gift of both friends and strangers. Thanks to the generosity of an anonymous blog reader, we rented a proper house in downtown Memphis, giving us a material incentive for the Brothers to return as soon as was practical. And we were making friends from new, non St. Jude–related families like Jimmy and Margie Lackie, who opened their guest house to give us a quiet, comfortable home to rest and regroup outside of the ambiguous environment of patient housing. Brennan's story was affecting others, revealing that goodness does exist even in the confusing world of war.

Within a couple of weeks, a tenuous ANC began to emerge, offering signs that engraftment was possible. The counts wavered daily, and at times success felt more elusive than possible. Tara and I lived on adrenaline and instinct, often getting through the day only because of the hands that had been extended our way. Our capacity to chronicle our lives through the blogosphere allowed us a medium through which we tried to articulate our reality without revealing the cracks that were becoming more and more evident in our daily armor. Indeed, but for the blog records, I am not certain I could adequately recall the details of that period. Our diaries reflect confusion and the shock we were enduring. But we had to hold it together as we hunkered down and fought for our child.

We Stand Alone, Together
Posted Feb 24, 2010 1:36am
(Day Plus Twenty-Seven post-transplant)

The innocent young man accused of a capital crime, on the eve of his verdict, gets little sleep. The mother and father of that young man would trade places with him in a second if it would eliminate even the risk of his life being cut short. The fear is too raw and overwhelming to describe. Suffice it to say that with every muscle trembling to hold on, each second that ticks by is painfully precious.

We have been on pins and needles since last Thursday when the doctors began to express concern about the lackluster progress of Brennan's ANC, and therefore the transplant itself. Dr. Leung was very upset on Friday when the bone marrow biopsy was delayed. "I need this information in order to move forward! We cannot make decisions in the dark!" He expressed this on more than one occasion.

With Brennan's ANC floundering at 100 for a few days, the team of experts who designed his protocol were growing impatient. Their impatience, while tempered by cautious optimism that the leukemia burden would be minimal, signaled to us that we had reached the point where the rubber was either on the road or not.

Our nerves were on high alert. At times they were off the charts. I prayed volumes in milliseconds. Looking back now, as much of the sense of urgency conveyed by the docs was rubbing off, we were way guilty of reading too much between the lines. "Is the fever graft-versus-host or the fungus? Is the rash now where doctor Leung wants it, or does it need to get worse? Why is the ANC flat? Why is it dropping? Why is he sleeping so much? Was yesterday's ANC increase an anomaly?"

Throughout it all, I must admit that Brennan was strong and, as long as we were around him, we were too.

One evening, I had been up literally for the last two nights with occlusion alarms ringing constantly on Brennan's IV pole while Brennan had been wavering between fevers, demanding either attention to play games, or simply needing a father's hand. It became my turn to get some sleep away from the hospital. And with inconclusive daily reports as to whether or not the ANC was improving, I needed some rest, bad.

Yet back at the rental house while Tara monitored our soldier, I was unable to keep my mind off of things. With ice dancing as the main winter Olympic coverage event, I switched over to a late-night airing of *Forrest Gump* in an effort to divert my mind from wandering, and often times taking me to dark places I would rather not consider.

Watching this movie, I recollected the first night over a year ago in the mountains when Tara and I first knew something was wrong with Brennan. The scene arrived in which Forrest runs to his mother's bedside, where she tells him, "Son, I am dying."

"Why, Mama?" he asks, triggering the famous line, "Honey, life is like a box of chocolates, you never know what you are going to get."

With this, I switched off the TV and threw the remote, ran upstairs, and screamed, "Stop it! It is not a box of chocolates. We know what we want, and we are begging!"

To distract myself from that distraction, I started reading the nearest bedside table book. It was *The Guns of August*, about the beginning of WWI, which I had picked up in fits and starts for several months. The Germans had just routed the Russians on the eastern front and were about to rout the British and French for an early end to the war when the tide started to turn. And as I read, I realized, "Hey, the good guys end up winning this thing." The demons began to slip away.

Think of life as an arch with the apex representing the midpoint between birth and death. Then imagine a second curve superimposed on it, one whose apex comes much sooner, with a much longer downward gradient on the back end, more like a wave than a bell, gradually washing onto the beach until it trickles away. That curve represents one's capacity for experiencing each day with vigor and zeal: "seizing the day," "carpe diem," "smelling the roses," whatever the cliché. With most of us, there is a definite point where we cease dwelling in the moment as a habit. Our present experience is eclipsed by earthly pursuits.

But occasionally, life throws us a challenge in the proverbial box of chocolates that, I believe, suspends that descent for a time. Sometimes it is bitter and hard to swallow, but it is real, it is raw, and it is life. While our initial response may be of regret and sorrow, shouldn't we also try to feel gratitude, deeper understanding, and appreciation for the love that we all share despite our challenges? That's the part we must cling to.

I arrived from my night of confusion to find Tara up early and at our soldier's side, all anxious, like me, about what was about to be the most telling bone marrow aspiration yet. I walked in to find Brennan up early! He was sitting up in his hospital bed with the alacrity of someone who has just returned from the spa, freshly pampered and clipped and full of color, intently working a jigsaw puzzle of a golden retriever. He was smiling and, with the exception of his haircut, was 100 percent Brennan.

Glancing at the Winter Olympics coverage on TV as we wheeled him down the road for the procedure, he said, "Man, even in the Olympics those Germans are still pretty tough. Aren't they, Daddy?" He was cheerful, beautiful, and strong, gripping my hand tightly and calling our names as he drifted off. The results would not be available until the next morning, when Mimi was to arrive for the overdue return of Nat and Christopher.

• • •

As soon as they touched the ground, Mimi took over at the hospital, allowing Tara and me to welcome the boys at their favorite Memphis restaurant (the Flying Fish). Their smiling hugs immediately anchored my shifting focus, even as they went straight for their mom. It was clear Nat had been afraid to leave Augusta, and before we started eating, he asked some hard questions about Brennan and what "could" happen. Leaving his friends and St. Mary's is always tough for Nat, and I could sense the strength and compassion in his return.

Although they could still not visit Brennan because of his isolation status, they could get a glimpse of him via the "fishbowl" waiting room just outside of the BMT unit. This is the little cylindrical-shaped glass room where the sisters of Cassidy Clark (a fellow AML warrior and transplant patient, and from North Augusta, South Carolina!), Mackenzie and Savannah, have effectively been spending their days doing homeschool and playing games in an effort to be close to their sister who is undergoing her transplant. This family refused to allow "isolation" to totally separate their kids from one another. It seemed appropriate to bring the boys here first, introducing our boys to these girls and for them to learn that "feeling distance" is better than long distance.

As we waited for Brenny to get wheeled out to his side of the fishbowl, the boys bashfully walked up to the Clark girls. Not much eye contact was involved as they timidly said hello. But within minutes, they were playing cards and chatting. We were grateful to see these two sets of siblings in identical boats, getting to know each other in their home away from home. And as soon as the walls were down, Brennan and Cassidy rolled up almost simultaneously, acknowledging one another shyly across their little blue face masks. Rolling to the windowed partition that separated them from the fishbowl, each child placed their hands to the glass to receive the warmth from their siblings' palms on the other side. Our boys were back together. There was a new energy about.

The next morning, I dropped the Brothers off at the Montessori school. They left the car smiling and happy to be back (what a relief!). After putting things at Target House in place for the boys' return, I absolutely crashed, feeling almost delirious from anticipation and exhaustion. Napping restlessly, my mind once again began to wrestle with Brennan's unknown verdict when Tara called: "He's in remission!"

It was almost unbelievable how Tara received this news. A Eucharistic minister from St. Mary's church in Memphis had walked into Brennan's room to offer Communion. Brennan happened to be awake and alert, playing with Legos and feeling good. His grandmother Susan was also in the room, and as the minister was delivering the host to Tara, the nurse practitioner peeked her head in and said, "I hate to interrupt, but Dr. Leung wanted me to tell you that Brennan is in remission!" News delivered with Christ present.

Everything since has been a whirlwind. Phone calls, email, texts, blog updates, all of the positive commotion that comes with the thrill associated with announcing the unbelievable. But while celebrating tonight in the reserved but warm comfort of our two other sons, we are trying to temper our sense of accomplishment. Having lost what seemed to be a surefire remission once before, one can get gun-shy. But, I honestly admit that it feels different this time. It is too unbelievable not to be true.

And then there is the step of getting Brennan out of the BMT unit and reunited with his brothers. He's got a long row to hoe. The fungal infection is still there. The kidney function is still woefully off course. The high fevers must subside before he can be discharged back to Target House.

It was quite an announcement to Nat and Christopher as I picked them up from their first day back at the Montessori school. I waited to tell them until after they were in the car. Driving over the bridge back into Memphis, they were not initially jubilant as I had predicted to myself. Instead, they seemed to sit back in their seats and sigh in relief. Quietly gazing across the reflection of the city buildings in the river below, the afternoon light brightened Nat's little face.

It is as hard on them as it is on us. But the band of Brothers fights together. They have emerged from another long, cold battle to face the next challenge. Hopefully, the worst is behind them. The war wages on and these boys stand alone, together.   —NTS

Behind the Night
Posted Mar 5, 2010 8:00pm

Faith is much more easily summoned the day following hopeful bone marrow biopsy results than the days preceding. I won't go into any more redundant detail about the agonizing mix of emotions on the clinical days of a remission's retrial intended to confirm the judgment from two weeks ago that Brennan is in remission. Hopefully, as time goes by, Brennan's prognosis will give substance to a proven pattern of improvement, rendering these trials to routine and relatively stressless procedures. At the same time, having had such regular and recent firsthand disappointment, if we did not admit being a little gun-shy, we would be much less than truthful.

This is particularly true when the biopsy, which was to have been part of a routine schedule, is moved up two days because the doctors see symptoms as "discomforting."

The discomfort was triggered because Brennan's ANC dropped suddenly and sharply to a level that was well below the comfort zone for a transplant patient thirty days out. He was therefore back in the hospital. On the morning of the biopsy, I was sitting alone with Brennan, sleeping in his room, when the doctor came to look him over and confirm the agenda. His comment was: "He looks healthy. We feel positive the cold is the culprit

121

here, but the ANC level is not good." The alarm unleashes the reflex to hit the foxhole.

In such situations, Tara tends to listen and absorb the down and dirty medical information with a much less paranoid sense of interpretation. At least she does not show it, as far as I can tell. For some reason, my nature is to try and read between the lines. "What does he/she know that they are not telling us?" It is truly more of a reflex than anything, representing what I assume to be a reversion to some sort of ancestral survival instinct. Whatever its source, it produces feelings that run through the veins with coarse and arrhythmic regularity. The net result is little rest and zero comfort. The mind wanders and obsesses about things that have nothing whatsoever to do with the circumstances, wandering from where it should be focused: on Brennan and our family.

Despite his beautiful company, it is awfully quiet in his room. Considering his fevers, he is asleep quite a bit, or when briefly awake, quietly watching TV. But when he is lucid and alert, he is who he has always been, grounding me back to the state of being a dad and a friend, laughing up recollections of old practical jokes, talking about what we are going to do this summer.

Pondering a book of fish, he asked, "Daddy, did Pops catch a stingray one time?"

"Yes, he did, Brenny. A big one, too."

"Daddy, has anyone ever caught more than twelve fish in a day? You know, I caught twelve fish at the river one time. I think that might be a world record?"

"Yes, Brenny, I think so too."

He is weak, but he is strong, and he always brings me back.

On a brighter side of the coin, we are comforted with the presence of the Brothers back in our daily lives. No coincidence in timing of their return, as far as I am concerned. All I can say about these two guys is that they are awesome. Their friendship is deep, and their capacity for entertaining one another is tremendous, despite their age differences and often times conflicting interests. Nat is the sports guy. Christopher is James Dean.

Nonetheless, their quiet understanding of why we are in Memphis and why they are relegated almost exclusively to one another's company and spare time spent in hospital waiting rooms (the fishbowl with the cafeteria being the highlight of post-school social life), as well as the gravity of what is happening to their brother, eclipses the territorialism that would exist under ordinary circumstances.

From Christopher's signature outfits to the beaming pride he expresses when we pick him up from school reporting that he is learning to write in cursive, or that he and Mr. Fletcher are building a raft to float on the lake, he shows such a strong and independent spirit that comes totally from him—certainly not from our instruction.

Nat, our serious and quiet elder statesman, is mastering the hula hoop! Telling me that he could do it for thirty seconds at a time when he arrived here last week, I now have lost sixty dollars (wagers are over) and he is up to close to thirty minutes without stopping. He smiles and waves to me when he gets out of the car, a mannerism I feared had been lost since first grade, when he would exit into the carpool population with too much grown-up coolness to say goodbye.

They make us smile. We need to smile. Our little windows of time with them suspend fear and, although we often worry about how they are dealing with everything, the comfort that we are all in this together is perfectly understood.

Occasionally, one of them will ask a tough question about Brennan and the consequences of leukemia and cancer. Tara and I have consciously not forced the subject, but this being a world where apartments become vacant because of other kids dying, this realization is compounded.

I do not want to even imagine where we would be had we listened to the experts that day in Atlanta and ignored our hearts. One thing's for sure . . . we would not be here.

Wednesday night, the evening after the biopsy, Tara and I drove back to the hospital with the Brothers following an early dinner. She and I were to relieve Aunt Susie so that we both could spend the remainder of this symbolically important day with Brennan. He had specifically requested us both to be there, and we complied, despite the clear disappointment of Nat and Christopher that they were, once again, being passed down the line.

We were driving onto the St. Jude campus through what we call "the back gate," entering from the north and providing a gateway adjacent to the BMT building. Looking up from the car as we drove past, I could see lights on in Brennan's room and the flickering colors of his TV through the broad plate-glass window. Being in "isolation," he had a large corner room that could be observed from two sides.

I knew he had been asleep for most of the day, mildly hung over from the biopsy anesthesia. But noticing movement through the glass, I felt a jolt of mild surprise and announced to the car: "Hey, guys, look at Brennan's room up there. You can see his TV, and someone's walking around."

Nat and Christopher immediately said, "Stop—let's get out of the car and yell up to him so he can see us."

My conditioned reaction was to ignore the pleas and drive on. We had to coordinate with Aunt Susie, who was here helping; we couldn't be distracted by things like this. But instead, I said, "You guys have not laid eyes on one another in weeks. Do it!"

Pulling over to the yellow curb, we called Susie's cell phone. I could hear her telling Brennan that Nat and Christopher were out on the lawn. At that point, I thought the chances of him coming to the window were less than 50/50. He had not been out of bed for anything but the procedure and the restroom in several days. He was weak and hampered by at least a half dozen IV-related connections. But before we could walk out of the car and position ourselves on the dormant grassy road shoulder, waving our arms and shouting to our partner up in the window, his silhouette stood above us with arms raised, waving his reciprocal fidelity.

The passion was more than enough to imply his smile. We could all feel Brennan's gratitude and happiness. The Brothers cheered. Partitioned by two stories of bricks and mortar, we were all back together for a moment and we were all good.

The mood continued Thursday in Brennan's sunny little hospital room. Tara and I felt we were going to get some good news. The "other voices" had been absent until I looked up to see the doctor and PA walking into Brennan's room, washing up before entering with the verdict. I admit skipping a beat or two and reaching over to hold Tara's hand when we saw smiles on their faces. Their response was, "Things are good, and Brennan can leave the hospital for Target House this weekend." The final analysis about residual disease presence wasn't complete yet, so I had been reluctant to even begin writing this entry. I do not want to build up a fever of accomplishment, knowing that an infinitesimal presence of disease in his system is too much if we are ever going to declare true victory. It only takes one little weed to ruin a promising garden. But he was being discharged!

And here we sit. Brennan had a great night. He is back in Target House for the first time in a week, not having had a fever of any substance for two days. And he just looks better. He got up early today and received the best measure of medicine money can buy, nestling into his first dose of *Beverly Hillbillies* reruns from his new DVD set. He loved it, belly-laughing hard.

It is dusk on Friday night. I am standing at the threshold of our little halfway house; the boys, Tara, and Aunt Susie are inside. The blue skies of the bright blessed day have passed the baton to the evening light, and all is good. The blue is still up there behind the night. I just saw it, and it will be here tomorrow.   —NTS

Something's Brewing
Posted Mar 12, 2010 3:20am

The Minimal Residual Disease analysis (MRD) still shows microscopic bits of disease in Brennan's system. He is back in the hospital, and we are still on the roller coaster. Between the arrival of Lego packages mailed to Brennan from grandparents, I had been taking trips to the Walmart in West Memphis, Arkansas, almost nightly, texting Brennan photos of Lego boxes from my cell phone to ensure that I would be delivering the right product. His fevers were incessant at that time. He was nauseous more than not. And as his fevers burned, his work too was heated. He began to build, working on his projects feverishly. And then . . . he started to paint.

While our firsthand experience relates to only a handful of facilities, I am confident that there is not a pediatric hospital anywhere without an abundant arsenal of art supplies. Kids like it. It distracts them from the more uncomfortable issues at hand and, in many cases, offers them a medium through which to express themselves. Every single wall at St. Jude's is decorated with artwork from patients—some childishly rudimentary, some very sophisticated. Others deliver powerful and often heart-wrenching messages, some obvious and others more enigmatic.

Brennan, and indeed all of our boys, has enjoyed painting as an activity since preschool. While none of them ever fully put it aside, Brennan's interest was more than rekindled with the onset of cancer. The interesting thing that Tara and I noted during the "early times" was that each painting he created was identical. A single tree alone in a field. We never asked him about it or directed him in any way. He seemed called to it. It is just what was transposed from his heart to the paper or canvas.

Almost immediately after the first transplant, the subject changed slightly. Instead of one tree, there were two. And as his expression evolved, we never talked with him about it or attempted to encourage any variation in his work. As the trees multiplied and took on more detail, so did our hope and confidence.

Freudian symbology or not, we both thought this transformation represented a breakthrough with regard to Brennan's subconscious, telling him and those around him that things were better inside.

But after relapse, he not only slipped physically, but his creative side suffered. Efforts to focus on Legos resulted in many half-completed endeavors. Whether coloring, drawing, painting, building with Legos, etc., he was tired. His efforts were still there, but listless. Along with his taste buds, hair, and appetite, they just seemed to be gone.

On the day he started to paint again, we were too distracted by the medical stuff to notice any difference in his new creative endeavors. We were simply satisfied knowing that he was semi-active. After focusing on a presentation pad with his colored pencils for an hour or so, he pushed the work table away and sat back, arms confidently behind his head, and began to watch

TV. Tara noticed the change in his demeanor and walked over to see what he had done.

She slowly lifted the paper, smiled, and turned to reveal a picture of a volcano erupting. Gracefully whisking reds with yellows, purple with gray, an effusion of meaning emerged from his heart to ours.

Tara and I have talked about the volcano a lot lately—something potentially destructive, but with all of the ingredients necessary to deliver new life to a planet. A volcano, of all things, has become a new symbol of hope for us. The drawing resides on the wall of his new room in Target House today, reminding us that we are close to the tipping point of this journey.

On the day of the volcano, I stealthily left the hospital to the brothers' school around one-thirty (two hours before final bell), collecting them for a surprise field trip courtesy of our new good friend and landlord, Jimmy Lackie. Jimmy called me earlier in the day to let me know that the Memphis University basketball coach had given clearance for the Brothers to attend an afternoon practice.

Stealth was required for two reasons: (1) I was taking the guys out of school early for an unscheduled event and wanted it to be a surprise for them, and (2) when we first got the invite, we were under the impression that Brennan would be getting transfusions all afternoon and would not know anything about it. Unable to participate in basically anything that the others guys do for fun, particularly in public places, he often feels left out and different. I am embarrassed to admit, therefore, that much of our conversation about outside activities is censored, obviously in an effort to eliminate any unnecessary emotional injury for a boy who has had more than his fill of it. You can throw all the chemotherapy in the world at this guy, push him literally and physically to the brink with pre-transplant conditioning, poke him, prod him, make him exist in a world of vomit, diarrhea, fevers, and fear, but leave him out of the mix with his brothers, and you better stand back. When word gets out about them going to a basketball practice or Chick-fil-A, he erupts.

But keeping the Brothers completely quiet about their activities was impossible. With people in and out of Brennan's room, news about the basketball practice leaked out. He shut down on the outside and started brewing on the inside. One will never know if the emotions contributed, but by 7 p.m. his fever was over 100. By midnight, his fever was 102, well beyond the maximum threshold of 101.3 that required hospitalization. For three straight days he fought fevers and slept. Few smiles. No art. None of the cultures revealed infection; organ functions appeared to be sound. But inside, he still brewed.

The physiological phenomena occurring is all a sign that the real fight for Brennan's life is underway, well below the surface, and that his spirit is as strong as it ever was. The occasional burst of flames and lava reveal themselves in the form of fever or a bedpan full of vomit.

And through it all, the drawings and paintings are coming forward at a furious pace. This afternoon, we stumbled across a drawing he did early today. It was of a heart. It was accompanied by the following words: "St. Jude loves you. WE WILL help you."   —NTS

4

REPRIEVE
FEBRUARY TO OCTOBER 2010

A loud, hollow silence permeates the brain after the bombs have fallen. The bullets are no longer thwacking into the dirt around you. You are no longer lagging behind in the mud, screaming for your soldiers to "KEEP MOVING!"

Ears are ringing; feeling is coming back to your fingers. The divergent dimensions of time are converged as one again. You are in one place. There is suddenly slightly more time to think about what has just happened— what you've missed, what you have to do, what could have been. And you pray that the next path is layered and reinforced from the humility of the way prior.

Initially, you feel the reflex to hit your knees and offer devotion to something much greater. But another reflex rings as an intuitive warning not to allow oneself to forget the servility through which the reprieve was granted. On your knees one moment, begging God for strength, you don't want to be someone who simply stands up, says "thanks" for a moment, and then shrugs it off for the next chapter. There are plenty of emotions that must be shed in order to get back up and live again, but one must be careful not to lose the understanding that every moment experienced with awareness and gratitude is a gift that cannot be rejected.

We accepted the news of remission with exhaustion. We felt surprise, as well as sincere yet deferential thanks that our war may be winnable. And while Brennan may have been the one with his life on the line, I felt like I had been the one called into the office of the Almighty to beg for peace, forgiveness, and another chance. Emerging from those imposing, awe-inspiring halls back to the everyday world was like stepping through a portal from one world to another. While the rest of us weren't taken to the physical brink Brennan was, we all felt equally exhausted.

We had been doing everything in our power to deliver normality to the boys since our arrival in Memphis, but between the sterile environment of a leukemia patient and the remote likelihood of another remission, it was clear that, despite my best charade, I was far from walking the confident path. I cannot imagine how the Band of Brothers could have looked at me during that time and not sensed a manic nutcase through the façade of their father. One day I am dragging Nat and Christopher to Beale Street for fun, the next day I am dragging them to Mass. The next, I am holed up in my chair, staring blindly across the yard in deep thought and prayer while they simply do their own thing. And in the hospital, one moment I am building Legos with Brennan in deep concentration; the next I am at his bedside, clutching the relics of St. Therese and her parents; in another I am in the parent room, weeping after a brutally honest conversation with Dr. Leung, trying to compose myself so that I can appear strong at Brennan's bedside.

Yet a day or so after receiving the remission news, I was walking with Nat and Christopher across a cold, wet downtown Memphis side street, talking about getting Brenny back with Mommy, all under our new little rental home's roof. And I smelled barbecue.

I ordered a fresh homemade brisket sandwich at our new neighborhood corner grocery while the Brothers jostled from aisle to aisle, intently musing over whether to invest in candy or chips. The man behind the counter studiously prepared my sandwich as someone would for himself. We knew each other from sight, as I had been shopping there since Brennan was admitted for his second transplant. I watched quietly, peering over the deli case, when he turned and pleasantly handed me the finished product. "How's your son? You know I know about him because of your other boys out there, and I just want you to know that I knew a kid who did not make it, and that I pray for your family."

The boys held their little bags of candy while this man and I talked about the life and death of children.

As I walked outside, the sun was reflecting in the wet streets, and I somehow felt happier and more awake. Similar sentiments had been related to me in countless mediums over the past year, and I had often accepted them with poorly reciprocated platitudes. But looking in that man's eyes, I felt his emotions. I physically understood that to whatever meaningful degree, his life too had been affected by our experience and Brennan.

The man who made my sandwich really told me nothing new. I was just listening without the immediate burden of fear. How many times had we made acquaintances and friends with other families with equal or worse chances for survival? And how often did I allow my heart to open for them as this man had for me? I was in my own foxhole; they were in theirs.

Yet that day, I began to feel the sun again. And while still quite winded and uncertain from the days and weeks prior, I felt that I could look in the eyes of the stranger passing me by. Having been focused totally inward toward the survival of my son and on his potential departure, my capacity to reciprocate emotion had been choked. Yet finally, there was some respite.

Looking back, I could see how much of my time and energy had been consumed by fear. Fear is revealed in selfishness. Faith, I decided, is realized through love.

Yet this man's reference to that one nameless child who had not survived forced me to finally recognize that the battle never ends in everyone's favor. Some walk away. Many more do not. Yet all, presumably, prayed to survive through whatever medium or faith instruments they had. But when the shells stop flying, regardless of whether our personal wish list to God has been obliged, all walk away with an abundantly more open conduit to the unknown.

Moments of awareness do not always occur on some vast mountaintop. As we made our way back to the apartment, the sun had emerged long enough for the boys to sit on the porch steps and eat their treats. Sitting back in a weathered and faded porch settee at our new little neighborhood abode still damp from the long, cold winter, I noticed couples pass by with their kids and dogs, some nodding "howdy." Life was starting to flow again in both directions; the circuit breaker of constant fear had broken. Soon all five of us would be together again, away from the heat of battle and, presumably, closer to home.

While Brennan's post-transplant little body had withered into a sickly shell of his physical self, he too was looking forward to a game plan that got him out of this hospital and into a normal living environment. Unfortunately, the new little place we had rented in downtown Memphis was off limits to him for the foreseeable future, as the St. Jude housing had been designed specifically for kids with his immunological deficiencies. Target House offered air-filtration systems, handicap accessibility, and a community. The other house was simply waiting. Home was waiting. One long step at a time.

We had a boy to heal, fatten up, and get home. He was sickly, and yet he was emerging with all of his beautiful spirit intact. We had two other boys who had become deficient of love and attention and two parents deficient at providing it. Their spirits too were strong, but they had been neglected to a large degree and were long overdue for some normalcy. We were still reeling.

The adjustment would be gradual, particularly for Brennan, who for the most part was no longer an ordinary member of the community who could come and go as he pleased, eat what and where he wanted, play whatever and whenever he wanted. Like most returning from the battle, we were all coming back different. We had assumed many new lessons and rituals that, tested in the most trying of circumstances, should sustain us in the ordinary.

After transplant number one, we had expected to win and to get back on our ordinary tracks. To a degree we now feel more hardened, but abundantly more learned about the power of spirit and the staggering capacity for human knowledge to understand when it is called to fight.

Here Comes the Sun
Posted Apr 23, 2010 11:03pm

After dropping Nat and Christopher off at Maria Montessori school yesterday morning, I was feeling energetic and full of life. It's hard to put my finger on it other than to say that it was a refreshingly nostalgic sensation. The feeling was not too far from those special and liberating childhood experiences like exploring the beach on my bike alone, or the conscious sense of freedom I had as a young adult moving into my first apartment. While not a novel feeling, it was fresh in that it was overdue.

Earlier in the week I was home in Augusta for work purposes. Knowing that MRD analysis was due any time, which would let us know whether or not Brennan's remission had truly taken hold, and not knowing how I would react if the results were not fully favorable, I was uneasy being away. I needed to be at this meeting for just two days, but at the same time I really wanted to be with Tara and the boys when the results were delivered. But almost immediately upon arriving in Augusta, and diving into some relatively exciting work, it did not take long for the veil of vocation and service to blanket the emotions. Fortunately, so many people back home followed Brennan's situation with such sincere interest that I did not have to wander far without someone asking about him and how we were all doing, bringing me back to the fact that the future of each member of our family would be affected by the results of this one test back in Memphis.

Driving across the bridge to North Augusta on Tuesday morning, the cell phone rang. Having just spoken to Tara a few minutes prior, I hit the "talk" button nervously.

As soon as I said hello, she said, "Point zero one eight."

"What?" I said, being hard of hearing anyway, but not totally on the correct frequency.

"Point zero one eight. I just talked to Susan in the BMT clinic, and she said that Brennan's MRD showed .018 percent leukemia, down from .56 percent six weeks ago. Dr. Leung says this is close to a 100% decrease in the disease burden. Susan [Shelton, another one of Brennan's favorite P.A.s,] said she just received the email and had to call immediately. Everyone in the B Clinic is very excited about the news. His disease burden is considered negative!"

"What does it mean? Does it need to be zero? Will there be maintenance treatments? Is it low enough that the body will keep it in check?" I asked these questions even though I knew the news was very good. Just last week Susan told us that if Brennan's MRD ratio was the same or better, it meant that we would be able to come home soon.

On the other end of the phone, Tara was busy with Brennan cleaning out our storage bin at Target House, already moving him and his stuff to the little rental house downtown where all five of us could live together. "I am squeezing him into the car so tight right now that I don't know what else to say. Susan kept saying over and over that his leukemia was 'negative.' We'll talk to Dr. Leung later in the week."

I told Tara to give Brenny a big hug for me, hearing her saying, "This hug is from your Daddy." She got back on the phone and asked me if I could guess what kind of response he had. "I can see him smiling right now," I said.

The rest of my work trip was a formality from that point forward. The only thing that I could really think about was getting back to Memphis. I did have a couple of important meetings and needed to do a few errands. But the back-and-forth focus from work to Brennan was pretty much squelched. Just enough "back" to get through the day with enthusiasm and plenty of "forth" to fly back to Memphis with good vibes on all sides.

The next day, when Tara pulled up to the baggage claim at the Memphis airport, the tinted rear window of our car rolled down to show Brennan's little face smiling ear-to-ear. "Hi, Daddy," he yelled with his grin, his chin tilted up so he could see over the door.

I got in the car and squeezed him hard. He was visibly proud. Tara and all of the boys were big-time happy, giving knowledge that there was nothing to be afraid of right now. Driving into town, the conversation bounced between the prospects for playing on the junior golf tour this summer to hunting, fishing, and all things boyish and fun. For the first time since all of this started, all five of us talked openly and together about Brennan's disease as something that could be behind him soon, and that our family life would begin to take shape again.

The next day Brennan woke up, collected his little book bag, organized his things on the kitchen table, and asked for help doing his homework. He really didn't need my tutoring, just someone at his side. But with his mind focused on the mini word problem, his head leaning while it rested upon one hand (with the other grinding the pencil down on the paper the way little kids do) and his tongue sticking through his lips in deep concentration, I just stared at him and thought about his miracle. Not the miracle of a CURE, but the miracle of his being in our lives, the strength that he has delivered to our family, and the gifts that we receive every single day from people we love.

Settling into our chairs for a meeting with Dr. Leung about the MRD the next day, our question was simple: "What does Brennan's MRD mean long term? Can his body manage this degree of disease burden on its own, and will it ever get to zero?"

The clinical side of the conversation was pretty quick. The short answer was yes, his body can manage it. However, Dr. Leung tells us that he has had patients who have shown no traces of disease but who have relapsed ten years later. The bottom line is that the leukemia is not going to give up, but, if working properly, the immune system keeps it in check. And Brennan's newest one is off to a powerful start.

With the new immune system maintaining a strong graft-versus-leukemia effect, our job as caregivers is to keep him healthy so as to avoid chronic graft-versus-host disease (GVHD), which is effectively a hyper-reactive graft-versus-leukemia effect. In other words, in addition to attacking the leukemia, it attacks its own body with life-threatening consequences. According to Dr. Leung, transplant patients must maintain a healthy system for two to three years before chronic GVHD can no longer be considered a threat. In Brennan's case and at this point, it is to be avoided at all costs because treatment would necessitate the use of high-dose steroids and other immune suppressant medications, which would weaken his immune system and thus present opportunities for the leukemia to break through the barriers holding it in check. We must carefully consider various environmental

135

factors that might trigger an immune response. In effect, the entire outside world threatens as a trigger in some form or fashion.

Heavy exposure to the sun is a major one. Dr. Leung has had too many patients come back in for treatment and even die because they went on a cruise or a family trip and the patient couldn't bear not being with the siblings. Other triggers include basically the same things we were to avoid after transplant number one: detergents, extreme dryness and humidity (particularly in situations that he is not used to), pets, mold spores, and of course viruses, bacteria, etc. Every detail of every daily activity must be considered with extreme care. It was a good meeting, but a serious one.

In one way, we had received beautiful news that Brennan was allowed to participate in life again. In another, all of the conditions were very frightening. So while we may have crossed from the heat of battle, we also know that we have a long way to go before we are free from this war. In Dr. Leung's words, "While I will not say that Brennan is cured, he now has a fair chance."

When we met Dr. Leung last October, most doctors were giving Brennan no chance. At that point in time, Dr. Leung's exact words were, "Your son is at the bottom of the barrel of a bad batch of apples. What we need to do is to get him into a new barrel. From that point, he has a chance to get cured."

Looking at Brennan feeling so strong and so happy today, I think we can say "mission accomplished." Over the next several weeks, he will undergo basic organ function evaluations and some physical therapy, and then we can pack things up for good ol' Augusta, GA. The timing will be perfect, as the Brothers will be getting out of school at about that time and can finish things up here in Memphis with their new friends and enjoy their Augusta buddies over the summer.

We are looking forward to our last month here in Memphis. No treatments, no terrifying verdicts. Just me, Tara, and our three boys, living life and being together. We are not compelled to live like we are dying anymore . . . at least for now.

It's been a long and lonely winter. But I can say, it's all right (ta da da, ta da da, ta da da, ta da da, ta da da, ta da da da da daaaa). —NTS

Find Me a River
Posted May 18, 2010 6:01pm

An awesome guitar music playlist helped us float down the late afternoon highway. It was both shady and sunny, under the kind of billowy and colorful skies that emerge when there is almost a thunderstorm. I would peek in the rearview mirror to see Christopher looking out at the fields clicking by, army helmet bobbling from side to side, and murmuring his own personal lyrics to the music.

Suddenly he began to pepper me with questions: "Why does the river flood?" and "Are we still in the 'country'?" and "Why is there an Augusta here in Arkansas? . . . Is this home?" and "When will Mr. Fletcher and my friends get to the mountains?"

Christopher was outfitted for our adventure, which was to take us through uncharted countryside for our first Ozark Mountain experience. Having packed all of his essentials, which included a WWII helmet (complete with captain's bars and the "Easy Company" spade on the left side, an essential feature of the Band of Brothers uniform) and a blue plastic rifle, he was finally in a place where he could be the focus of my attention; no discussions about hospitals, no shared time with Nat, no interruptions on my phone. Alone in the backseat, he personified everything about a little boy that was worth fighting for.

It is fair to say that while Tara and I conjured every ounce of energy and tapped every resource we could find to save Brennan, the other boys had been somewhat unfairly pushed to the backseat. For the first few months of his existence in Memphis, Christopher literally lived in the hospital with Brennan. No days outside. No riding his bike. No soccer team. No golf. The wingman goes with his lead, and Christopher's life was that of an inpatient on the leukemia wing, sans treatment.

Tara and I remained confident that, after Christmas, Nat would make the adjustment to being a fourth grader at a new school despite his tearful reluctance to. And he did. He just buckled up and fit in. Nat's fundamentals were sound enough for him to adjust to just about anything.

But when Christopher (aka "the Babe") first became a student at Maria Montessori, we had been concerned that he was falling between the cracks. The first graders there, all of whom had been part of the Montessori experience since preschool, were years ahead of Christopher with regard to the unique teaching methods that would be impossible for a child to adapt to in such a short period of time, much less halfway through a school year.

He was still trying to read *Go Dog Go*, and these kids were writing in cursive. At first, we kept him with the pre-K and kindergartners (who were also writing in cursive). With his inborn sense of humor and unconventional knack for fashion, he quickly established himself as a sort of "new boy" icon. But they were simply too young for him, and the way they looked up to him made it hard to identify with his classmates.

A student without a class, Christopher became something of a general school mascot, jumping in with the pre-K folks one day and the older kids on others. But from the very beginning, he began to gravitate more and more to the school's outdoor education teacher, Mr. Fletcher.

Christopher's adjustment rallied through his time with Mr. Fletcher and with the responsibility he assumed through his instincts as wingman, particularly through an outdoor education project where the children hatched a school of rainbow trout, an annual tradition concluding in their release into appropriate waters. As progenitor of this little hundred-gallon microuniverse, Mr. Fletcher and his kids cared for everything related to the growth and well-being of the little fingerlings until they could be liberated into the wild. Christopher not only took an honest interest in the fish, but in the garden and the various school improvement projects that fell under the jurisdiction of Mr. Fletcher. As the fish matured, the garden grew, and the projects emerged, so did Christopher.

We used to joke that while Nat was adjusting to his new fourth grade class, Christopher was migrating toward a vocational education. But as Christopher assumed his new roles with Mr. Fletcher, he began to shed other inhibitions and insecurities about school. His reading improved, he began to show off his prowess in math, and his critical thinking and creativity flourished.

Most of this, of course, we attribute to this school in general. It was the right place for this little boy who had been taken from home to battle his own little baby demons as he fought alongside his brother. But most of it we attribute to Mr. Fletcher and his unique gift for listening to kids and sensing what it is that they require.

Getting to know Fletcher Golden over the past however many months, we learned that he had played his own role of wingman back in the mid-1960s. Fletcher did not talk about it much, other than to let us know that his little brother, who was less than a year apart from him (the reverse scenario of Brennan and Christopher), was diagnosed with leukemia and treated with the chemotherapy drugs of the day (which, shamefully, have not changed much at all since). Like Brennan, Fletcher's brother too relapsed. They lived in Memphis then, but St. Jude had not yet been established, and his care options were very limited. As a result, Fletcher's brother did not survive. While the brother suffered, Fletcher's dad told him to stay by him and protect him. And that's what he did. He stood by his brother.

Today, he is standing by and protecting a seven-year-old wingman who has been thrust into the role at a much earlier age. But Fletcher stumbled upon this little boy who is currently bearing the same cross he carried forty years ago. And Christopher, at a crossroads that could have directed him upon a path with unpredictable pitfalls, has stumbled onto the one guide who has traveled this road before. Coincidence?

So with two weeks to go before school is out for the year, and roughly two weeks to go before Brennan is given official clearance to go home, the "trout release ceremony" was scheduled. Punctuating the end of an amazing school year, it represented a rite in Christopher's life that both celebrated this unique student/teacher relationship and delivered symbolic closure to this amazing time of physical and spiritual growth.

On the day of the release, Tara, Nat, and Brennan were in Augusta, preparing for the big move home. Hopefully, Brennan's current leave from the hospital will be his final one from major treatment, with trips back to St. Jude only for checkups and potential maintenance. We are praying that he is now positioned to declare full-fledged victory someday. Regardless of the future, this milestone is worthy of celebration—a celebration that is proper only through the acknowledgment that the war still wages on long and hard for many.

For a number of days, Christopher debated going home with Brennan to see his classmates from Augusta, but Tara and I agreed that the trout release represented much more than an outdoor education experience for him. Our decision to stay was the genesis of our road trip. We would spend the evening and day together until the trout delegation arrived from the school the following morning.

When we pulled into Heber Springs, it was sunset. The place reminded me of a small Georgia farming town in the mountains. The main street was relatively intact, with just enough antique and knick-knack stores to let you know that this was a true middle America tourist destination. Checking in to the white clapboard Anderson House Inn, we found that the proprietor was across town chaperoning the high school prom. His fishing buddy was filling in; and being unfamiliar with the credit card machine, he gave me a key to the room and told me that they would "deal with the money stuff sometime over the weekend."

Christopher sherpa'd three bags up simultaneously, bouncing off the narrow stairway as he struggled to lift himself without complaining, a true soldier. Our door at the top of the stairs was closed, but with no real latch, it was rigged so that it could be pushed open. When we told the front desk guy later that the key didn't work but that the door did, he said, "Most of 'em don't. I wouldn't worry about it."

We were feeling happy to be together and were invited by the hotel chef to our own little father-son dinner in the dining room. It was perfect. Christen, the manager, took a strong liking to Christopher and indulged him with Shirley Temples, home-battered chicken strips, and the dessert of his choice. He barely made it back to the room before he was dead asleep, ready for the big day Saturday. We slept with the windows open.

Fletcher and his wife, Jean, met us at the Highway 110 bridge over the Little Red River around 11 a.m. They were a little late getting out of Memphis, having waited on some release participants who ended up not being able to make the journey because of Mother's Day weekend obligations. We were disappointed that there were no other students there. But Mr. Fletcher was there, as were the fish, and he was a pretty good friend.

While our greeting was warm, Fletcher and Jean seemed to be concerned about the fish, many of whom had apparently perished on the way up due to either mechanical malfunctions or temperature issues in the tank. Nonetheless, some were still fighting, and we quickly toted the survivors to the riverbank.

There were just the four of us walking into the water on this fine spring day; but there were a lot of serious people already fly fishing at this destination, well known for its trout fishing. They watched with strange curiosity as we walked into the water with a cooler and a net.

It was freezing. The sandbar to which we walked was halfway into the river, which in this cold almost seemed too far; but the baby trout needed to be in the channel. Christopher toted the net while Fletcher and I lugged the big cooler over the deeper pools.

The first wave of hatchlings floated downstream in flaccid stillness, so Fletcher's concerns were clearly warranted, but they were mitigated by a handful of seemingly healthy fish who swam off quickly, darting across the stream with vigor. Swoosh . . . welcome to your new world. A few stragglers lethargically barrel rolled in the shallow water until righting themselves and swimming away, but most did not make it home alive. Christopher reported confidently that fifty-eight fish were strong. His optimism helped ease a little of Fletcher's heartbreak.

Then the three of us, much to the chagrin of the fishermen around us, dove into the freezing water, baptized by Christopher's positive perspective on the day and its accomplishment. We felt invigorated, and dried ourselves hastily with only our dirty clothes behind the car. Our ears burned from the cold. The peaceful easy feeling clung to us as much from the deed as from the river water, and we drove off feeling good from a job well done. No regrets. Just hope for next time.

For Christopher, his little graduation ceremony was officially an accomplished sacrament, although I am sure he was still feeling energized and relishing the many great new experiences. For me, as we drove homeward into the sun, I could only think about the fact that we were exactly three weeks from driving all five of us to Augusta, pending the results from a final batch of tests. In between lay all of the logistics of organizing the move: packing, shipping stuff, trying to organize things on the home front, delivering reasonable expectations to the boys about life "back home," and managing Brennan's new lifestyle restrictions.

But even greater than the anxiety associated with moving is the pending sense of emptiness that we know we will experience when we leave this place. It is very hard to explain, but having lived in the middle of the childhood cancer world for so many months, sharing so much with so many other families who are dealing with the same issues and fears, the notion of leaving the predictability of our little aquarium for the unknown and often cold waters of the real world outside weighs in a powerful way. It is really over.

The biggest unknown, of course, is with regard to Brennan. There is also the fear of getting back into the game of making a living and balancing that with so many new priorities in our lives. First and foremost, however, there is the strong desire just to be with these boys under normal circumstances and live even a little bit of a normal life. See some sights. Smell the roses while they still bloom. Celebrate this gift.

Being somewhat in tune with the natural cycle of things, we are noticing that many of the families with whom we have become close are also on their way home and have expressed a shared anxiety about leaving St. Jude. It seems peculiar that there is such strong attachment to a place that one struggles to leave. There is always the gravitational effect of family, regardless of its eccentricities or unorthodoxy, so I guess the sense of kinship and love that has developed between these kids and their families is not surprising. But a lot of it has been due to the fact that we have been living this experience, day in and day out in the same aquarium, shoulder-to-shoulder with so many others who were/are driven by the same proclivity to press on.

As we enjoy our final days in Memphis, Brennan gets stronger every day, and with his strength grows our ongoing belief that he may indeed be the first statistic with regard to a cutting edge new therapy for AML bone marrow transplantation. Every day he takes it upon himself to write a letter to someone or to make a "God's Eye" out of yarn and popsicle sticks to help brighten someone's day. This morning, he took it upon himself to make a batch of brownies (start to finish) with absolutely no supervision whatsoever. He read the box, cranked up the oven (much to our surprise), and baked the darned things. I found out about it when he walked upstairs and delivered two hot brownies to me while I wrote this journal entry.

So there continue to be many reasons to believe in what is possible, and countless reasons to be grateful. As we approach the last pre-departure hurdle, we continue to pray constantly and to hopefully prepare ourselves for life in our rightful habitat. After all, we are not jumping into the river for the first time. We've been in the water the whole time. We're just out of the tank and headed home.   —NTS

Gratitude for a New World
Posted Jul 11, 2010 11:02pm

We made it. 2103 Gardner Street looks the same, despite quite a few unpacked boxes begging for relief. It feels the same, despite the surreality from having not been here for so many months, and it smells the same, too, which to me is the most poignant of the senses.

The back door remains unlocked almost around the clock. To the pleasure of houseflies and moths, it is open more often than not, as the boys scuttle in and out on a seemingly constant basis, visiting back and forth with the Berry boys next door. These kids are so happy to be reunited that a revolving door is under consideration. And the bugs . . . I do not even have to open my mouth anymore to drive this point home. Both the neighborhood kids and our own boys see the vented frustration through the volume of my door slamming, after which time someone blurts out, "Sorry, Daddy, we forgot to close it."

But as I catch myself scolding the guys about the little things, the sternness of my delivery is more often than not concluded with an apology. When I find myself slipping into the role of taskmaster, fuming about the inconsequential, I am now more inclined to catch myself and ask, "Is it really worth getting angry about?"

We are home, away from the daily war on cancer. We are grateful, and despite more than a few lifestyle adjustments, we are all party to a miracle that reminds us every moment of the day to be conscious of this privilege, even if for a fleeting second.

All of our lives and schedules are driven by Brennan. "All for one and one for all," we have embraced the rule of "lowest common denominator." Until the new lifestyle controls that keep his remission on track become second nature, everyone is making sacrifices for the common cause that pale in comparison to what Brennan has done and must do. Compared to the things we were doing in Memphis, we feel liberated.

Brennan's routine, while rigid and far from the liberal summertime lifestyle he was used to pre-leukemia, is mostly indoors and delightfully slow. Same rules as before regarding fast food, sanitation, etc. With public places out, we find ourselves sitting around the table as a family at least twice and even three times a day. How often do we lament the absence of the family table in today's world? Now, it is the welcome by-product of nothing much else to do.

His fledgling new immune system is keeping him alive. From this perspective, he is like a newborn again; his system is only as old as the transplant itself. And while his hair is back, and he once again looks like just another skinny little boy, we must think of Brennan as a baby who must be constantly monitored. Fortunately, most of the precautionary measures taken to avoid chronic GVHD are things that he is already used to, such as face masks in public places, the constant washing of hands, eating at home, and redundant lectures to grandparents and guests to cover their mouths, use hand sanitizer, etc.

The most hyper-cautionary approach to any of these changes, particularly since we live in the hot South, is with regard to the sun and the heat. Since his central line was removed, he is able to swim (and loves it!), but we are only able to do so around dusk or at night, and we must be somewhere where we know the conditions of the pool, who's been in it, etc. So when we find a pool we can use, it is not exactly what the boys have in mind. The few choices we do have are rarely bestsellers.

As parents, our biggest challenges are related to the Brothers and the illogical reasoning behind the residual nature of these restrictions on their lives. The lowest common denominator rule is not something we expect to follow forever, but we find it helpful and even necessary until we can ultimately find balance between the old world and the new. Therefore, Nat and Christopher are spending an extraordinary amount of their summer inside, too.

Being home is in many respects harder than being at St. Jude. Having work obligations right around the corner, but a kid at home who has earned time with you, creates anxiety and feelings of foreboding that are hard to explain. Tara and I have hundreds of people to thank here in town, many of whom we should embrace and hold tight, yet at the same time, I find myself avoiding crowds. We are slow to find the groove.

When you look at Brennan's lifestyle changes . . . When you sit back and think about all the kids and families we have met and grown close to along the way . . . When you think about the kids we've met who have not made it home . . . When you know others we are close to who will not become adults . . . When you sit at your desk and don't feel the passion . . . When you go to a party and have a hard time carrying on a conversation . . . When you fight every globule of your brain to stop thinking about side effects that Brennan will most likely have as a result of his treatments . . . When you find yourself on your knees every single morning of every single day . . . You know that it's just never going to be the same. But you also know that you could never be more grateful for anything.

While each week is a little easier, the experience gets no less profound. Two weekends ago offered up one of those wonderful spontaneous times when we all gathered with old friends at a family farm near Sylvania, Georgia. There were close families, fresh tomatoes, hamburgers, sweet corn, watermelon, homemade ice cream, and a clean pool with late afternoon shade. And at twilight, it meant we (including Brennan) could fish for red-bellies in the cool, dark water of Briar Creek. The enveloping canopy of ancient moss-covered hardwoods has embraced this beautiful little stretch of paradise for centuries, and for a couple of days, we had a taste of summertime the way it's supposed to be.

That Sunday morning, Tara and I intended to make it home by noon. But a plentiful supply of pecan waffles and fried fish kept us lingering a bit too long, so we decided to join our friends at the charming 1827 Red Brick Methodist Church along the old country road.

Folks park along the sandy lawn adjacent to the old church cemetery, but we were a bit late in arriving. Walking up the worn stoop, the muffled sound of "How Great Thou Art" on an old-timey sounding upright piano could be heard from outside. Our clandestine efforts to slip in during the last verse were blown, and twenty or so smiling nods greeted us after the large wood door let out a slow, loud squeak, almost as conspicuous as the waft of hot air that was blown inside. Some were in their Sunday best. Others, in coveralls, represented people who had work to do, being in a farm community. But freshly groomed hair or a crisp shirt offered a sufficiency of Christian reverence.

About the only noticeable change from our last visit here several years ago was the steady hum of an air-conditioner. Last time it was also summer, but we were relegated to using funeral home fans made from cardboard cutouts of Jesus, stapled to tongue depressors. I cannot forget the Rockwellian comfort of ordinary-looking old folks harmoniously sweeping their paper battens to and fro. But today the sanctuary was pleasant, and, despite the heat and our earlier stress to get home "in time," it delivered an immediate sense of comfort and relief. Quoting the gospel of Mark, the short but stern-looking female pastor, Kitty, sweetly reminded us, "Whatever you ask in prayer, believe that you have received it and it will be yours." She preached about the necessity of truly believing in the fulfillment for which we pray. As we listened, Tara pointed out to me in the bulletin that "Brennan Simkins and Family" was on the prayer list. I looked around at all of these simple good folks, most of whom we did not know, and thought about how many others we had never met.

I looked into Tara's eyes and was overcome with the realization that, throughout this entire experience, we had never not believed in Brennan or in the hope for his treatment options. And while I often articulate my fear for his life, my spiritual wavering—the ways in which I have been emotionally affected by all this, his prayerful connection to me—has never trembled. Wiping my face, mingling tearful eyes with a sweaty forehead, I considered the promise that his most recent treatment is now offered to others, an odd yet purposeful prayer for those fighting leukemia who we may never meet.

In our case, the obligation of the present is to share the confidence and love that has been bestowed upon Brennan and our family to others we meet along the way. We must accept the love directed to us and consume it while sharing it. And while we may struggle to focus in our own efforts to pray, we know that the love directed toward us must simply be accepted. That is the belief that is necessary within the power of prayer. Acceptance is the only thing we have the capacity to control. The rest of the cycle is in God's hands.

While the person we pray for may be afflicted by a terminal illness or find themselves in a situation where survival is unlikely, we need to remind ourselves that we are all terminal. Like the soldier who knows he may not make it to the end of the day, the bottom line is that, whether it happens today or long after the war is waged, the gig will be up. Why not, therefore, focus our energy on what we can accomplish right now?

Like the soldier who finds himself frozen because of fear, our obsession about the "what ifs" of tomorrow can be equally debilitating. I know because I have cowered in that foxhole and have brushed up against the temptation to quit.

I remember sitting with Father Jerry Ragan in his office with Tara before leaving for St. Jude last year. I was a basket case, finding my mind slipping into awful mental screenplays about funerals and how different members of my family and Brennan's friends would react in the worst possible circumstances. I was obsessing about these types of thoughts almost every minute of the day. Who would the pallbearers be? What music would we play? Keeping my composure for several weeks prior to departing for Memphis was one of the most difficult assignments I had ever faced.

After I told him this, Father Jerry turned to me and said, "I cannot imagine a more difficult cross to bear than that of a parent and a terminally ill child. And when you look to God for answers, the most difficult thing we must embrace is, 'Thy Will be Done.'"

But if we reconcile ourselves with the fact that God's will is what it is, then I believe that we can focus our prayer and our energy in changing our perspective about the amazing gifts that every single human being has, and to share each and every day that we take a breath. Not the gifts of privilege, but the gifts of love that can only be experienced without the burden or fear of what we cannot control. These are the gifts that we can share regardless of our station. This is the gift that delivers us from the foxhole.

Brennan's spirit is a gift. Over the past many months, it has proven to be his most valuable asset. It has allowed him to face so much adversity with courage and an appropriate amount of naiveté for him to avoid subjection to doubt and cynicism. He believes in his family and his friends. He believes in his peers who have supported him so wholeheartedly. He believes in his doctors. He knows of tragedy with regard to other kids he has met along the way, but he sees himself as a kid who is fighting his own fight. All of this mindset represents the aggregate of many things from many people and many experiences. It is the product of prayer.

I write this with apprehension that my point will somehow be misconstrued, that people will assume that I have it all figured out. Far from it. Almost every waking moment of every day for me right now is dominated by my own struggle to fend off the selfish thoughts and doubts about what has happened here and to accept the love directed my way from others. Tara and I happen to be living between our old lives and the new life that has been granted our family; consequently, we spend a lot of time with one foot in one world, one foot in another (and our thoughts in another one altogether).

But as anyone who has fought alongside a family member or friend in a situation like this will tell you, my eyes are more open, my ears more receptive, and my tongue more at bay as I fight to accept God's will, knowing that I cannot afford to waste my time fretting over that at anyone else's expense. I am not going to waste my fear of a brief remission at the expense of accepting love.

• • •

On the fourth of July weekend, we had plans to visit friends for the fireworks celebration at the lake. But one of their kids had a virus, so we found ourselves home in Augusta with no real direction or plan. It was a pretty weekend, and unseasonably cool, so we talked about getting our own fireworks, playing some golf, cooking out on the grill . . . It looked as if we were being handed an awesome, spontaneous weekend, with both feet in a world that we knew and appreciated.

But halfway through an afternoon round of golf, Brennan hit the ground in pain. Literally carrying him off of the golf course to the ER with the other boys left standing, mouths agape, in the vacant fairway with their Aunt Martha, Tara and I were instantly reinserted into the dreamlike world of frenetic hospital activity. A little morphine later and well past midnight, he came home, albeit upon my back as we traversed our way backward through the turbulent logjam in the hospital waiting room, overflowing with holiday emergencies. Seemingly filled with distraught parents and children crying, some in splints and others vomiting and bloody, the room was a stark reminder of what we had yet to escape. It was as if we were making our way backward through the Styxian marsh to solid ground.

But the solid ground was short lived, and maybe not so solid after all. The next morning, the pain recurred in church. He withdrew from a junior golf tournament two days later, screaming in front of a hundred-plus concerned kids and parents as we whisked him away while the two Brothers stood, once again, mouths agape on the golf course.

As a precautionary measure, Tara and I left for Memphis the next morning with Brennan to rule out our unrelenting worst fears. It sounds hard to believe, but walking back into that hospital delivered to me the most unexpected sense of security I had felt since we left in early June.

Don't get me wrong, we have been far from homesick for St. Jude. But there is something about being there. The natural light everywhere, familiar faces, and just being around others who understand life in two worlds. Part of us will always be there anyway.

Of course, we would rather have been returning for something scheduled; however, within what seemed like a few minutes of arriving, even before the triage folks could see him, Dr. Leung happened to walk by with a couple of his colleagues in deep conversation. After we flagged him down with a loud, "Hey there!" he immediately turned to us with a smile, leaving his colleagues stopped in their tracks so that he could greet Brennan. Bending over so that he could talk at eye level, he said, "I told your parents that you were supposed to take it easy, and I hear you are playing golf and swimming all the time. But you look good."

The ultimate affirmation came this past Saturday when the MRD analysis showed that Brennan tested negative for leukemia. His remission is still solid. But the bone issues he's experienced are real and remain. We will manage the osteopenia at home in Augusta. It threatens his quality of life, and therefore, his beautiful and happy outlook; but, as parents, it is the kind of problem we prayed for.

Both feet straddling two worlds, seeking balance in a third. I guess it is what we've been doing all along. Brennan has just given us the capacity to see it a little more clearly.   —NTS

5

BATTLE OF THE BULGE

FALL 2010

The improbable summer had come and gone. The war seemed distant. Our leave had opened our eyes to a much broader horizon, which gave prominence to the fragile balance of peace.

Another season may have simply passed by to many in our community as they put away the things of summer and prepared for a new school season and the last quarter of a productive work year. St. Mary on the Hill had reconvened, this time with an unexpected yet anticipated participant at the annual First Day's flag raising ceremony. Distinctive in his floppy khaki anti-sun hat and blue face mask, but proudly reciting the Pledge of Allegiance, hand firmly across his heart, in unison with the assembly, he was the same: a peer, a classmate, a brother. Yet also a survivor.

Nothing in life ever turns out exactly as one dreams, but this was pretty close. We had made it further than anyone predicted. The battle lines of old were way in the rear, and like the 506th in the fall of 1944, we were facing what appeared to be a guardedly confident march forward, toward victory.

Our big guns, no longer necessary for our daily life, had been mothballed to make room for the tools of a more civilized routine.

And then the horizon erupted, and the tanks came rumbling out of nowhere.

I can look back on the calendar and give a more exact number of days between the touchstone of school starting and the "routine" appointment at which we heard that the leukemia was back, but it was no more than a couple of weeks. We could not have been caught more off guard than we had been even at the beginning of this entire conflict, almost two years prior. But when it came, we stripped off the civvies for khaki almost unconsciously. And while we felt as if we may have been ambushed, at least we were rested and tested enough to don our fatigues and pick up a rifle.

I am convinced that we would have collapsed from depletion but for the brief respite. As we drove back to St. Jude, shifting gears for round three, Tara and I thought back to how many kids we knew who had fallen subject to such detestable fates. When one considers those we just knew would survive, those who have not, and those who still fight, the body literally aches. Fate is at hand for us all, but on this battlefront we walked toward the fray with blind faith and accepted its reality, again, with sickening fear.

The nature of cancer is war. And while the inherent behavior of all life is to thrive through the adaptation of newer and often more aggressive traits that improve the capacity for survival, the cycle of life inherently requires the destruction of something else in order to continue. Animals eat, and nearly everything we consume was alive at some point. That which seems abhorrent preys on the innocent. Weeds thrive in gardens. Vines consume forests. Insects feed on the wounds of harmless mammals. There is murderous behavior, ruthless competition, war, cancer. The history of life is generally a chronicle of changes in behavioral traits, and it is a portrait of Being as affecting other beings.

In war we see humans in their raw essence, and life at its microcosmic core. But simultaneously, the promise of peace, as experienced through the spirit and the acceptance of love, is also possible and real. The powerful desire to achieve this is reflected in how we dedicate our hearts to beating something so unmercifully in the simple biological sense.

Death and tragedy are never not there. But in such blatant and overbearingly aggressive mediums as childhood cancer, we struggle with both through the fight and our ability to live simultaneously as we struggle.

As Abraham grudgingly climbed the hill with Isaac, feeling the end, he still believed that God would deliver his son and absolve him from his decided path. Lee, sending Pickett's boys up the hill into certain death, was faithfully performing his duty to, hopefully, finish the war once and for all. And the same commanders from Normandy fed troops into the Bulge so that they might hopefully hold long enough to regroup, establish a valid plan, and win. They knew boys would be sacrificed, as in the battle before that, and before that, and before that . . .

It seemed that with every major setback, we never had time to doubt ourselves. I think the urgency in the question to try again when even the attempt before was deemed impossible was as much related to our medical team's knowledge and their capacity to offer a real option quickly. Had we been given more time to think, as with the three weeks of planning prior to transplant #2, we might have become more doubtful. The issues of dropping out of our recently reacquired and comfortable lives back home, or the collateral potential and concern of hard fiscal disappointment, were never considered.

So we left it all behind again. Not yet knowing what was in store, we effectively went from the flag ceremony to Target House, for what we deemed to be an ordinary checkup. We moved the kids from St. Mary's back into the little Montessori school seemingly overnight. And for the next six months, we did it again. And again.

Once back in battle, it was not necessarily painful. But the fighting was intense, and we had to make decision after impossible decision to "take the hit" and "keep moving." It was all or nothing. It was an overwhelming time of physically intense prayer, extraordinary personal doubt, and a fierce commitment to each other. And through all this, we were numb enough to keep it going.

"Here we go!" . . . explosion . . . "Keep moving!" I can't see, where do I go? "We are here, this way . . ." Light. "Heads down, move forward!"

I don't know how our spirits absorbed it. No one knows how Brennan made it day-to-day. Reverberating concussion after reverberating concussion, we held on to our boys, we told them we loved them, we prayed, and we did our best to inspire.

The spirit experienced a place where, in the heart of the maelstrom, there is a ringing, senseless absence of sound. So you move forward through the char-flattened wasteland to the light that glints ahead.

And one day, with ears still ringing and the morning sun beaming to our prostrate minds in the grass, we felt life caress our spirits like a melody from nothing.

> Half a league, half a league,
> Half a league onward,
> All in the valley of Death
> Rode the six hundred.
> "Forward, the Light Brigade!
> Charge for the guns!" he said.
> Into the valley of Death
> Rode the six hundred.
>
> —Alfred, Lord Tennyson

And one was our eight-year-old boy.

The Long and Winding Road
Posted Sept 15, 2010

Just days ago, I was generally hopeful and feeling a taste of the old normal. Brennan has been and is feeling strong, and he looks great. More and more, we find ourselves reining him in like a regular ol' eight-year-old boy. He's climbing trees and fences. Football is now something from which he must be restrained, where just a month or so ago it was something he simply could not physically handle.

With the relief of fall in the southern air, the last scheduled trip to Memphis was to have been the kickoff to this promising new season away from the hospital. While the primary purpose for the trip was for medical checkups, it delivered our family a small opportunity for reunion with our Memphis friends. We planned this particular trip as one would a holiday. The medical stuff seemed an obligatory sidebar.

We headed west down US 78 through the beautiful Mississippi hill country until the serenity of the countryside was broken by the outer sprawl of Memphis.

"Are we in Memphis?" asked Brennan, to which we both replied yes. "Yeah!" screamed the backseat simultaneously. The convenience stores and shopping centers began to flip by at a more regular pace, letting us know that we were truly closing in on our old home. Suddenly, Brennan asked, out of the blue: "Am I going to die from leukemia?"

"No!" yelled Nat and Tara simultaneously.

Engrossed in my iTunes and not having heard the question clearly, I asked him to repeat himself, but everyone told me to drop the subject. When Tara and I had a chance to talk about it later, she told me what he had asked. It was the first time he had asked a question in this way. It was the first time he had ever acknowledged his mortality. It came from nowhere.

That first morning, I dropped Tara and Brennan off at St. Jude on my way to the Montessori school with the Brothers to reunite and visit with their old school buddies and teachers. Mr. Fletcher was in his customary carpool line spot, greeting each child as they scuttled from the car to the school house, and Nat and Christopher arrived happy and eager to visit.

Back at the hospital, I found Brennan and Tara in the BMT clinic just prior to his physical examination and biopsy from Lisa, one of his favorite nurse practitioners. Lisa was raving about how good he looked. She said his weight had returned to a normal percentile for his age group. Rubbing his new crop of wavy black hair, she said, "Everything looks fine; you're doing great, Brennan."

"His blood work looks great, although his platelets have dropped a bit," she said to me, "but we do not expect anything abnormal on his pathology. It is the MRD that is the important test."

"You don't expect any surprises there, do you?" I asked, knowing that she was required to give me the party-line response. But she said, "Anything but a good MRD would be a surprise."

While Brennan underwent the bone marrow aspiration, we had lunch with Jeni Clark, Cassidy Clark's mom. The Clarks had recently learned of Cassidy's second AML-related relapse, and they were already back at St. Jude, following "Brennan's Protocol" from his second transplant. It was great to see Jeni, who is always cheerful and full of moxie, despite the intensity of their reality.

Afterward, in the recovery area, we found Brennan awake, sipping a Coke and eating Oreos. It was his most energetic post-recovery effort to date, and within a few minutes, we were exploring the hospital in his wheelchair and shopping for St. Jude T-shirts and such. The rest of the day was splendid, and when we arrived in the parking lot of the Montessori school, Tara received a call telling us that the morphology report from the aspiration "looked good, and Brennan showed no signs of leukemia." Just the news we needed for a celebratory afternoon at the little school with the boys and their old friends along the banks of the river. The whole trip was going exactly according to plan.

As I was shaving the next morning in the hotel after hitting the snooze button at least twice, my cell phone rang. I walked into the room to answer it in my towel, shaving cream still on my face.

"Mr. Simkins, this is Ruth from B Clinic. Do you have a moment to speak with Richard about your son's MRD?"

"Uh . . . sure," I said. In a flash I recalled the last time I had received this call in July, and how the nurse practitioner, rather than diving straight in and saying, "Good news!" had dragged the subject out. "Mr. Simkins, we have reviewed the morphological data associated with the MRD analysis, and the report is negative. Congratulations." The five seconds it took her to say this seemed like an eternity.

This morning, I got the same mantra, only the ending was different.

"Mr. Simkins, we have reviewed the morphological data associated with the MRD analysis, and the report is positive. Will you be available to meet with Dr. Leung at 10 a.m. to talk about your options?"

I was speechless. Hesitatingly, I replied, "No problem," and hung up. The weight pushed me down onto the bed to the extent that I noticed Christopher's feet were being smushed under my rear end.

"Get up, boys, we have to go to school," I shouted, feigning impending tardiness. Nat quietly slipped out of the covers and into the bathroom, confused as to why we would be taking them to school again (they had just visited yesterday, but it was the only thing I could think of to keep them occupied and away from what was going to be a brutal conversation at St. J). Christopher said he would get up if I dressed him. As Nat did his thing in the bathroom, I slipped into the hallway to call Tara in the room with Brennan.

What a difference a day makes.

I said nothing to the boys at this point. Loaded up and on the road to school, then the hospital, I found myself nervously tapping my foot and slapping the steering wheel, waiting for the light to change. I was reminded of the time last January when Nat and I sat at this same red light on our way to the grocery store when we received news that Brennan's chemo protocol had failed and that we could be out of options. Like then, Nat was talking away to me, oblivious to my mental state of affairs.

The boys greeted Mr. Fletcher, who looked concerned about this unannounced visit. Tara and I waved "good day" to the Brothers like any other ordinary school day, while trying desperately to calmly leave for our meeting at St. Jude. Brennan adamantly refused to be left there with his brothers or to leave us for a Childlife specialist. He did not want to leave our side, as if he sensed something in our behavior.

When we arrived, Brennan was (thankfully) removed to an examination room to have a cough he'd developed checked out, serving as a minor blessing to me and Tara, as Dr. Leung otherwise has no qualms about speaking frankly in front of him. He is a "say it like it is" kind of guy, which we admire greatly; but it just was not what we needed at that time. Tara and I adjourned to the consultation room with Dr. Leung to talk in more detail. Brennan's MRD report showed that he had 2 percent abnormal cells and a drop in the number of T cells. (This would have been undetectable by conventional laboratory methods, and therefore would have gone unnoticed by the vast majority of cancer institutions, very few of which have MRD technology.) The test results represented that a relapse was imminent.

As of now, we had two options. The first was to do nothing. Dr. Leung explained to us with very careful and deliberate language that Brennan had far exceeded the level of treatment that most kids would ever receive in a lifetime. Therefore, many families at this point would choose not to subject their children and families to the stress and inevitable complications associated with any further level of treatment.

The second choice was what they called a "haplo-transplant," wherein the cells of a parent (who is a half match) would be used in a very risky third transplant. He spoke with confidence and with a lap full of copious documentation revealing what appeared to have been a very methodical strategy. I assumed he had been up all night figuring out what, if any, weapons we retained to keep fighting. In actuality, he had been working on this, just in case, for months. Tara and I had given blood samples the previous year, and it had already been determined that my blood, should we choose this route, was his best option. With only one half of the cells compatible to his, however, this method would ensure a significant graft-versus-host situation and establish a full-scale immunological attack against this uncompromising disease.

In other words: Brennan's cancer does not respond to chemo, and the last two stem cell transplants were too closely matched to keep it under control. We need new weapons. We need to invent weapons.

Dr. Leung explained the extreme risks of this procedure and that, indeed, St. Jude was the only institution in the world that would offer it as an option at this time. Having had some success with haplo-transplants in the past, he offered us comfort that their experience was such that, should we choose this, we were in the best possible place to attempt it.

He also explained that, as with any transplant, we had advantages and disadvantages. The primary advantage was that Brennan was strong, much stronger than he had been in January when, according to Dr. Leung, "Our backs were truly to the wall."

"To be quite honest," he said, "last time I was not optimistic for success. But we had no choice. Brennan's heart has gotten much stronger since having had a full summer's respite, and his liver and kidney functions appear to be significantly improved since he was here last. The disadvantages are the simple risks associated with the GVHD after transplant, for which he will be more susceptible. And of course, there is significant risk with transplant itself. But know that St. Jude's is the best equipped place in the world to handle these risks."

Once again, the confidence that brought us to St. Jude to begin with was convincing us that we were among the best qualified people to make the impossible fight with us.

As we numbly left the verdict room, Tara fetched Brennan and took him to the cafeteria while I talked with the transplant coordinator about my schedule, travel plans, etc. I happened to bump into our old buddy Cameron Varnell's mother Allison, with whom we had grown very close during our first days at Target House. Cameron had become buddies with all of the boys, and Allison and Tara had remained in touch since. It was a true gift to find her smiling face, as well as to see Cameron and Brennan break away to drag race wheelchairs down the aisles.

Having just completed Cameron's own bone marrow aspiration earlier that morning, Allison expressed concern. His platelets were also dropping. We quietly confided in her what had just happened, so she offered to hang out with Brennan and Cameron while Tara made some calls and I walked myself to triage to give what looked like about twenty vials of blood for the donor matching process. Our heads were spinning. We needed a friend at that exact moment, and there she was.

When I emerged from triage with a big Band-Aid on my left arm, Tara was in the lobby of the hospital with Brennan, Cameron, Jeni Clark, and our friends Kim and Carissa Barnett. Carissa has been battling adrenal cancer for years, and all of her family have been close to us and within our daily prayers. Everyone in our pitiable little group was hugging and consoling Tara when a nurse from A Clinic pulled Allison aside to inform her that

Cameron had also relapsed. With fresh teary eyes, Allison then looked to me to reciprocate by taking Cameron and Brennan away somewhere so she too could have "the talk." As I ushered the boys out the door toward the gift shop feigning "adventure," I noticed the front desk attendant, who was crying as she witnessed the whole scene.

For such a weirdly terrible day, it appeared to have been oddly designed by providence. If Brennan hadn't had an emergency biopsy in July, our appointment would have been a full month later . . . and who knows to what extent the leukemia would have progressed by then. And what were the odds of so many fellow warriors standing there with us and for him? Cassidy was already here for her third . . . The fact that his trenchmate Cameron was diagnosed simultaneously with a relapse was also uncanny. Now they would fight together again; and even if divided by hospital walls, Brennan, Cassidy, and Cameron would be stronger for one another.

Before picking the boys up at school, Tara and I sat Brennan down in the cafeteria for a Coke and to explain to him that we would be coming back soon, possibly for a long time. Noticing the "blood bracelet" on my arm, he asked, "Why are you wearing that, Daddy?"

Once again, Brennan was making things easy for us. "The doctors wanted to see if my blood could help yours," I said carefully. "The test results show you have some abnormal cells. They are not leukemia at this point, but they want to make sure it does not come back. So we are going to get more bone marrow from you next Tuesday in order to determine if another transplant would help you. I would be your donor."

"OK," he said, taking a sip from his soda.

We planned not to tell the other boys right away, but we pretty much hit the road for Augusta immediately after picking them up from school. As Christopher and Nat told Mr. Fletcher goodbye, Tara asked the school director, Maria Cole, if they would accept the Simkins boys again, soon. She understood and told us that they were loved and always welcome.

Driving down I-55, we finally told the Brothers that we would be back in a few days for an indefinite stay. There was silence. There were hugs to

Brennan, who sat in the middle, and then somber glances to the passing countryside.

My grip on the steering wheel was firmly directing us toward Augusta when Tara looked at me and said, "Turner, first of all, you need to slow down. We have precious cargo here. Second, what's the hurry? We are together now, and we are still on vacation, so why not ask the kids what they want to do?"

A vote was taken. Brennan's arm shot up first as he yelled, "Target store!" Nat yelled, "Oxford!" Oxford, Mississippi, had become one of his favorite places during his past residency in Memphis. He also knew that the University of Mississippi sometimes left Vaught-Hemingway Stadium at Hollingsworth Field unlocked and accessible to kids like him to throw the ball, kick field goals, and generally immerse themselves in the feeling of being a big-time football player.

Tara's usual calm demeanor delivered the appropriate salve for my generally irritated state, so I declared, "We shall do both!" So, what could have been a straight shot to Augusta in order to get our affairs in order transformed from a tense race into a more relaxed, although significantly clouded, return trip.

We are praying for a lot of specific things right now, all of which probably exceed any sort of reasonable quota. Mostly, I am asking for strength and the ability to see God's will as something that will allow each of us to press on in our own way through our own lives.

As we prepare to leave home yet again, we do so knowing that this summer has been the greatest possible gift. We were once told that it would never come. Last night—representing our last Friday night in Augusta for potentially a long time, maybe even forever—Brennan, Nat, and Christopher led the Aquinas High School Fighting Irish football team onto the field for what has become their best start in recent memory. The team wanted to honor Brennan, who gives them the fighting spirit they need, and so the boys and a strong group of buddies thundered through the big paper "GO IRISH" banner as everyone cheered and the team roared onto the field. No obsession about the future, or cancer, or death. They were absolutely beaming.

After the game, a newspaper reporter who knew nothing of the relapse approached me.

"Your boy looks remarkably strong," he said, taking out his notepad.

"You are absolutely right," I said. "He is." —NTS

Move Forward!
Posted Sept 26, 2010 5:09pm

I think I understand the mentality of the marine who has been at it for so long that he begins to feel the odds working against him. Thoughts overwhelm me as I lie in bed fearing how the Brothers would be affected by Brennan's death. It would certainly be more than just a blow to the family. What about all of the other kids who are so emotionally committed to Brennan's fighting spirit? How would all of this affect their lives?

Again, I make mental plans of funerals and think about going through all of his things and keepsakes. The mind drags you into the worst places and away from the here and now. I was at my nadir earlier this week. It was Wednesday. Brennan's platelets had dropped from 211,000 to 165,000, a 25 percent decrease from a week prior. I was angry.

I had read *Flags of Our Fathers* recently, coming off of a good, long summer of Pacific Theatre movies with the boys. The book made reference to several of the veteran soldiers who, despite myriad decorations for valor and formidable reputations, walked onto Iwo Jima knowing that they were going to die. It was the observation of the survivors that any marine who fell subject to this mentality could not survive, regardless of their fighting history. Once a marine started talking this way or revealing weakness of will, his comrades wrote him off. And according to the majority of those interviewed, he ultimately proved himself clairvoyant.

As we are unexpectedly swept back into the fighting cycle, reindoctrinated into the incredible risks associated with yet another, even more dangerous, bone marrow transplant, the challenge as a parent is to fight the commonalities of anger, fear, and doubt, a difficult task when you are the one who is scared. I think a lot of my scattered-mindedness and fear must have its roots in the fact that it all happened so unexpectedly. One day you're high-fiving doctors for having a kid who appears so strong. A day later, you're in a vortex of conflicting energies that will take you in one of two directions: fear or love. Which direction you take seems more a matter of will than of choice.

I am sure it was a combination of everything, but the straw that broke my camel's back was related to a mistake the attending surgeon made in installing Brennan's central line when he first returned for pre-transplant conditioning. Two sub-clavicle arteries and both lobes of his lungs had been nicked and were causing him a lot of pain. To make matters worse, he had developed a hematoma and had air pockets around his lungs. Two X-rays revealed that their condition was stable but that there was no improvement. No improvement or a worsening of the situation could result in a significant delay in the transplant, or even disqualification. My mind, of course, went to the worst possible place, conjuring scenarios of losing this one last shot, like dropping your last bullet in the river as the enemy shoots down from above. For God's sake, we can't lose this game because of a fumble!

My anxiety began to double down that night before going to bed. The boys were milking the last few minutes of common-area time playing the Wii in the Shaun White Room at Target House when Brennan really started to complain about chest pain and asked for morphine. I was spiraling.

Brennan's pain was affecting me as much as him. I took this as a potential sign of depression, sensing that he was being affected by doubt and fear. After all, he is much more attuned to the terminal nature of this disease than he was a year ago. But he was just dealing with discomfort, and before the night was over he proved to me that he was still the same old Brenny.

After the resident common areas closed for the night, he wanted to leave the apartment and do something. He asked if he could go with me to the garage apartment. This well-kept little guest room of Jimmy and Margie Lackie had become our home away from home during previous visits. This was our overflow abode after transplant #2, introduced to us by an old college friend when we exceeded the occupancy quota at Target House (four people per apartment). The first day we met Jimmy Lackie, almost a year ago, Christopher and I drove over in the rain to introduce ourselves. I was afraid that my first impression had been tarnished when my car conked out in his driveway, requiring a jump-start, and for the next several months we rarely saw either of the Lackies, arriving late at night and leaving early. But over time, we began to walk into their kitchen to talk about our day and catch up a little bit about the real world of Memphis, and gradually we became close friends.

With Brennan's request, I called Jimmy to ask if we could come. Last year's "Relax" CD was on the car CD player, and as we silently drove east on Poplar Avenue, I noticed Brennan singing quietly in the backseat. Sarah McLachlan's song "Hold On" was playing, which to me has always been one of the most beautifully heavy songs ever recorded, presumably from the writer's perspective of losing a loved one to illness. Being affixed to our car's player, the children hear it regularly; however, I have no indication if they have ever taken the time to listen to the lyrics. But as I have said many times before, Brennan is a listener. The beauty in his voice as we drove down that nighttime stretch of four-lane road could only emanate from someone who felt what he was supposed to feel.

When we pulled into the Lackies', we saw Jimmy through the window. Emerging from his Archie Bunker chair and turning off the TV, he came outside to greet Brenny, who smiled and ran to him with a hug as he would a member of the family. Jimmy grabbed him by the hand and said, "Come here, Brennan, I want to show you something."

Jimmy led him around the back of the house with me following behind. The home is beautifully landscaped, with a collection of perfectly proportioned Japanese maple trees surrounding a black-bottomed pool. In these trees hung what appeared to be dozens of glass lanterns lit with candles. A subtly brilliant aura filled the entire yard, establishing a framework of firelight for our guest bedroom. Somehow, between when we called and when we arrived, Margie Lackie had made this yard light up just for Brennan. It was beautiful, and I could tell that Brennan was quietly touched.

Before we could head to our room for the night. Brennan was thrilled to tell them all about his hunting accomplishments earlier in the fall. As he pridefully recollected the drama of his dove and armadillo shooting, I observed the confidence with which he spoke, simultaneously recognizing the similarity between his confident demeanor now and the last two times he embarked upon a journey into the unknown. Brennan has always found refuge and reinforcement in life's little accomplishments, whether catching a fish, draining a putt, scoring a goal in soccer, or successfully completing a complex set of Legos. Because of his innocent and natural capacity for embracing positive experiences, he is predisposed to solicitude and therefore, I assume, more resilient to suffering.

Because of my own weakness and foreboding, I was unintentionally conveying my own depression about his circumstances. Brennan was not depressed. He was just sore from his surgery. Any angst over what was happening was my problem, not his. Because he chose me to stay with that particular night, my perspective began to turn a corner.

We awoke early, scheduled for a radiation simulation appointment at seven thirty, to see the candles still glowing in the early morning mist. Later that day, I received a voice mail from Jimmy expressing surprised exuberance that he and Margie also woke to see the trees still lighted.

"Turner, I just had to call you and let you know something. Margie and I have put those lanterns in the same trees with the same candles many times over the years, for parties, special guests, and so on," he exclaimed. "But never have they stayed lit through the night. That was the first time we have ever seen it."

Driving into town, we got caught up in our share of morning rush hour. Brennan slept in the backseat while I did my best to carefully maneuver quickly without risking my precious cargo in the back. I also reminded myself of Dr. Leung's warning that for at least the next week, I too was precious cargo and did not need to be doing anything that would jeopardize my status as Brennan's donor.

My tardiness resulted in more delay in triage. I found myself slipping again, worrying about the chest X-ray and whether or not the surgery problem was going to disqualify Brennan from the protocol. The perceived gravity of the things beyond my control pulled the demon door on me. There I was, sitting alone with Brennan in the waiting room, and my mind started racing.

One of my reflexive responses to the mood swing is to surf the news headlines on my handheld. Recession, Afghanistan, BP, Lindsay Lohan . . . all the usual headlines were making me feel worse. So I switched over to email.

A lot of work-related messages yet to be attended still lurked in my inbox, reminding me about how friggin' far behind I was on everything.

But then Brennan lay his head in my lap, grabbed my right hand, and wrapped it around his chest, holding my hand tightly as he attempted to nap. I clicked off the Android and peered up through the skylights of the radiology waiting area to see crisp blue sky and clouds raining brightness. I started to stroke Brennan's black wavy hair with my other hand. I took a breath and recalled Sarah Young's daily devotion, which I had read before leaving the Lackies' guesthouse but was in too much of a rush to give much thought at the time:

> Trust Me and refuse to worry for I am your Strength and Song. You are feeling wobbly this morning looking at difficult times looming ahead, measuring them against your own strength. However, they are not today's tasks, or even tomorrow's. So leave them in the future and come home to the present.

Is this not the pattern from which we have strived to face each of these challenges? The cycles of negative energy may be spinning furiously for the time being, but the love that radiates so strongly from this kid is immutable and always present.

Suffering may be inevitable. But so is love. The cycles of negative energy seem to fight for my spirit, but the hopefulness and love are simply there for it. One comes to you. The other we must seek. With only a few appointments the next day, the load was lightened further as Brennan's chest X-ray confirmed that the lungs were healing properly and that the hematoma was subsiding.

No alterations to the protocol would be necessary—obviously a tremendous relief knowing for certain that he would be admitted to the BMT unit that evening. Tara and Brennan arrived back at Target House around lunch, in time for all of us to hang out and be a family for the remainder of our last day before the commencement of this great new offensive.

Brennan's energy levels were still high from the night before. Nat was waiting very patiently, yet eagerly, for his return, and for a solid couple of hours, Brennan and Christopher stalked one another in the lush parklike lawn shared between Target House and St. Peter Manor. Dotted with hedges, walls, and many mature trees, the two little brothers played in joyful concentration on their imaginary battlefield as they would on any other day. Unlike me, who was fighting away thoughts about "the last afternoon together," trying my best to enjoy the day, the kids were just kids.

Nat and I threw the football as we observed the one-on-one skirmish between the two little guys, occasionally interrupted by a climb up a tree or directions from Tara, who served as the official war photographer, chronicling what seemed to be the entire event. A breeze blew our hair, and the magnolia leaves clapped to the first noticeable sense of autumn, shaking their limbs in declaration of a new season. It represented by concession that this summer was over, and we were truly beginning a new cycle.

With Brenny's little bag packed, we headed for BMT, the arrival to which was considerably more somber. As we waited in triage and registration, the reindeer games continued on in the hall, but as we approached the elevator up to the BMT unit, a hush fell. I could see the red mark on Nat's right cheek darkening, which has been a telltale sign of his emotions since he was a baby.

With hospital quarantines back in full gear, the boys had to say goodbye at the entry to the unit. Christopher cried, "I want to go with you, Brennan."

Brennan replied, "I'm sorry, Christopher, but I have to go."

And that was it. When would they see each other again?

Tara was on duty with Brennan in transplant for the first two nights. On the way back to Target House, the Brothers asked some pointed questions about his treatment. I explained the notion that my cells would recognize his bad cells and attack them, and that the doctor's job was to make sure that they did not attack his body in a bad way. They listened to this explanation quietly, but heard and therefore understood its implications.

"Brennan's not going to die, is he, Daddy?" asked Christopher.

"Brennan is where he is because we are doing our best to make sure that this leukemia goes away once and for all," I said as confidently as I could. Before getting out of the car for the walk up to our apartment, I pulled the boys aside and said, "Guys, you understand that regardless of all of this, we are all going to die. Our job as Brennan's wingmen is to keep him positive. Promise me that you will not let your mind wander to bad places. If you do, please come talk to me and Mommy, but Brennan needs nothing but positivity and smiles from each of us." They nodded. We all held hands and went up for bed.

That night, Brennan immediately started his pre-transplant chemo-conditioning. Due to the extraordinary amounts he has received already over the past year plus, his chemo cup runneth over; therefore, the remainder of his pre-transplant conditioning will be managed with total lymphoid irradiation (TLI). Dr. Leung determined this to be the best tool to help knock down Brennan's current immune system to make room for the new donor cells for his transplant this Friday.

I pray that my cells deliver him refuge from this terrible disease. They will either save him, or the leukemia will win. I think I am OK with all of this, knowing that at the present, they are his only option. Our relics of St. Therese and her parents, Louis and Zelie Martin, and now those of Pius X remain on his bedside. Every morning we pray for intercession on Brennan's behalf. We already feel God's grace, as our dispositions and commitment to him and to each other grow stronger while we transition into this new season.

I think it is clear from my confessions above that I am far from conquering fear. But I pray fervently to recognize only the hopeful similarities between this cycle and the last and for the capacity to remain strong in Brennan's presence and to continue feeding from the love that pours from his being.

The love is there. It is with Brennan now. It is in his smile, his voice, his song, and his joy. It always has been. It always will be.   —NTS

Day Zero, Part Three
Posted Oct 1, 2010 4:54pm

Yesterday (Day One), I could hardly participate in a conversation. With my looming role as donor, I felt heavy and was fighting tears throughout the day and night. I snapped at Christopher for things that, while maybe worthy of correction, did not warrant the severity of my tone. Same thing with Tara. I felt nervous and disagreeable with everything. The grandparents were in town and we all eventually gathered for dinner, and everyone, except for me, was loose and grateful for this rare time together as extended family. It was a precious opportunity, of which I was acutely aware; I tried hard, but nerves simply prevented me from being present. I finally found rest in Brennan's hospital room, sleeping at his side, briefly.

Waking up around 4:15 a.m., I took a shower, went through my backpack to ensure that I had a change of clothes, Dopp kit, etc., for the hospital. Eventually I found myself with an extra forty-five minutes before needing to depart. I grabbed the rosary that was given to me by a new friend, as well as the relics on Brennan's shelf. I knelt at his bedside, held his hand once again, and said my gratitudes, doing my best to conjure up everything I could be thankful for on this day. I prayed to St. Therese and her parents, as well as to every friend and relative I could summon. I prayed that my cells would treat Brennan with care. I prayed that my focus would be on the love I was feeling from the sleeping hand in mine. And then I was off to the hospital.

The bone marrow harvesting procedure was short and easy. A little pain afterward, but certainly less than getting my wisdom teeth out. I was in the recovery room at Methodist Hospital during the requested noon prayer (11 CST) with my dad and Jimmy Lackie at my side. We had asked all of our blog readers to pray at noon (EST) and again at 5 p.m. to inspire the collective energy from as many as possible. At the scheduled time, we all held hands and prayed for Brennan, Patrick, Cassidy, our families.

I find it no coincidence that this day, Day Zero, also represents the Feast Day of St. Therese of Lisieux, who has literally remained at Brennan's side almost from the beginning: the "Little Flower" whose simple and humble ways teach that God exists in life's most basic and simple experiences.

Still groggy from my procedure, I arrived at Brennan's room feeling goofy but lucid enough to feel the welcoming arms of him and Tara. I puttered around there all day, offsetting my exhaustion with the fact that he was just so happy and fun. Still, I was ready to see this transplant through from the harvest to the last drop. When my cells had been cleared, and when it was confirmed that we could begin the transplant precisely at the moment of the requested evening prayer vigil at 5 p.m., I finally let go.

Brennan feels terrific. Waiting on his new stem cells, I am amused watching him teach his grandfather how to play Call of Duty on the Xbox. The ultimate mismatch, his grandfather's video-game character stumbles aimlessly as easy prey for Brennan's sniper. Brennan laughs his way through the afternoon, eating lollipops and enjoying the clear skies of fall through his hospital room window. His view offers a direct line of sight to the Great Pyramid of Memphis (a full-scale glass replica of the Egyptian pyramid, originally constructed for the University of Memphis Tigers basketball team and special events). Other than some mild nausea from his radiation treatment, he complains about nothing and does everything to make the best out of his seclusion here.

With his Aunt Susie, Brennan has embarked on a gargantuan art venture, painting and creating early Halloween cutouts of bats, black cats, witches, ghosts, pumpkins, and the other conventional symbols. Just yesterday he had me taping fake spiders inside the linen storage area and placing rubber snakes behind couch pillows in order to shock nurses and visitors. A remote control tarantula arrived yesterday, which creeps me out, but which adds to his refreshing—although mildly twisted—outlet of fun.

He is not in isolation as we were for the entire treatment protocol last time around, so he is able and even encouraged to walk the halls of the BMT floor. He takes physical therapy once a day, shooting baskets, throwing darts, and balancing—confounding the therapy staff with his amazing hand-eye coordination. The grand finale of this little workshop was celebrated with a couple of laps around the floor on "the wiggle car." When we pass Cassidy Clark's room, he waves to her through the glass (if she's up, as she continues to make progress on her third transplant).

I notice that I am able to relish the moment, joking with him while he is awake and holding his hand while he is asleep, praying that his gentle spirit will continue to grace our lives for years to come.

Looking back, the looming surgical procedure associated with collecting a sufficient quantity of my bone marrow had to have been weighing on me, less because of what I was to experience than because of the physical consequences for Brennan.

My "half-match" will ensure a sufficient graft-versus-leukemia effect to keep the disease in check, if not to eradicate it altogether. With my cells in his body, we are effectively starting the physiological equivalent of a "back burn," similar to forest firefighters who start new fires in an effort to eliminate the fuel that feeds the destructive force of their opponent. The flip side is that fire is fire. It is an aggressive means of addressing a desperate situation. In actuality, two situations with equally destructive potential now exist. It must be managed with absolute precision, assuming that the fire we are starting can be managed.

This was the choice. Two months of life remaining with no transplant. I see no dilemma here. He has done it before, twice. And by golly, this time around he is as strong as a baby ox. His strength, combined with the energy we feel from the events on Day Zero, have given us much peace in this regard.

We've been posting our struggles and hopes for going on two years now, the sentiments surrounding the weight a parent feels surrounding a bone marrow transplant for their child can only be expressed so many ways. But still, each time it seems like it is harder and harder on the caregiver.

I mean, there it is, right in front of you. The very thing that you hold dearest. Your child . . . life itself right there in your hands. And you're scared. The epitome of the universal question: "What are you going to do when you find out you've only got an hour left?" Are you going to focus on the regrets or the things undone, or are you going to soak in those last sixty minutes? While it seems as if I know the answer, I am having a damn hard time locking into it. Kind of like the words to a song you know and love but can't conjure no matter how hard you try. And then, there they are.

Yesterday was clearly the culmination of a lot of subconscious fears. But at the same time, my conviction to fight for Brennan and to express my love for him, to him, and for everyone around him directs the struggle through the fog of doubt to the clarity of belief. Seems like it should be easy. Seems like you'd start to get better at it the second time around, or the third. But at least there is comfort knowing that despite the doubts, belief always prevails.   —NTS

Two Worlds, One Heart
Posted Oct 11, 2010 8:01pm

Our apartment windows face the west, yet the morning light is bright. Weekday nights, the blinds are left open. We need to wake early enough to rouse the two Brothers for school, and there's no sense in prolonging the darkness.

Last year our apartment was on the opposite side of Target House, so mornings came early on clear days. The blazing sunlight reduced the alarm clock to an anticlimactic bother. Being a one-parent/two-kid engagement, I can't confidently speak to Tara's perspective on the nuances of getting Nat and Christopher up, dressed, packed, and out of Target House barely in time for school in the morning. But our punctuality record reflected the relative effectiveness of each of our "rise-and-shine" methods.

But bringing up the rear while the other kids were already in class provided me an opportunity to walk the boys to class, pass the baton with a real hug, and, more often than not, allow myself a little time to hang around the schoolyard for a while to chat with Mr. Fletcher or Ms. Maria before heading over to the hospital to see Brenny.

This year, our apartment faces the setting sun. The opposing façade of the adjacent five-story building harnesses the morning sun, returning the dayspring in warm reflection. With this exception, little has changed in the realm of life at Target House. We've hardly had time to develop a routine, but we are dealing with the same two boys, the same two parents, the same pre-school routines, the same desire to hold these guys hard and close while keeping our commitment to the soldier on the front line.

Brennan's new room in the BMT unit faces west this time as well, again offering a direct line of sight to the Great Pyramid of Memphis just a few blocks away. Thus the "all-seeing eye" delivers the reflected light to which we awake and begin our day, an accidental portal to this ancient symbol of immortality, renewal, and regrowth. One of us is always in the apartment with the Brothers. The other is always with Brenny. Two daily routines in sync with two different worlds. Their orbits seldom intersect, but they cross paths enough to preserve the essential function of this little solar system. In the right rhythm, Tara and I feel that we are capable of balancing sufficient time for both, ultimately reminding the boys and ourselves that these worlds will be joined again someday. One world, one orbit, one family, two roofs. But despite the separation, comfort, warmth, and energy emanate from the core.

Weekday mornings here at Target House are typically filled with boys shuffling about locating shoes and belts under couches and behind chairs before racing to school. Be it me or Tara at the helm, lunch boxes are hastily packed for each kid. Since both Nat and Christopher have their own personal eating idiosyncrasies, each lunch box is filled with totally different items. With the exception of the standard bag of Goldfish crackers, Nat has his stuff and Christopher has his. Should these standards be compromised, we'll face an intense discussion following school. It's a pattern that we should have broken before Christopher started first grade. But he started school about two months before Brennan's first relapse, and we just haven't gotten around to it.

Lunch box contents are typically not details one expects to read about in a story of this kind, but I mention this as an example of how, in Target House world, there are probably a number of parental standards that, while maybe unthinkable to do without in the real world, are set aside in this one. One of our priorities is to ensure that the Brothers do not regret anything about their absence from Augusta, and if a little indulgence can make a day more special, allowing a kid to open his lunch box with a surprise smile, I can't think of a more appropriate time or place.

These two guys are such an important part of this equation. A lot has been asked of them over the past twenty-plus months, and for the time being, it does not look like the demands are going to get any easier. So Tara and I treat our time with them with as much importance as we do sitting bedside with Brenny and a throw-up bucket.

Afternoons are now becoming routine. Usually we hang out after school for an hour or so at the Montessori parking lot, which becomes a huge play area for kids of all shapes and sizes. The older boys love playing ball, while the younger ones scoot about on Big Wheels and scooters, darting in and out of the game du jour. The older girls watch, and a lot of them sit and participate in conversations with the moms, many of whom enjoy watching the kids play from the comfort of a nice bench.

Back at Target House, evenings usually consist of dinner before heading back to the hospital for an exchange of chaperones and, if Brennan is feeling up to it, a quick glimpse/"howdy do" with the Brothers through the fishbowl. Unlike last time, Brennan is not in isolation for adno-virus; consequently, he continues his physical therapy and making his daily laps around the BMT unit hallways. He can therefore make it to his side of the waiting area, separated from the visitor side by thick glass and encircled with built-in cushioned benches, giving the little guys outside a ledge on which to stand and communicate. Brennan remains inside with his tree of IV pumps (usually two pumps on one tree with somewhere between four to ten meds and nutrition pumping through at any given time). If the boys raise their voices, they can understand one another. One of these days we will follow the lead of Cassidy Clark's family and get some walkie-talkies, replicating a sort of prison-family visitation scene.

The weight of these visits usually renders quiet drives home to Target House. As I walked to the elevator with Christopher yesterday, holding his hand despite the green cast he still sports (having broken his arm the week before we learned of Brennan's relapse), he said, "Daddy, I would give anything just to sit with Brennan in his room for a minute. It's all I want to do."

Fortunately, Target House is filled with friends these days. We are often greeted at the front door by Carissa, who has been fighting her battle with adrenal cancer here a lot longer than Brennan, but she always has a smile, a hug, and a sincere interest in how everyone is doing.

Also, Cameron finally moved into Target House, having been in the hospital for his pre-transplant chemo cycle. The boys all love his high spirits and are looking forward to Xbox games and planning mischief with him before he checks into BMT. His dad, Lonnie, and I have become quite close, sharing a strong bond in music and, of course, our boys.

And then there is Markell. He and Nat became really close last spring. He has been battling osteosarcoma, and he just received some promising news that the spot on his lung has cleared up. He is beginning his last chemo cycle this week.

This past Saturday, Christopher and I spent a good deal of the day with Markell and his mom, going to the Memphis Zoo early in the morning with my mom, who was in town for the weekend, and rounding off the day at the movie *Secretariat*, to which the boys clapped and cheered. On the way home, I sat in the backseat with Markell and Christopher. It was then that Christopher asked, "If you could have anything in the world, what would you get?" Markell pondered this one for a while.

During his silence, I chimed in and said, "Now, Markell, we are talking about 'anything,' not just stuff. I know a lot of people who may choose something like 'peace' or 'happiness.'" He quickly responded while staring out of his window at the lights flashing by in the opposite lane, "I don't need happiness," he said. "I already got that."

Markell's happiness, Cameron's free spirit, Carissa's smile, the fraternal bonds that grow stronger every day at the boys' school, the steadfast commitment to see their brother every day, even if it is through a wall of glass for less than a minute, a smile that comes from a surprise bag of gummies in a lunch box for a kid who is too young to truly worry about whether his brother lives or dies. Every promising element within Nat and Christopher's world has a source. Every morning, that source greets our day through the reflection off a building over a church outside of our bedroom window.

I say all of this because, while our lives back home may be suspended and most likely transformed forever, the world we inhabit now revolves around a fragile state of equilibrium between belief and fear. Clearly my writings of late reveal chinks in my psychological armor.

In writing these entries, I believe that I should, to a reasonable degree, let people know about the real fears and concerns of a parent in this situation. Likewise, I try my best to articulate what motivates me, Tara, and the boys. What are the hopeful signs, how do we interpret them, and how do we balance them with our doubts? My concern in writing this stuff is the "balance" part. I have written plenty about my wrestling matches with the dark side. Should I attempt to write it all down, though, I risk portraying someone overly frightened, dangerously insecure, and morbid. Those thoughts do me no good in thinking them, so what good is it going to do in writing them down?

Believe me when I say that I latch onto every good sign that comes our way. I believe that the collective energy that comes from so many, particularly so many children, can have an effect on the world. But as hard as I try otherwise, I also understand that the effects associated with my specific prayers for something so relatively small in the grand scheme of eternity may not necessarily jive with the ultimate will. Therefore, I want people to know about the many good signs we experience, particularly the promising signs associated with Brennan's spirit and the goodness he exudes with every breath. Even the mundane is refreshing. But never would I wish to convey a naive sense of certainty. I commit enough sins without presuming to know what God has in store.

Walking into Brennan's room, the world is different. But the morning sun wakes us here, same as it does in the other little world in our lives. The Pyramid lights up like a flame at a certain point every morning. I have yet to see the light reflect back on us directly. Like a Mayan sundial reveals the sun's zenith for the purpose of managing future events, I wonder if it's possible that one moment every year, the alignment of the sun, the Pyramid, and Brennan's room will triangulate to complete the circuit.

As Brennan sleeps early in the morning, Tara and I both have a routine of quietly focusing on our gratitudes. In my case, I usually pull up the little rollaway couch adjacent to Brennan's bed and hold his hand. I focus my energy from him, through me, outside the window, toward The Pyramid, and back again. Having this time every morning in this room is a blessing. It is always how Tara starts her day, regardless of where she is. In my case, when at Target House with the other boys, I'm usually scrambling early in the morning and do not take the time until later in the day. Regardless, I make it a point to make the time.

Brennan still feels pretty good. Up until yesterday, his energy level and cheerful disposition have brightened the face of every nurse, doctor, and visitor to room 12. Endless games of speed, rummy, and blackjack have established a productive learning platform in the area of cards. Practical jokes have also been big on his list. Just this past week he left a plastic snake in the linen bin adjacent to his room, the effectiveness of which was proven by the scream of the innocent victim. All of Brennan's distractions are good for the parent or grandparent spending time with him. Just being around this kid is strong medicine for the rest of us.

But as Nonnie left from her brief visit yesterday, Brennan lost his smile. Playfulness and mischief have been eclipsed by pain and nausea. Since yesterday afternoon, he has been complaining of acute headaches and neck pain. As the night wore on, he also developed a fever that breached 102.

We were told that the source of the muscle pain could be signs of early engraftment; but his blood counts, while stable and consistent with what the doctors want to see at this point, have yet to show such activity. It should be noted that Dr. Leung's prediction of pain was also accompanied by his observation that Brennan's progress thus far is good and that he would hope to see him discharged from the BMT within a week.

Of course, Tara and I are taking this comment with a grain of salt. At the same time, Dr. Leung's encouraging disposition was helpful. For the first time since conditioning began, every minute of the day has not been tarnished with distracting fears. Like a switch, my time was not veiled with regret, but with hope. Even now, with Brennan feeling as lousy as he does, I honestly can say that I am feeling more hopeful than not.

Like the sun that reflects into his room from The Pyramid, or the reflective morning glow into the boys' bedroom at Target House, we are physically and mindfully lifted from darkness to the light. This is the week that will tell us about Brennan's engraftment, so I am going to talk about living for a change. We pray that he feels better soon and that all of his pain now is just part of the gut-wrenching process of winning.   —NTS

Seeing Through Walls
Posted Oct 18, 2010 11:33pm

Walking off the elevator to the BMT unit, I saw a new family hanging out in the fishbowl. The full group was comprised of about eight people, all of whom sat silently, most of them staring at the floor, arms crossed and otherwise not engaged with each other. As I walked by I threw out a "howdy," which was received with some eye contact and a wave, but I was generally ineffective in my effort to extract a smile.

Most folks around here have their own sort of walls. Some are thin. Many are deeply rooted and unshakable. I try my hardest not to have any, but it is difficult. Acknowledging others, passing smiles, simple interchanges about where someone is from or how they are coping are often met with a wall.

A cross-section of people represented at any hospital could probably be seen as a cross-section of the world in general. I've sat by myself in the cafeteria numerous times, surveying the cash register line and assuming that, when it comes my time to request entry into the pearly gates, that line is going to look a lot like this one. This hospital is a veritable patch-quilt of humanity, and while representing a rather common type in this part of the world, I represent one of many threads in this community's fabric. As an observer, it is interesting to see people change day-to-day. Often, with the parent's mood, so moves the mood of the patient. There's the depressed-looking dad pushing a depressed-looking kid in a wheelchair, and conversely, the super-pumped mom high-fiving and congratulating her kid after an irradiation recovery situation. It makes a big difference when the wall is up or when it is down.

For me and Tara, being alone with Brennan is the best remedy. All last week, she and I were either at bat or on deck with him the whole time. Game faces only this week, meaning "knock the walls down" and keep them there. Brennan's energy draws us to him like a moth to light. It feeds our souls and breaks down our walls. His invitations to work on one of his airplane models or play yet another game of rummy are sacred.

Looking back over my adult life, how many times has the impulse to check my email trumped an invitation to play a game, read a book, or just sit and talk with Tara or the boys? When you get right down to it, outside of the fact that one of my kids has a terminal disease, nothing else has changed. Why, then, has the immediacy of this threat grabbed me by the neck and stuck my nose in the rank uselessness of my shallow priorities? Things that consume time, emotion, labor, and money quietly and methodically gnaw away at the framework of my spirit like termites, gradually whittling away at things until the substance, the intensity of belief is no longer of any use. The interim nature of childhood itself should be sufficient to hold every one of them tight for every possible second, to share with them the things that we hold sacred, to say that we love them and to only ask that they love in return. We should not need cancer for this.

The same thing goes for the times when he is miserable—retching endlessly, crying, begging to go home. Fits of anger when he discovers that his brothers are back home this week doing real boy things trigger comments like, "It's not fair! I just want to feel good again."

Even in the depths of this misery, the emotion to participate and be a kid is enough that Tara and I know that we could never choose "comfort care" over treatment when he still wants to fight. We still have faith in our doctors and, ultimately, in the chance that he will feel good again.

When we're with him in either scenario (fun-loving, practical-joking Brennan or miserable little soldier), the walls are dismantled, delivering the capacity to see, even for a brief glance, the infinite beauty of the other side. His life and his suffering deliver the channel through the wall in which hope of reconciliation exists. The overintellectualization of it all—"Why me, why him, why now, what next?"—serves the opposite effect, strengthening the barriers that not only prohibit trust but that prevent us from sharing with others the love and understanding to feed their spirits.

This notion was driven home to me yesterday afternoon after the Brothers arrived from a weekend grandparent binge. First thing they did was show up at the fishbowl where the conversation at the glass wall was upgraded with our own new set of walkie-talkies. Brennan felt decent enough to walk around the corridor and see the Brothers.

"I see your hair is starting to fall out again," Nat commented in his opening remarks. Brennan responded with a quick, firm grasp to the top of his head, from which he quickly and easily snatched out a big golf-ball-sized clump of black hair. Nat screamed and ran down the corridor while Brennan and Christopher belly laughed.

This morning there was a new family in the fishbowl. They also seemed frightened, but they were smiling and greeted me after I dropped the Brothers off at school. Good body language. Good result. Walking into Brennan's room, I felt hopeful.   —NTS

Pick a Direction, Any Direction
Posted Oct 21, 2010 9:27pm

We awoke Monday with mild encouragement, but were also informed that Brennan was scheduled for a CT scan of his brain to try and rule out anything of concern as related to his severe headaches. The hopeful presumption was that it was a by-product of his intravenous cocktail mix, and the scan was "just in case."

At Day Plus Twenty, engraftment (is it happening, is it not?) remains issue number one. Today was the first day that Brennan's ANC maintained a threshold 100 for two days in a row. It is the closest thing to a positive trend we've had to date. The minimum count for a healthy human being is above 1,500. Dr. Leung tells us that the average time for engraftment is usually around 18 days, but that beyond Day Twenty-Three or so, the likelihood of a successful graft diminishes considerably. It is tense right now.

Returning to the hospital with the Brothers after a covert putt-putt match on a beautiful, cool fall day, Tara was at Brennan's bedside. "What's up, guys?" I saluted as usual. She smiled in response but said, "You just missed Dr. Laver and Lisa outside doing their afternoon rounds. Why don't you go track them down and talk to them?"

This meant there was something she did not want to talk about in front of Brennan, so I briskly searched for Dr. Joseph Laver around the corridors. After a full circle and a half, I started looking through the blinds of other patient's rooms until I heard Dr. Laver's voice two doors down. I simply hung out in the hall and waited.

"So I guess you are here to talk about the cyst?" he asked as soon as he and Lisa emerged into the hall.

"I guess," I said. "I am here to talk to you about whatever is going on."

They proceeded to tell me that the scan showed a mass on the rear right side of Brennan's brain that extended down into his spine. After studying the films, the radiologist assumed it was a simple cyst.

"Not to worry," Dr. Laver asserted. "We are fairly certain it is a common abnormality, probably not related to his headaches and most likely requiring no action. But we have to be sure. So we have scheduled an MRI for tomorrow."

I stayed with Brennan that night, playing cards and watching James Bond flicks until we both fell asleep around midnight. We had fun. Just being around him prevented any new walls from emerging in my troubled inner world. But we woke up to hear that his ANC had dropped back to zero. Dr. Leung's tenor escalated to "We now have real concerns about the engraftment."

If I were to pick an example of a trigger phrase at a place like this, "real concerns" would be in the basket. Dr. Leung explained to Tara that if we pass Day Twenty-Three without a concrete engraftment, we will need to begin talking about plan F, or wherever we are right now.

Since an aggressive new immune system, particularly in a half-transplant, presents a real risk of death, they have had to err on the side of caution, and therefore have been using a blend of immune suppressant drugs. Now, they are taking him off of two of the three suppressant medications to see if they can jump-start the process. The day before, we were looking good, or so we thought. Now we are fielding two curveballs. No matter what the doctors say regarding the cyst, there is no way that news of a mass on your child's brain is something not to worry about. And then there are the "real concerns."

181

Brennan and I went to the MRI suite midafternoon to begin dealing with the cyst. I held his hand as the anesthetist gave him the "push" and his eyes began to glass over. In the split second before he went down, he gripped my hand, locked eyes, and said, "I love you, Daddy."

Those words stuck in my mind all night. While Brennan slept peacefully in the dim luminance of the IV machines, I was fitful and awoke several times to read on the couch. Staring fixedly at The Pyramid's silhouette outside of his dark window, I was in deep communication with the Almighty, wondering what in the world was happening. Reaching over to Brennan's little bed, I rested my hand on his head. With the vast unknown unfurled beyond The Pyramid to my back, I knew that this child beneath my hand represented a rightful link to heaven and earth, a small yet palpable validation of eternity's goodness.

Signs in the morning. ANC back to 100! The MRI revealed an arachnoidal cyst, which in the grand scheme of things is not a problem. Located in the outer layer of his brain, it is a benign growth that will simply be monitored.

Brennan inexplicably awoke with the happiness and good cheer of a kid on Christmas morning. He read through volumes of new jokes, encouraged from a Facebook challenge put on by Tara yesterday. With full-fledged belly laughs, he recited them to anyone who ventured into his room. We see his energy as a sign that the war in his little body is turning in the right direction.

I'm telling you, this stuff is hard.   —NTS

Lifetime in a Day
Posted Oct 23, 2010 1:07am

On the way to school, Tara called me to tell me Brennan's ANC was 350. The Brothers sang Beatles songs in the car, and I opened the windows to feel the cool, crisp air of the Mississippi. We crossed the Mud Island Bridge on a long overdue beautiful morning. It looked like a good day was in the cards, so Tara asked if I could relieve her at the hospital so she could make a 9 a.m. yoga class. I arrived to find Brennan in an eye clinic examination (looking for post-radiation and -chemo side effects), sitting up straight in one of those huge optometry chairs decked out with various retractable arms, lights, and viewfinders. He grinned at me from ear to ear as he welcomed me.

"Hey, Daddy, listen to this one!" He recited new jokes from one of the many emailed to him. His energy was high, and my spirits lifted. We were interrupted by a phone call from Tara. In her rush to make yoga, and in mine to meet her in time, I had left her car running during the exchange. We have a keyless remote, and I'd failed to hand her the fob before she drove away. She was halfway to yoga class when the alarms went off. My heart sank when I realized I'd just preempted her one weekly form of escape and relaxation.

"No worries," she said, exhibiting her remarkable flair for forgiveness. "I will just turn around and hang out with you guys."

Brennan thought the whole thing was funny and went back to the jokes. But not five minutes had passed before a nurse from the eye clinic came in and said, "I need to speak with you outside." The tone of her request was certainly unexpected, considering where we were, and I felt very strange and conspicuous leaving Brennan in the room alone. "Dr. Leung needs to meet with you and is on his way down," she said sternly. "Where is your wife?" I told her Tara would be here soon and walked back into Brennan's room to continue the joke volley, but my heart was suddenly in my throat. I forced my best composure and did my best to laugh at Brennan's jokes and feign enthusiasm.

Within a few minutes, Dr. Leung and Mary, his transplant coordinator, knocked on the door and asked me to come out.

"This morning we were celebrating with the ANC of 350, but then the lab reported that there are a number of blast cells," Dr. Leung said. "Given Brennan's history, they are typically a telltale sign of disease."

In order to determine for sure, a bone marrow biopsy was ordered for noon. In the event that the worst case was confirmed, the solution was to begin donor lymphocyte infusion (DLI), effectively a means of jump-starting the immune reaction against the leukemia cells, by extracting additional cells from my blood. This represented a fairly significant change in the protocol.

Dr. Leung did his best to put me at ease. "It is possible that these blast cells are simply immature good cells. I am guessing we have a chance of this, because I have seen it in others. But we are fighting the clock. We do not expect to get the results from the biopsy until three, but we are moving forward with all of the preparation to begin DLI this afternoon. All of the paperwork and consent forms are underway now. We need to make sure that you will have Tara here, because it looks like Brennan will be taken down for his bone marrow biopsy at the same time that you will be in the donor room for your blood harvest."

Tara was headed back here right now because I accidentally kept her key. Had that not happened, she would have been on cell phone silence and unreachable until after twelve. Coincidence?

I did not call Tara to tell her what was happening, but waited for the BMT nurse to escort us back to the unit to tell her in person. We sat in the little eye clinic room for an eternity, waiting. I was struggling, feigning amusement at Brenny's jokes. At this point it was almost surreal. Brennan was having the time of his life, laughing about his little joke book, and I was choking.

Finally I had to call Tara to see where she was. "I'm in Brennan's room waiting for you guys. One of the PAs is here and she's filled me in on everything. I love you."

Brennan remained in a great mood and enjoyed the wheelchair ride up and across the glass pedestrian bridge from the main hospital to the unit. It was a beautiful morning. I remember walking across the bridge with Brenny and looking out across at The Pyramid, but I have absolutely no recollection of what we talked about—only that Brennan was happy and that I didn't mess it up.

DLI was the non-curative option proposed by Emory. Maybe we had passed the point where a cure was still in the cards, I fretted. Had Dr. Leung just implied that we were now past that option?

As we reached his room, Tara, Lisa, and I sat Brenny in the bed and told him that he was going to be put to sleep in a little while. We wanted to make sure that this rather radical change in his day's schedule did not upset him and that he was not alarmed at all by the secret conversations going on around him.

"Brenny, we need to do another bone marrow biopsy to see if there is still any leukemia in your body, 'cause if there is, we are going to give you some more of your daddy's blood to try and fight it, OK?"

"OK," he said with a shrug of the shoulders as he flipped through a book. "Do we have time to make some paper airplanes and fly them before the biopsy?"

For a solid hour and a half, we manufactured about a half dozen airplanes using the famous Nakamura Lock, known as the finest paper airplane technique in the world. The nursing staff came out to watch him fly the planes. The BMT coordinator who had come to get my consent for the procedure stayed with us for at least thirty minutes, laughing and joking with Brennan as he challenged me to make the longest flight down the corridors of this place that defines his fate.

We finally packed him and his new planes in the wheelchair and proceeded back across the glass pedestrian crossway to the surgery suite. Brennan asked the nurse to stop. He got up out of his wheelchair and threw two planes. The one I had manufactured stalled and crashed into the glass. His flew in graceful waves down the entire hallway, landing in a gentle slide. He looked up at me with a wry, competitive smile.

Tara and I held both of his hands as he went under anesthesia. He drifted off, saying, "I love you" before closing his eyes. We then made our way over to patient registration and the donor room for my part of the deal.

Tara said, "I think this is all amazing. A year ago at this time, we were given no options. Now our team is creating options by the hour."

I thought about this quite a lot as I lay on the blood donor couch. The assembly of experts, administrators, nurses, etc., all gathered in the room for my harvest was larger than the staff of most emergency rooms. Brennan and this DLI procedure were priority number one. And to think that on some days, these guys have multiple cases with equal or greater degrees of urgency.

185

As the blood pumped from my arm into the collection bag, I stared out at the wall. Alone for a while, I reached into my pocket, grabbed my rosary, and tried to focus on all the positive things that reared their heads above the many horns of fear in our way. I prayed boldly to Jesus and every saint I could conjure, to make this kid part of a miracle. Seeing so many kids with equally grim prognoses, I have always been purposefully more humble and self-effacing than I was today. But we had as much riding on the decisions of today as we have had all along. Just after three, Dr. Leung walked up to the room and asked us to come outside.

"So we are moving forward with the DLI thing?" I asked. "I guess you didn't like what you saw in the marrow?"

"No, actually, we are moving forward with DLI despite everything. There is no reason to wait on results. The fact of the matter is that, regardless of the blast cells, we do know that Brennan's immune system demonstrates cells from three places of origin: you, the last donor, and Brennan. What we have here is a race, and we need to make sure that your cells, which have now engrafted, are given the greatest chance possible to win the race."

These comments were not exactly what I had envisioned moments earlier, but it was still an answer to my earlier prayer. We were still in the race.

On the way back to Target House, I grabbed the Brothers at school and pit stopped at a costume store to find a Confederate officer's hat that Christopher required for his school's "Historic Halloween" recital this coming weekend, where he is to portray Robert E. Lee. Once he was fully dressed, he admired himself in the mirror, adjusting himself crisply, and asked to visit his brother.

Brennan was waiting for his brothers on his side of the fishbowl. Christopher stood proudly in his military regalia, and Brennan reciprocated with a paper airplane that he managed to get through the cracked door. They talked on their walkie-talkies for about half an hour, the longest engagement to date, before telling each other, "I miss you." "I love you." Then he said, "Mommy, the only thing in the world I want right now is to grab Nat and hold him." He placed his hand to his brother's on the glass and was wheeled back to his room.

The lady covering the front desk observing everything said, "I've got to move from this place. I don't know if I can handle watching these kinda goodbyes or I'm gonna lose it. Either that or I'm gonna open that door, give them boys a mask, and let 'em hug each other. This is too much."   —NTS

Signs of Change
Posted Oct 27, 2010 2:03am

"It doesn't rain here anymore," Fletcher said as his golf ball bounced along the deadpan fairway under the base of a towering white oak. Nat, Christopher, and I rounded out the foursome, which was effectively a nice walk through the links of Overton Park. It had been blustery and threatening, but the dark clouds delivered nothing more than a single drop on the tip of my nose.

As we rested under the canopy of the ancient woods, we talked about it for a while . . . the reluctant changing of seasons. As I'm always looking for signs from above, and sometimes drawing unhinged conclusions from causes with no relation whatsoever to their supposed effects, the anemic threat of rain left me worried about Brennan's engraftment and about what would happen if these new life-dependent blood cells never emerged.

The Hunter's Moon—also called the Blood Moon—lighted the skies on our way home. This moon guided Native American hunters on their final kill before winter, and it heralded a change ahead. Indeed, it was followed by a morning ANC of 800, the most solid sign to date.

At last Brennan developed a rash, which according to the doctors looked like "textbook GVHD, exactly what we are looking for." The BMT team concurred to the extent of completing discharge papers late Monday afternoon, trusting Brennan's immune system to be stable enough to enjoy life at Target House with his family and fellow soldiers.

Another checkpoint in the battle. Another overdue respite. According to the doctors, this week will tell us a great deal about which way the protocol is going. Another confirming biopsy is scheduled for Thursday.

The Brothers were chomping at the bit to give their brother a hug, having endured acute spiritual malnourishment away from him for so long. Before discharge papers arrived, Brennan dispatched me and the Brothers to Target House to fetch his tennis shoes. He checked in in bedroom slippers, but he told me that under no circumstances was he going to leave in them. So we rushed to Target House, as Tara instructed.

When we arrived back at the hospital, the nurses burst in, showering Brennan with confetti and congratulations for reaching this point in transplant yet again, wishing him luck and best wishes for the next stage. Scooping confetti up in one of the little plastic nausea troughs, we ran out of the room in full civilian gear, surprising the Brothers in the fishbowl. The spontaneous burst of cheers was resolved with bear hugs, laughter, and a "let's get out of here" sense of approbation.

Once again, I made the ride down the elevator at the BMT facility with all three of my children, a feat that I had nearly given up hope of one month ago. I then followed each of these kids out of the hospital and to the car, Brennan in his requested tennis shoes.

The difference between this exit and that from transplant two was night and day. Brennan was so frail then. Having lost so much weight, and having endured a grueling five months of treatment, including transplant, his little body had been literally pushed to the brink. Now that I think about it, transplant pretty much takes your body to the brink and back again all by itself. But Brennan is amazingly strong now.

Something else appeared different, and I realized that his tennis shoes were spotless. Buckling him in, I considered that, living in a clinical environment, these kids don't have the opportunity for their shoes to look broken in and normal.

Arriving at Target House, he was the first inside and upstairs to our apartment. But he proved to be fueled more on inspiration than raw power, and by eight o'clock he was out like a light.

Tara and Brennan's Aunt Susie went to the Lackie's apartment, leaving me with the boys for the night. Christopher slept in the bed, and after finishing our bedtime story ritual, we were all sacked out before ten.

• • •

It started with a dream. Around half past midnight, I startled myself awake with a nightmare that I could no longer breathe. I got out of bed for a glass of water when something told me that I needed to check on Brenny.

Tiptoeing over to his bed, I felt for his sleeping head. He was on fire. I held Nat's head in the bed next to him as a comparison, not having any thermometer. Kicking myself for forgetting such a standard tool, I got the nerve to call my friend Lonnie on the third floor to borrow his son Cameron's. The rule of thumb at this stage is that any fever over 100.3 requires hospitalization. Bacterial infections or viruses can be tragic. Lonnie understood and had no problem with my late call.

Brennan's underarm temperature read 100.7. I then woke him. "How do you feel?" I asked. "I am fine. What are you doing?" he pleaded, trying to go back to sleep. But after an argument of a minute or two, he relented and let me stick the thing under his tongue: 101.4.

I called Tara, who immediately arranged for Susie to stay with the Brothers while we escorted our soldier back to the BMT unit. Packing enough of Brennan's gear for a day or so, I flicked on the TV while I waited for her. "Heavy Rain & Winds—Gusts to 50 Miles per Hour," read the weather alert caption.

When Susie walked in, I woke Brennan to carry him outside. He was still being fed intravenously, so I had to juggle my backpack and his, which included the IV food and pump. Tara greeted us at the bottom of the elevator, and we walked to the car. Stepping outside, we were almost blown over.

Stoplights twisted side to side in the wind as we drove to the hospital, red to green, green to red. Like armless men rotating back and forth, street signs twisted in the wind. Surges of leaves rattled across the street as the gale pushed our car from one lane to the next. Had it not been the middle of the night with no traffic, it would have been too dangerous to drive. But they were waiting for us at the BMT unit.

We were greeted with surprise and concern. We had been gone for not quite six hours.

Back in his old room, Brennan's temperature had dropped below 100; but he suddenly began to scream with pain from nausea and headaches. Finally, he drifted off to sleep around two-thirty or so. More bad dreams. Restless sleep on all fronts.

This morning, the Great Pyramid of Memphis could hardly be made out through the rain outside Brennan's window. The weekend's storm had not been enough. Mother Earth thirsted for more, and rain it did . . . all day long.

The Blood Moon was indeed a foreshadowing. Brennan, too, is quenched for new life blood within a barren landscape. We no longer pray for water, but for mercy.   —NTS

Tug of War
Posted Nov 9, 2010 3:54pm

The Brothers were fully occupied with *Charlie and the Chocolate Factory*, two eating dinner from their little folding TV tables, the other sucking down IV food. Brennan's fevers had broken and he was back at Target House, curled up with his IV backpack. All seemed numb to the clinical nuances surrounding the fact that a nurse was in our kitchen training their parents how to administer lipids via an intravenous feeding pump. Nat and Christopher laughed and fought over ice cream, but Brennan's fading eyelids revealed a child unmindful of the many little things that normally would have drawn out both his ire and his funny side.

About halfway through the little training program, Brennan's eyes bolted open from his slumber. "Mommy!"

Struggling to sit up as his brothers watched on, mouths agape, he said, "I feel weird, Mommy. I think I have to go to the hospital."

As I carried him and his backpack down the elevator with Tara and Christopher, who was not going to let his brother leave without walking him to the car, he seemed lucid and himself. Christopher told him to "have a good trip."

"Don't worry, Christopher, I am going to stay with you and Nat," I responded. I gave Brennan a hug, but once I buckled him in, he seemed to just stare absently out of the windshield. Once again, in less than a day, he was back in the transplant unit.

The medical team is trying to get their arms around everything. His oxygen levels were slightly low, which will hopefully be remedied with another transfusion this afternoon. Tara left in the morning to manage a few things. Since I arrived, Brennan has been talking nonsense, asking his buddies Reab and Gray from Augusta to be quiet while he watches TV. He has been telling Christopher, who is at school, to come in the room and talk. He then changes psychological channels to say something about Saturn or what people have to eat in Antarctica. At first, the docs chalked this up to the fact that he's taking a lot of drugs, but he's been taking these drugs for a while without talking crazy. Things are getting weird.

Fortunately, it's not 100 percent gibberish. In between the nonsensical, he asks for water or tells me that he's really tired. His organ functions are all looking good, even better than yesterday. There is the possibility that his cranial cyst is growing or that it has created a predisposition for him to have hallucinogenic reactions to the combination of immune suppressant meds.

We are probably looking at a couple of weeks before the next bone marrow biopsy, which is the ultimate barometer of the internal tug-of-war. Now, with GVHD probably brewing, there are other new side effects; therefore, we are bringing in some barometric tools that we have not needed as of yet. Despite his looking worn and the clear signs of dementia, we know he is holding on tight.

Standing by his side throughout it all, we owe it to him and to the many exceptional people helping him every minute of the day to keep a grip on our own fears, pulling hard when we can't and showing the strength of faith to believe in this miracle.

A few minutes ago, a Eucharistic minister who frequents the hospital and has become partial to Brenny came by the room. She asked him how he was doing. He looked absent and responded, "I am not sure what you mean."

Noticing he was not himself, she proceeded to go through the Eucharistic liturgy with me in the corner of the room. Brennan started to sleep. But as we said the Lord's Prayer, I looked over to see him mouthing the words behind his closed eyes. "Our Father, who art in heaven . . ."

He said every one of them. He is clearly not absent, just pulling his weight when it counts.   —NTS

Ain't Nothin' Over
Posted Nov 11, 2010 1:31am

Brennan is in ICU, which appropriately is located in the epicenter of the hospital building, the design for which represents a Coptic Cross. While renovated and reordered over the years, the shape is recognizable from the old photos. The Pyramid is visible from here too, but from the periphery. While farther away, it still serves as a conduit for hope. Only one floor above Brennan's BMT room, the air here is noticeably thinner. Here, our soldier is supported with much different fighting equipment and a team who will either keep him alive or help usher him homeward with grace. This is the last place of hope for many, and therefore, it is the last place for many. We struggle to comprehend what has happened so quickly, and we pray for deliverance from this room. The battle has reached a climax.

Concerned about Brennan's cognitive detour yesterday, his team quickly ushered him to MRI to check his lungs and to get detailed pictures of his brain, specifically the cranial cyst. It was the logical culprit for his mild delusions.

Preparing for MRI, Brennan's oxygen levels were noticeably low, triggering a debate about his capacity for handling anesthesia. Not only were his levels unusually low, they were dropping. The procedure had to be postponed.

By this time it was three-thirty, well past the time for me to get the boys from school. Assuming everything would be worked out before I returned around six-thirty or so with Tara's belongings for the night, I took off to Maria Montessori, arriving to find Nat and Christopher playing stickball in the parking lot with their friends. I had no real plan for the afternoon other than to get Christopher to a cookie party at Target House at six o'clock. With the boys still occupied, I decided to slip across the street for a very late lunch at the little neighborhood market.

As I was sinking my teeth into the first juicy bite of a Reuben sandwich, Tara called. "The X-ray technician thinks Brennan has toxemia."

Toxemia . . . I thought I recollected the term as a lung condition obtained from breathing pigeon poop, but not certain, I started Googling things on my handheld. But the fact of the matter was that the mere notion of it was keeping me from thinking straight, and I had to get away from the school playground before I revealed the propagation of cracks in my psychological armor. I don't know if I said a word to the boys all the way home about what was starting to happen to their brother. Driving home, Nat was his usual sweet self, throwing out Georgia football statistics and commenting about which bowl game they were headed to. I was listening to Charlie Brown's teacher again: blah, blah, blah.

Home, we all puttered around our three rooms for a while waiting for the cookie party when Jimmy Lackie called, asking if we could attend a U of Memphis basketball game. It was a kind and generous offer, but I responded abruptly, shocked that his telepathy was not sufficient to recognize my feelings of urgency. The audacity to ask such a question at a time like this! "I can't do that, Jimmy. I need to be with Tara and Brennan," I snapped.

I hung up, but after thinking for a minute about what I had said, I called him right back. "You know what, if you would be willing to take the boys, it would be great. I could visit with Tara and Brennan, and these guys could have a little more fun than decorating a cookie."

Jimmy happily agreed, even to the extent of offering to keep them for the night in the event that I needed to stay at the hospital. So I packed their little bags, took them for half an hour or so of the cookie party, and then kissed them goodbye.

I called Tara to let her know the change in plan. "I think this may be a gift from above," she said. "There has been a change in plan here as well. Brennan does not have toxemia, but they suspect an infection of some sort because he is having a very difficult time breathing. And it is getting worse.

It is possible he may have to be in ICU, and I am afraid you and I may be put in a position to make some tough decisions very soon."

"Is there any news about what's happening?" I asked.

"Until they can get the MRI, they do not have the information necessary to make a diagnosis," she responded.

My knee-jerk response was to fume. Were there no other tests if we were worried about infection? I emailed Dr. Leung asking him why this seemingly critical situation, with time of the ultimate essence, would not allow faster solutions.

He called me on my cell phone as I drove to the hospital. Simultaneously, Dr. Asha Pillai, the BMT physician on duty, attempted to call in. Incapable of a three-way call while driving, I accidentally hung up on Dr. Leung and spoke to neither.

Finally at the BMT floor, both doctors were in the hallway talking to Tara. They were worried about me and concerned that I knew everything as I should. It's really pretty amazing when you think about it. It's 9 p.m. and two doctors who are on duty for the sole sake of assessing a game plan for a single child had taken time out of their pressing medical and family duties to deal with a confused and emotional father.

Both doctors confirmed that toxemia was not the issue. However, regarding his delusions, they were concerned about potential fluid buildup in his brain. A lumbar puncture would be necessary to assess that and other potential viral issues. But anesthesia would be required for both that and the MRI, and so they found themselves in somewhat of a quandary.

It was possible to schedule emergency procedures in both cases that night, but general anesthesia had been ruled out. Brennan would have to be physically restrained for an MRI and could be offered only local anesthesia for the spinal tap. The whole procedure sounded rather inhumane to me, and Dr. Leung inserted, "We already have Brennan on all of the antiviral, fungal, and bacterial agents to manage the potentially major enemies. I would wait until the morning to perform these procedures. If it was my kid, I would not do it tonight unless it was an absolute emergency."

Everything relating to the bone marrow transplant and GVHD at this point had been pushed aside until this emerging emergency issue could be addressed.

Brennan was still in room 12 at this point. Tara and I retreated to his bedside, where he was resting very restlessly. He was having an awkward time with the little oxygen probe inserted into his nostrils, trying to watch TV but not appearing to be focused on much of anything. He was coughing regularly and obviously uncomfortable.

For a while, Tara and I did not even talk, about anything. But as Brennan interacted with us to the extent that he could, our ice began to melt.

Tara wisely said, "You know what? Rather than freaking the Brothers out with such a sudden move, why don't you call Jimmy and ask them to stay with you back at Target House. Let's not make things worse by alarming them."

Brennan coughed, looked me in the eyes, and smiled. "It's OK with me, Daddy."

I kissed them both and headed back to Target House. The boys were already there, thrilled to see me and sporting their new U of M jerseys, courtesy of Mr. Lackie. We fixed bowls of Oreo ice cream and sat down to watch the last half of *Seabiscuit*, which we had started a few weeks before.

Obsessing about ICU just a few hours ago, I was so relieved to be with these guys in our pajamas staying up past curfew. But before we could settle into a groove, the phone rang. Tara was on the verge of tears. "Turner, if it's not too much, can you please come be with me? It is getting way worse, and I am scared."

I called Jimmy and changed plans again, and then I walked into the boys' room and told them that I needed them to pack and spend the night with the Lackies. Christopher started crying. "Why?"

"Remember, I told you that Brennan was having a hard time breathing. Your mom really needs me to help with him tonight," I said. Still, Christopher refused to go until I told him that I would make sure that the Lackies did not take him to school until after ten.

Nat was ashen and appeared to be close to crying. I could not help but want to hold him, but my "wall" held me back. As we waited for the elevator, I turned to the boys and asked them to look me in the eye. "You guys need to promise me that you are going to be strong. Brennan is having a tough go, and we really need you guys to be there for him. But mostly, I want you to pray. Can you promise me that?" I expected tears. Instead they responded with confident and serious expressions. "We'll pray, Daddy. I promise," said Christopher.

When I got to the hospital, Brennan had lost the oxygen prongs and gone to one of those masks with the bag on the end. A respiratory therapist was in the room looking at his saturation counts, heart rate, etc. Tara looked like Nat when I told him goodbye. "Turner, I was terrified. His heart rate has been through the roof, and he is getting no oxygen. We just now got him stabilized."

He held steady, and we watched the monitor in silence for every heartbeat to show an increase or decrease in levels. I recalled my father's dear friend Bill Thurmond, intently focused on his O2 monitor when I saw him last, staring at the oxygen monitor levels and struggling desperately to get the numbers back up. This was just a week before he passed away.

While all of this was going on, Tara, the nurses, and I were doing our best to encourage Brennan to relieve some of the internal fluid pressure that was compressing his lungs. So throughout the monitor monitoring, about every half an hour I would wake him up to go "number one."

"I'm sorry to wake you, Brenny, but we really need you to go because it will help you breathe better." He never once complained or asked why.

I pulled the fold-out chair next to Brennan's bed and held his hand about the time Tara went to sleep.

For a while, the levels improved and he started coming around. He would wake up and take off his oxygen mask. "I don't need this; I'm fine," he would say. With my best calm dad impersonation, I would say, "But, Brennan, it will help you breathe easier and get you out of the hospital faster." With which he would just say, "OK, Daddy," and roll over to sleep for a few minutes of restless dreams. This routine repeated itself every fifteen minutes until about 3 a.m., when the coughing began in a big way.

It all started steady but took a quick and violent turn. The nurse and I held the throw-up bucket at his lap, which started to fill with a frothy, bloody substance every time he coughed. The monitor alarms started squealing, and he began to plummet quickly. The nurse at this point was in the room every minute. All three of us were holding him and doing our best to make him comfortable, but he had probably produced a pint or more of bloody phlegm in the bucket when the doctor came in. I could tell that he was dying.

"We are headed to ICU now," the doctor said. "He needs more support than we can give him here."

Without complaining or asking what was happening, Brennan was propped up in his bed. An oxygen tank was attached to the front, along with all of the relevant heart rate and oxygen monitors. One nurse grabbed his IV tree, and five of us escorted him out of BMT and across the glass catwalk that overlooked The Pyramid. When we arrived in his ICU room, an army of staff was there waiting for him. He was immediately re-equipped with a better oxygen mask, for which he once again exclaimed, "I don't need this!" as they forced it around his struggling little head.

With a dose of Dilaudid and half an hour or so under his belt, he began resting and maintaining about 91 percent oxygen saturation. The coughing persisted, though, and while he appeared more comfortable than he had all night, with each ping of the monitor it became more and more clear that a respirator was on his horizon.

With him semi-asleep, Tara suggested I slip over to the parent room across the hallway for a two-hour nap. On the way there, though, I left my father a message: intubation seemed imminent by day's end, and we did not know where things were headed. My head was swirling for lack of sleep, and I crashed until the morning.

With no windows, the parents' room is pitch dark day and night. When I woke up, I did not know where I was or what time it was, so fumbling for the light, I simply slipped on my old jeans and shirt from the night before, brushed my teeth, and ran over to see what was happening.

Tara was up and on the phone. The TV was on, but Brennan was having a difficult time, showing much labored breathing. He lay on the bed with his chest heaving in waves, neck to stomach. Each breath was accompanied by a little squeak from his vocal cords. He could hardly utter a single syllable per breath. "Huuu . . . Daaa . . . Huuu . . . Deee." He sounded like a broken bicycle pump hemorrhaging air. His little body looked like a slow motion video of an earthquake in a desert.

The entire staff was rushing to prepare for intubation before I had stepped a foot back into the room. Tara told me they were just about to come get me.

Members from the BMT team were present, including respiratory nurses and the new ICU team. Dr. Leung was present, as were Dr. Pillai and the on-call ICU partner, Dr. Lynn Frantz.

Dr. Frantz pulled me and Tara aside to explain. "The faster we can have Brennan intubated, the faster we can give his lungs a rest. They are clearly tattered from so much violent coughing."

The intubation is basically a ventilator. A flexible tube is placed into his trachea to open up his air passageways, providing positive airflow into his lungs and relieving his body from the tremendous stress it has been enduring to keep itself going. He will be kept on the ventilator until the cause of the pulmonary issue is resolved, or until it is determined that he cannot survive without it.

"Of course," Dr. Pillai added, "there is always risk in that some patients simply cannot wean themselves off of the ventilator, but he cannot support himself at the current time without it. At this juncture, we have no choice."

Tara piped in, "Can I make one request? Before you guys put him on the vent, can you give Turner twenty minutes to pick up Brennan's brothers from their school so that they can talk to him?"

Dr. Leung responded, "I think that is a great idea."

I dashed out of the hospital, cranked the car on, and was driving away before even buckling my seatbelt when the song "One Little Boy," which I had written and recorded for Brennan, came on the CD queued in Tara's car. I rolled down the windows and cranked up the volume, playing it twice before I arrived, believing it may somehow be heard as my prayer for Brennan's life. I walked into the school, probably looking rather tattered and dazed. "I would like to take Christopher and Nat with me to the hospital. Now, if you do not mind?" I really do not remember what else I said. I just grabbed Christopher's hand and left.

Nat, they told me, had already been picked up by Margie Lackie. Telling his teacher earlier that he did not feel well, he had called to be picked up. I called Margie, who said she was not far from St. Jude and would meet me in the lobby of the hospital with Nat ASAP.

Margie pulled up to deliver Nat, looking confused and dumbstruck, with tears in her eyes. The boys clearly sensed something important, so I just told them, "Brennan is having such a hard time breathing that he is going to be put to sleep, possibly for several days. They are going to put a tube in his throat, just like they did to you when you donated bone marrow, Nat. Once his lungs are rested, he will not need it anymore." Margie waited outside while I took them up.

When the boys arrived in his room, the anesthesiologists and respiratory people were all waiting for us. Their faces were all veiled with urgency. Most of the BMT doctors were there as well, as were several PAs from the BMT team, Childlife specialists, our social worker, and nurses and hospital staff who had nothing whatsoever to do with the procedure, but were there for Brennan and for us. Dr. Rubnitz from the leukemia team was there with his assistant Stephanie. The hospital CEO, Dr. Evans, came down. It was as if these very busy people, who had grown to love and respect Brennan so greatly, felt compelled to be with him as he fell asleep, possibly for the last time. No one wanted to say goodbye, but no one wanted to miss seeing him either.

The Brothers walked up to Brennan, who was sitting up in bed. "We came to tell you good luck and goodbye," said Nat. "We'll see you later, Brenny."

"Why are you saying this?" asked Brennan. Heaving one breath after the next and covered in lines and monitors, he acted as if it was just another day at the office. Still, the presence of all these people revealed to him that the battle plan had just changed and that he was the one to make the first step into the unknown. Instinctively understanding that he was alone for this fight, he looked as if he had just heard the sound of hope turning backward.

Christopher asked Brennan, "Can I give you a hug before I leave?" Walking up to him with his arms out, Brennan said again, "Why are you telling me goodbye?"

We hated to use the word, but it is what we did. It was what was happening. The Brothers all held hands with me and Tara as the anesthesia took effect. Christopher stroked his head, and we all stood, looking at him there peacefully. The Band of Brothers all together in that room as only they can be: talking, fighting, or in silence. I understood how fortunate we truly were to have lived together. God willed this beautifully difficult moment; he is fair and loving.

Neither Tara nor I cared to witness the tubes being inserted. We took the boys downstairs where Margie remained waiting patiently in tearful concern to take the boys home with her. As they drove away, Christopher's face seemed frozen in the window with his palm to the glass. Tara and I stood on the curb and cried.

Most of the staff people were very teary and almost apologetic. "We are so sorry that he has to do this but pray he will make it through," was the standard message. But many seemed encouraging and hopeful. One of Brennan's favorite nurse practitioners, Lisa, who was there for no other reason than to show her love for Brennan, gave us both a hug and said, "I have seen every miracle that can happen at this place. And I can promise you that I have seen kids walk out of that same bed Brennan is in right now."

We were talking with the doctors a bit more about what to expect when the anesthesiologist emerged and said, "I could not anesthetize him enough for the MRI." All of the procedures for the day had to be postponed and rethought. With more to be concerned about, Tara and I walked into his room to see him for the first time garnished with all of the tubes and the ventilator. With so much emotion in that room, and so many brilliant people staring at him as if they had nothing left up their sleeves, it was very hard to take.

After I do not know how much time, I sat in the chair next to his bed. It was a beautiful and clear day. I put on Brennan's guitar music playlist and we just sat there with him, holding his hand, stroking his head, and quietly praying. The panic seemed to slip away, the grace of peace taking its place.

A nurse suggested that since he would be sleeping indefinitely, particularly for the next few days, now would be the time for us to take a break. It was after eleven, so we both walked to North Main Street to a little pizza place not far from the hospital. We held hands and talked about everything, what had happened, what could happen. We cried.

It was a warmish, crisp springlike day. We both noticed that this was our first date together, without any children, since we could remember. We even laughed about that. It seemed to get our minds on the right plane as a couple, and it gave us the gratitude to talk about how lucky we were in general, and how particularly lucky we were to have had Brennan in our lives, even if we never talked to him again.

I broached the subject of what we would need to do if Brennan never came off the tube, the details we should be preparing for, etc. Tara would hear none of it.

• • •

Both of our parents dropped all of their plans and headed to Memphis as soon as they received word early that morning. Only two people can be in Brennan's room at a time, so it became difficult to arrange things once they arrived. But we knew they would be a big help with the Brothers, and we knew that their presence delivered Brennan desperately needed energy as he tried to pull this one off. Simple power in numbers.

Late in the day, Dr. Leung's team called me and Tara to give us a report about what was going on and what to expect over the next several days.

Because of the swift onset of Brennan's pulmonary condition, the doctors presumed that a viral or fungal infection was the culprit. Brennan continues to be treated with a spectrum of antibiotics and antifungal and antiviral meds, the combination of which cover most of the bases. But there are a number of rare diseases in these areas for which he is not being treated. Until a diagnosis can be confirmed, it is too risky to treat him willy-nilly for just anything. Therefore, tomorrow at noon a bronchial scope will take samples from his lower lungs, which will give more data than the fluids collected from the tubes already.

There is also concern about the psychological symptoms Brennan presented yesterday, and the MRI tomorrow will hopefully tell us more.

Finally—and totally out of the blue—Dr. Leung told us that the tests had showed that Brennan's immune system is now 100 percent donor cells.

Just two days ago, Dr. Leung was preparing to perform DLI again, on the assumption that the graft remained weak and that remission was in jeopardy. That is obviously not the case. Furthermore, Brennan's blood work this morning demonstrated about a fivefold increase in the number of white blood cells. The staff was initially concerned about this, as white blood cells can be a sign of leukemia, but today, these white cells were proven to be healthy. In other words, Brennan now has a real immune system. He is in third remission!

This not-so-little tidbit of information was given to us in the context of the assessment and treatment options, which will begin tomorrow. It may be just a baby one, but Brennan's immune system is fighting whatever it is that's attacking his lungs. Tara and I were floored. These next days and weeks are going to be tough, but he has a chance, and we believe in all possibilities. Our boy is wounded badly and bleeding. We've just got to get him the hell out of here.

All I know is that this morning, I grabbed my wife and cried like a baby. She grabbed me and cried like a baby. Maybe I'm just a delusional dad holding on to whatever scraps of hope I can put my hands on, but despite how awful it has been, I felt profoundly changed by the day in a positive and hopeful way.

Brenny is in a real tough spot right now. He has never been in one quite like this, but he has fought and skirted defeat before. He is already a miracle.

He is a living prayer for so many people. I will always love him for it and be grateful for him and all that he has taught me.

When his fight is over, it's over. In the meantime, we are going to pray, and allow him to fight, and give thanks for the opportunity he has to press on. —NTS

A Place for Miracles
Posted Nov 12, 2010 12:56am

I arrived at the hospital as they were preparing Brenny for MRI, finally. I had received no calls. No one had been dispatched to wake me, and fortunately, overnight, his body had evacuated enough fluid that he could tolerate the additional anesthesia necessary for the procedures.

We had been warned that simply moving his bed across elevator thresholds between ICU and the MRI suite could cause uncontrollable distress to his fragile lungs. Tara and I accompanied him down to the radiology suite, grimacing each time the bed rattled. I had to turn my back to his listless form as they moved him from one table to the next.

We didn't really know what the day would provide, but knowing he would not live without any of these procedures, we were braced for major change. We had no idea if he was ultimately moving forward or backward, and we would have been thrilled with a stalemate.

Back at the room, the anesthesiologist met us before the rest of the medical team. "The radiologist needs to confirm their report, but the MRI looked good," he said. "You all should be quite relieved."

There were few details at that point, enough for our nerves. As the day wore on, the tenor of each report improved. The CT scan revealed fluid between his lung sacs and his chest wall, but it also demonstrated that his body was beginning to purge things slowly but surely. With regard to the MRI, the cyst had not changed, but there did appear to be some change in the temporal lobe in the area affecting short-term memory. Whatever the cause, it appeared to have affected both hemispheres of his brain equally, whereas a typical viral infection would be present more on one side or the other. All of the big bacterial infections have been ruled out. And the bronchial scope told us that his airways looked very normal, all things considered.

And after all of the jostling, poking, and prodding, he never needed another boost of oxygen. His blood pressure is low, and his heart rate is down to 108 bpm (yesterday it was over 170 when he was first intubated).

It appears that prayers are kicking in big-time. At this point, the doctors believe that Brennan may have had a bug of some kind in his system. What it is, we may never know. But his new immune system, seeing a foreign invader slipping in, jumped out of the trench at it screaming, which more than likely caused the "engraftment syndrome" in his lungs. Now, with more than a little help from his ICU support team, his body is starting to regulate itself, calling off the troops and performing as designed.

The next several days will hopefully confirm that this is indeed the story, rather than that some weirdo infection is in there requiring a drastic new medication. If his body is starting to regulate itself, he can be gradually weaned off of the oxygen and breathe on his own. If this is the case, I could care less what bug started this whole mess.

Oddly, with this news, his transplant has been documented as a "success," and I started feeling an oddly assertive sense of determination about Brennan. I cannot begin to express how many times I have consciously attempted to "give it all up to God," as those of us in my culture have been taught to do. Particularly over these past two years, to say, "Whatever happens is your will, and I give glory to the blessings of life regardless of what happens"—and to truly mean it—is hard. I inevitably end up falling back into my habit of trying to outthink it all.

But yesterday morning, I honestly believe that I truly "gave it up." I thought we had lost him. I felt no other path than to just let it go where it was going to go. I was not strong enough to hold on. Tara is a much more capable person at managing her spiritual side, and truly living it, than I will ever be. But something happened that gave me more confidence in Brennan than I have had yet. And here he is fighting this thing on his own, with a good chance of making it.

I may have just rolled the transcendental dice one too many times in making this statement. Getting off of this ventilator is no easy task, and a lot of kids don't make it. If Brennan leaves this place, it will be a miracle. But has the miracle not already happened? He's already beaten the odds, whether he walks out of here or not. The real miracle is in what he has already done, but also in what I believe can be done because of him and what has happened in my soul, and many others, because of him.

Today, the Brothers were allowed to come visit him for the first time since they'd said "goodbye" and "I love you." To prepare siblings for what their brother or sister will look like with all of the tubes, the Childlife specialists provide a little dummy with a scale model breathing tube for its mouth and IG tube for its nose. In this case, they also took a picture of Brennan himself and showed it to them, giving them enough of a preview not to freak out. Believe me, it is really hard to look at your kid this way. To a kid, and a brother, I cannot imagine.

When they both entered the room at separate times, they asked, "Can he really hear me?" "Yes he can," we replied. "Tell him something about your day."

Both kids just held his hand and stroked his little bald head, staring at him intently. "I love you, Brennan," they said. "We can't wait to see you." Each said it all matter-of-factly, with pure childlike honesty. They believe their brother is going to walk out of here next week. I do too.

For now, I am following their lead, sitting at his bedside, stroking his head, and telling him I love him. Mostly I am giving it up to him, telling him, "Thank you."   —NTS

Damn the Torpedoes
Posted Nov 14, 2010 11:52am

Groggily shuffling from Brennan's room to the parent bathroom in order to brush my teeth after a long, sleepless night, I ran into one of Brenny's most amiable doctors, Dave Shook.

"I just stopped by to look at the boy for a while. I am glad it gives me a chance to talk to you on a personal basis. No doctor's hat . . . just me," he volunteered as he stuck out his hand in the ICU hallway. He was clearly there solely for the purpose of seeing Brennan.

Seeming exhausted himself, he looked me firmly in the eye. "He is looking better, although we still have no definite evidence of what caused his rapid breakdown on Tuesday. But last night I was home with my family and thought about him and how amazingly special he is, and I just had a good feeling. For what my karmic opinion is worth, I think he is going to be fine. He truly is special. I just feel it."

These feelings have been mutually expressed from a diverse group of experts here. From the nurses, ICU and BMT docs, and a myriad of healthcare professionals, staff people, and volunteers, the number of people here who outwardly care for him is mind-boggling. And seemingly every other one we see says, effectively, "ICU on a vent is a very scary place to be, but Brennan is different."

Although Brennan has been effectively comatose, his room has been restless. Both grandmothers have been here since "the day," reading to him while he "sleeps" and recounting stories special to him. Tara does the same, and had actually been planning my birthday party out loud to him.

For me, I hold his flaccid hand and tell him about my day, but also a lot about tomorrow. I tell him about our bow hunting trip that we have been attempting to arrange. "We" talk about the new golf season, which will accompany new clubs for him when he gets out of here. "We" talk about fishing, movies to see, what to get for Christmas, and just about anything I can conjure of a positive nature.

But "we" also sing. His two favorite songs (at least the ones that I play on the guitar here in his room) are "Sweet Baby James" and "You've Got a Friend." When he listens to these songs in my car, his little voice always delivers the perfect layer of harmonic innocence from the backseat. So late nights, usually after my blog entry efforts, "we" play and sing together.

At first it was kind of embarrassing, noticing the nurses glimpsing through the glass observation windows as I perched on the front of the mini lounge chair trying not to bump the back of my guitar against the IV poles. After a while I just stopped caring, focusing on how he would sing these songs after begging me to play.

And throughout it all, whether with me, Tara, or one of the grandparents, the ubiquitous sounds of divinity radiate from the iPod guitar playlist, which has been a part of his daily experience since the healing process all started.

I wish I could say with certainty that our efforts to keep his mind occupied with positive input have generated a response. But knowing, or having been emphatically told by numerous people, that people on ventilators have a surprisingly acute sense of hearing and memory, and that one's activities and statements in their presence are critical components to their blueprint for recovery, we feed him in this manner.

Friday night, I was staying with Brennan. Having finished playing the guitar, I turned to put my stuff back in the case and caught him trying to sit up in bed. His motions resembled a kid zombie from a seventies-era horror move, bending upward from the waist with his hands sticking straight out like Frankenstein. At first, it was rather frightening, but then I noticed him reaching toward the tubing in his throat.

Gently restraining his arms, I desperately looked for the nurse's page button. Afraid he would jerk either the NG feeding tube from his nose or, worse, the vent tube from his throat, I finally appealed for assistance by horse-kicking the automatic door opener while leaning over to hold his arms down. I yelled for help. He finally fell back down and appeared to sleep.

The nurse came in the room. I announced, "He moved! He tried to get up and grab his tube."

"I've just dosed him with more pain meds, so he should not be doing anything," she said. Feeling confident in my observation, I said, "Brennan, grab my hand." His little eyes struggled to open, shuttering up and down as his eyelids retracted to half-mast. He reached over, grabbed my hand, and squeezed.

I called Tara to tell her. "Happy Birthday!" she said as soon as I got on the line. To my surprise, I looked up to see the clock at 11:55, just five minutes before November 13. I told her the news. "You may have forgotten what day it was," she said, "but Brennan didn't."

· · ·

Birthday morning, November 13, 2010: The new ICU physician in charge informed us that Brennan's capacity for weaning from the ventilator has been truly remarkable. "Almost every patient we see from BMT who requires intubation is at least two weeks out before their bodies are even remotely capable of existing without it. Brennan is exceptional. Rest up today, for tomorrow will be busy. Our schedule is to begin the process of removing him from it at eight in the morning."

Happy Birthday for sure!

I have now spent two of my birthdays in a row in St. Jude hospital rooms. It was cold and rainy, but still one of those wonderful fall days that provided a sense of tranquility and the assurance of renewal. We had committed to a relatively early night. First, though, my birthday celebration was conducted in Brennan's room with both sets of grandparents, my sister Martha, and the Brothers all present. The ICU staff made a generous exception for this. It was short and sweet, and after the "Happy Birthday" song was over and the fake candle was blown out, Brennan raised his hands and tried to open his eyes.

The plan was to begin the process of extubation at eight the next morning. However, at 5 a.m. we got a call from Tara's mom, who had stayed in the room in order to allow us to rest, saying, "Come over! He's ready. He is sitting straight up in bed and directing traffic. The ICU nurse has called the doctor at home."

We arrived to find Brennan trying to speak to us around the tube, producing only hollow tones of wind, but clearly trying to tell us to get these things out of him. I asked the nurse if they had backed off on the anesthesia early, who replied, "No, we had him fully dosed so that he would rest comfortably until the scheduled extubation. This kid is calling his own shots."

At 5:45 a.m., the tubes were out. They had never seen anything like it.

Wednesday morning when he was put to sleep, I told myself that I was going to shout and cry if he ever woke up. Instead, I just hugged my wife, said a little prayer, and cried. On cue, the sun revealed itself from the reflection on the gold dome outside the window. The day of renewal had arrived.

Brennan's first words were unintelligible whispers, his throat having been rendered more than raw after his marathon coughing episodes and now having been stretched by the tube. Of course, he is still affected by the anesthesia, which will take some time to fully wear off. But talk he did: "Why am I here?" "Why won't you let me walk?" "Water!"

I know a lot of hands were involved in this recovery: from the astute BMT and ICU teams, to the behind-the-scenes experts, to the transplant, to the long-distance cowboy healer Tara's cousin Lorrie put us in touch with last week, to this weird virus, which may have caused Brennan's organs to fail, but that failure triggered the engraftment syndrome, and to Brennan himself. The hand of God has many fingers, and we accredit the miracle of this rare and phenomenal recovery to celestial grace.

But ultimately, I will take this life experience to my last breath as the time when the circumstances gave us the choice either to react with anger or to simply turn it over to the big man upstairs and trust in the outcome. Either way, the gift is graciously accepted.

Brennan held his ground, and the troops delivered. He will walk out of this ICU unit, albeit with a bit of a wobble. Next week, he will be back in the BMT unit and back to the business of beating leukemia. As parents, we will walk back onto that floor with a renewed sense of faith in the team, in Brennan, and in God up above. This week gave us all one hell of a test. But I am paying attention now. That I can promise.   —NTS

Keep Moving
Posted Nov 18, 2010 6:26pm

The Brothers were blessed with no school on Monday, which allowed them to spend one more day with the grandparents as Tara and I planned for Brennan's discharge back to a "normal" BMT room.

Everyone was exhausted but doing their best. Christopher and I had just watched our first *Band of Brothers* episode in some time. They had scraped through the Battle of Carentan, just after the Normandy invasion. Lying around the burned-out village, spent from the experience, the soldiers felt like they had won the unwinnable, yet they had no idea what lay ahead. How many grueling months and how much more would it cost to either achieve victory or suffer defeat? Resting on the cold, broken stones of the shattered town square, staring at the sky, catching their breath, ears still ringing from the explosions, the master sergeant piped in, "On your feet, boys . . . we are moving out!"

Exhaustion. While the adrenaline wears from battle and the taste of victory melts away with time, all the worrisome days and sleepless nights start to build up and weigh heavy.

I do not think there is a member of the clan who can claim exemption from this cycle.

Early Monday morning, Brennan's breathing had become labored again, and the ICU team placed him back on oxygen. While not requiring nearly the volume as he had the previous week, the ICU team informed us that they were concerned and preparing for treatment alternatives to prevent another intubation. Apparently the virus that caused Brennan's engraftment also causes severe disease in transplant recipients and can lead to graft rejection and other organ disease, particularly the liver. Brennan had pulled off a major victory with his fledgling immune system, but not without major casualties. The rest of the fight was going to be hard.

If there was any upside to the delay, it allowed the Brothers to visit a little bit on Monday. Since they were allowed in ICU but not on the BMT floor, this little window was received as a gift, knowing that even a few minutes at the side of their brother could replenish necessary spiritual fuel.

At home that night, attempting to take advantage of the last few hours before getting back onto a "regular" schedule again, the wear on their little minds and bodies became clear. Nat reacted emotionally to everything. Tears and hyperventilation were the response to just about everything we suggested as parents all day. From his mother's menu selection at lunch to reminders throughout the day regarding his reading assignments to the unsuspended bedtime curfew, he was clearly overwhelmed.

Tara was in the hospital with Brenny that night. Aunt Martha and I stayed with the Brothers. I walked into his room as Nat lay in his bed, quietly reading his assignment through tears. I crawled in bed next to him. "Hey buddy, there anything you want to talk about?" I asked. "I know you've had a long week and are sad to see your aunts and grandparents leave, but is there anything else you want to talk with me and Mommy about?"

"I am scared about Brennan," he said.

"Me too. We all are," I said. I began to talk as frankly with him about my fears as I ever had. But I tried my best to recall the most recent lesson Brennan taught me.

"Try to remember the message from your movie *Facing the Giants*. I know it is hard, but you have to let go and trust to the best of your ability and pray for help." Before I left, I looked him in the eye. "I know you are getting too old for me to say prayers for you, but I want you to promise me that you will do this every day. Your brother needs it." He nodded and looked up to me for a hug. "I need it too," Nat said.

Walking into the other bedroom, I got Christopher into bed after a lengthy dispute, and he curled up into my left arm while we finished our book together.

I thought about Brennan and how long it's been since we have been able to hold him and read to him in this way. Emerging from transplant the last time, he had been revealing signs of a big boy growing inside, seeking independence despite the many months that he'd been deprived of a typical childhood. He has always loved to sleep with me and Tara, reading with one of us before bed every night. But between the hospital life and simply getting older, those days were fleeting.

I guess it won't be long before Christopher reaches that point too, transitioning from someone who relishes his dependence to someone apart. In anticipation, I have revealed a lean toward overindulgence, partly to keep his mind happy and off of the threat that looms over us all, but partly due to my selfish desire to make up for the deficit I feel since Brennan's life has been altered by this crazy war. In either scenario, independence is near.

As for me and Tara, the cumulative exhaustion is occasionally offset in large part by the staccato spurts of adrenaline triggered by sudden and intense demands for care decisions. But sleeping at home with the boys proved as necessary for me as for them.

We awoke Tuesday with good news about Brennan. He was totally off of supplemental oxygen and officially slated for discharge back to the BMT unit. Suddenly we were back to the ho-hum life of bone marrow transplant and fighting cancer. As one can imagine, though, Brennan's fighting strength appeared sapped.

All day long, he just stared off at the wall despite our best efforts to entertain him with videos, games, music, etc. He redundantly requested *The Black Stallion*, the old movie with Mickey Rooney. It replayed throughout the day, but he would just stare in a seemingly indifferent trance. Tara reported to me that the night before, some of his delusional perspectives on things were starting to reveal themselves once again, telling her he wanted "to go upstairs to the TV room." The notion of a "TV room" (which is what we called it at our house in Augusta) remained his obsession the entire next day. All night long, Tara stayed up with him, doing her best to answer his questions and talk to him as normally as possible, but he never slept for a moment.

The ICU doctor had explained that intubated patients often experience "ICU psychosis," which is a temporary altered mental state brought on by the lengthy anesthesia and the frenetic atmosphere inside the unit. Made sense to me: His brain had to be cluttered with chemicals, confusion, and questions about what, where, and how? We hoped the new BMT room would be the antidote to whatever degree of psychosis he had been dealing with. Granted, it is still part of the hospital, but it is not part of the ICU wing. Therefore, we hope for improvement over time, as he is at least back in a place with familiar faces and a window he can see through . . . a window with a pyramid.

Before moving, however, some significant adjustments were necessary. The antiviral drugs can only be administered orally; consequently the NG tube had to be reinstalled in Brennan's nose while still in ICU as a means of getting these drugs into his tummy. The NG tube has been something that Brennan has prided himself in *not* having. Tara and I were worried that even the suggestion of sticking this feeding tube down his nose into his stomach would generate backflips of anger. But that was based on our reactions from 2009. This time, telling him firmly but gently that this would help, he just sheepishly nodded.

Back in the old BMT room Tuesday night, a few awkward questions and comments would pop up regarding where we were. Every fifteen minutes or so he would request things he had just received: hot blankets, medicines, lotion. The things he focused on were by-products of obsessive delirium. The real him just wasn't there.

It was a long night for me because Brennan, again, had zero sleep. I finally nodded off around four o'clock or so as he sat up in bed to watch what seemed to be the one hundredth rerun of *Phineas and Ferb* on Disney Channel. Around 6:30 a.m., he poked me up again to help him with the bathroom and to get some water. I was so pleased that he was requesting fluids that I groggily got up and did not even notice that he had ejected the newly installed feeding tube from his nose by himself sometime while I was sleeping. The nurse pointed it out to me when he arrived around seven, to which I shrugged my shoulders and said, "Thank God for you guys." Meanwhile, the NG pump had been slowly dripping the formula for his gut onto the bed in a smelly, sticky puddle.

I awoke from my couch to a blinding reflection through his window. The crisp morning sun had enveloped the great glass pyramid in tea-colored stains of orange and red. It was a new and odd sense of awakening, as if the sun had risen from the west. I felt jolted from a dream of Brennan alone in a dark place. I moved from the couch to his bed and stroked his hair, feeling that wherever he was, he was my light. Relieved that we were safe for the moment, everything became quiet and peaceful. My head lay on his sheet, and the room hummed with muted electrical white-noise.

At that point, I cannot begin to recall what I was thinking about the end to this superfluous struggle. I knew that, moving forward, we had to saddle up with whatever energy we had left and encourage Brennan to scrape up whatever he possibly could. The problem was that at this point, our soldier was truly scraping the bottom of the barrel, and so were the strategic minds behind this whole operation.

The lack of answers concerned me heavily Wednesday morning. The questions about moving up "to the TV room" changed from simple requests to pleas to leave the hospital. I requested that the nurse bring the doctors in sooner than later, as I was getting antsy. Within about half an hour, the entire medical team came in. They had been talking about Brennan all morning. Concerned about the lack of improvement on the mental side of things, they had decided to bring in a neurologist to help determine if the symptoms were long-lingering side effects of the virus or some other form of seizure. They tried to assure me that although this loss of cognitive function became permanent in about 5 to 10 percent of patients, Brennan would beat the odds. They also told me that the donor cells in his system had dropped to 96 percent, which meant his graft was slipping, and that the team had agreed to proceed with DLI.

My short response was, "So, we are supposed to place all of our chips on the long shot for the leukemia cure and bet with the odds for the mental problems?" I started to suggest we consult a bookie, but bit my tongue. I was tired, and I felt like I needed to escape the oncoming wave of emotion before it enveloped me and spilled over onto these kind and gracious people, who were truly doing everything they could.

Brennan had finally fallen asleep for the first time in forever when an EEG technician arrived, closing the door with a bang and speaking loudly as she entered. I once again was short, telling this unsuspecting woman to be quiet in a less than pleasant tone. Tara and Martha happened to be right behind her to witness the whole exchange, for which I eventually apologized before actually biting my tongue, grabbing my backpack, and walking out to Target House for what was clearly a long overdue nap. I had to regain my self-control before coming back for the night.

Arriving back around 8 p.m. or so, I found Brennan sitting up in bed with about two dozen electrode leads and wires extending from every corner of his cranial globe. They were tied in the back into a long ponytail to keep them out of his way while he slept. With the electrodes poking out on top and the ponytail in the rear, he looked like a cross between Avatar and

Pinhead. It looked strangely surreal and entirely ridiculous, but he seemed to be relatively unfazed by the whole setup.

I assumed my night watchman duties, rested from the nap, and was actually excited with Tara's idea that we settle in for an all-night movie marathon. The movies started, but the night sort of floundered along. Brennan catnapped in and out of mild sleep for fifteen minutes or so every now and then, but he was clearly unable to sleep. Because of the EEG exercise, he did not qualify for any sleep meds. I felt terrible for him, watching him sit straight up only to slouch his encumbered head into his lap and then back up again.

The doctors made their rounds today to let us know that the DLI is tentatively scheduled for Saturday to jump-start the graft again. They do not want to start it any earlier, allowing his lungs as much time as possible to grow stronger from last week. His graft is slipping, and he needs the DLI in order to once again gain the upper hand on the battlefront, which is exactly where we were pre-ICU.

There are many battles, but the graft and its capacity to beat the leukemia remain the heart of the war. Each of these battles in itself is terrifying. Each renders an excuse to quit, to stop the torture. But the miracle of last week proves that Brennan is strong. The question is just how much stamina he has left. We have to remain aggressive, but not so aggressive that we lose our sensitivities. And he is certainly weaker than he has ever been.

This fight has been a balancing act since the beginning. The stakes just get higher and higher. It is hard to believe that this is even possible after last week. But we believe in the finish line to which we set our sights and in the power that drives us to it.   —NTS

Trust, Faith, and Creamed Corn
Posted Nov 20, 2010 4:49pm

Brennan awoke yesterday a little stronger, but he seemed to be stuck in the same psychological rut. When Dr. Leung examined him, he showed very little response to very basic and simple questions. "Where are you, Brennan?" Dr. Leung asked as he performed an eye exam. "Do you know why you are in Memphis?" With each wrong answer, the long road ahead was getting longer.

But even with the memory lapses, and behind the vacant looks and absence of smiles, sweet Brennan would occasionally raise his head through the fog. When the nurse told him "thank you" for allowing them to reinstall his NG feeding tube, he responded with, "You're welcome."

Occasionally, his little hand would reach over and hold mine or Tara's, or he would bend over and scratch my back and say, "Does that feel good, Daddy?" followed up with a genuine Brennan hug. And then he would seemingly disappear for a while.

I don't think we were ever worried that he was lost inside there, but I must admit feeling worried about whether we would ever see the real Brennan smile again. But then that voice inside would say, "What are you thinking? This kid was on a ventilator less than a week ago. Give him a break, for crying out loud. Give him some time."

Later in the afternoon, the entire BMT team came by to talk with me at Brennan's bedside, but they requested we adjourn to the hallway for what was looking like a heavy conversation. The body language from each doctor in the group was serious. Hands in pockets, eyes toward the ground, Dr. Leung's generally less-than-relaxed humor made both of us feel that we were in for a tough one before the first word was uttered.

But the gist of it all was less related to Brennan than to us and our commitment to riding this thing out. Dr. Leung explained that the DLI was scheduled for the morning, pending the positive results from the CT scan of his lungs. He explained to us, however, that he was worried about making up the ground lost last week in ICU, when his donor cells were distracted from taking root because of this blasted virus.

According to him: "While Brennan looks like himself, and while we know he is not totally himself from a mental perspective, we think we can wait no longer for the DLI boost if we want to maintain a reasonable chance of getting the leukemia back in check."

But he also wanted us to understand in no uncertain terms that with each DLI infusion, new risks are introduced, particularly in a patient who just days ago was experiencing significant pulmonary inflammation. "As with cancers that demonstrate increasing resistance to chemotherapy, so too do the leukemia cells respond to the infused lymphocyte cells. Therefore, each infusion represents approximately twice as many cells as before."

The long and short of this is that with more cells, there is proportionate increase in the risk of severe GVHD, and thereby a potential major organ failure such as we had just witnessed. The same big guns that almost lost our soldier to friendly fire were being pulled out again.

"If you want us to proceed tomorrow, we need to make sure you are still in this for the cure," he said matter-of-factly. "As an alternative, we can create a bridge to buy more time for him to live a little longer. But I need to understand with complete confidence that this treatment option falls within the parameters that you and Tara have defined for yourselves and for Brennan."

I don't know if I could have processed all of these issues on a rational level even at my fighting peak, but I do know that being tired all the time is not the way to interpret complex and emotionally sensitive matters about your child's life or death. Tara and I both explained to him that regardless of our fatigue or the strain that this experience had on this family, we had no goal less than complete cure for Brennan. If the point comes that there are no other options available to us, or that the treatments introduce anything that appears inhumane, we are willing to talk about alternatives. But for now, we have faith in our kid. We know we are in a corner, but we have to press on.

Heavy stuff, but not anything we do not ask ourselves and pray about every moment of every day. As the chinks are revealed in our armor, it is comforting to know that these professionals maintain a strong sensitivity to both the kid and the family. This is not a journey that can be easily managed alone. One's faith is weakened by the lack of faith of even a single member of the team. Therefore, checks of reassurance are imperative. A year ago, these were quarterly reassurances. Then they become monthly. Now they are daily, or more.

Walking back into Brennan's room, I found him to be quiet and withdrawn. He had been like this all day. He seemed pensive and silent, like a timid little mouse who sensed a cat. I was sensing that he may have somehow heard our discussion and that he was having second thoughts about the things we had just discussed outside. That would have been the only reason to stop and pursue the "quality of life" measures. But then he suddenly sat up in bed. Alertly, he pointed across the room and said, "Daddy, I want to work on that Lego set."

I tore open the box and delightfully began to sort each little package by color as he diligently thumbed through the instructions. In an instant he seemed a different person, and after working on the model for over an hour, he was ready to play cards. I emailed the doctors with news of a "breakthrough."

Dr. Shook came to witness. "Dr. Leung said that he heard Brenny was building with Legos and back to his old self again," he said. With a caring look at Brennan, he looked up at me almost tearfully. "That kid inspires me," he said, and he walked out.

The lymphocytes arrived at 9 a.m., once again about a thimble-full inside of a syringe. I said the Lord's Prayer to myself and five Hail Marys in the amount of time it took for the cells to be infused. I thought about the intense focus of what we had been praying for and how in the blink of an eye, things seemed to be moving in a new direction. "I smell creamed corn," Tara said. I did too.

"Yep, that's the smell of the cells," said the nurse. "Everybody says the same thing."

I thought about corn and what it has meant to people over the years. Googling its etymology, my instincts were confirmed. Corn, to Native American culture, represents the symbol for life and what sustains it. Back in our new room overlooking The Pyramid, I realized that we were finding meaning in everything.

Holding the faith and trusting in outcomes are hard. Just last night I received an email about a fourteen-year-old kid in Augusta who was diagnosed with hemolytic anemia just a few days ago and who passed away last night. It weighed on me heavily throughout the night. How do we maintain consistent faith with such inconsistency in this world? How do we trust when children we know and pray for die? Why did that boy die so quickly? Why is Brennan still fighting?   —NTS

6

SCORCHED EARTH

WINTER 2010 TO SUMMER 2011

No one foresaw the massive offensive in the Ardennes forest that Christmas in 1944. A "defeated" enemy turned out not to be so defeated after all, uncovering its true unrelenting substance as it organized for a ruthless counterattack. And while our guys were caught off guard and thrown into what some have deemed the most brutal fighting conditions of the European theater, they rallied, dug in, and fought. They were outnumbered, undersupplied, and unprepared, but most were proven soldiers by this time, and their instincts kept them focused on the goal.

Coming out of ICU, Brennan had effectively endured a relentless pounding from some very big guns. When the smoke clears and the ear ringing subsides to a lower key, one feels, "This has to be over." But it is just another beginning—in this case, a brutal renewal.

With a war-weary fighter and a desperate support team, all the stops had to be pulled out from that point forward. Whatever principles or "ethical" idiosyncrasies I may have subscribed to were eclipsed by the reality of experience. One often says to oneself (or at least I do), "In XYZ circumstances,

I would undoubtedly do A"—but the pudding reveals the proof on a platter for everyone to see. Living in the realm of the Dark Angel, one is stripped of vanity, yielding our human exterior to that of any other animal who simply exists at his mercy.

But our trust in a greater being remains, like that of a child in his father. Just as the shell-shocked soldier gets up and fights despite fear, we throw ourselves at God. There we can grasp the present, appreciate the past, and surrender the future to its rightful owner.

We were facing the enemy on multiple fronts, dealing with the viral situation and its unknown ramifications both for the transplant and for his body in general, as well as the leukemia itself. New drugs were thrown in, seemingly daily. Platelet transfusions became constant. Food intake dribbled to zero, with Brennan becoming totally dependent on NG feeds and ultimately IV nutrition. Constant monitoring of organ function, including potential long-term effects to the brain, became routine. Everything had a role in pulling Brennan out of the ditch and moving forward.

And anything could play a role in sparking a disaster. To think that a year ago we were Googling the potential ramifications of antifungal medications! At this point, almost everything on the medical front had a double edge. Brennan had proven what he could take, though, and we had no choice. Carefully, we began to throw more and more dangerous things into the mix. We started fighting fire with fire, with treatments that reflected the tireless efficiency of the disease itself. While radiation, toxic drugs, and novel transplantation technology may affect the cancer, the risks introduced are termed "acceptable" if they can win the war. Their potentially disturbing aftereffects represent a case study on human morality, rationalizing the lesser of two evils. If more lives can be saved than lost, in comparison to mindless holocaust, it is, we decide, worth the risk.

But the researchers—like the rocket engineers of the second World War—hone their skills under pressure and continue to learn. With children's lives literally on the line, they create new ways to manipulate a human immune system to its limit. And thus, like the eventual decision to bomb the major German cities, we kill the bad guys and burn the good.

These were the ethical gymnastics we wrestled with, both waking and in our sleep. If not for the perseverance of love and innocence in Brennan, his Brothers, and the other kids in our world, I think I would have become hardened beyond repair. With tight-fistedness, Nat and Christopher hung on to us despite what had to have been a clearly shaken composure, and their demeanor and abundant love for one another shined through Brennan's fight to live. Their example was our gift. It was everything.

A Light Shines
Posted Dec 13, 2010 1:30pm

Sitting on the second pew with Christopher asleep on my lap, the priest noted the pink advent candle during the homily and told us, "The point of it all is pretty simple. Keep your mind and your hearts open to the light. Feel the miracles. Try to experience the day not as something you control, but as something you receive. Then you will truly experience the miracles, which are so abundant."

Christopher and I had attended evening mass at St. Patrick's in downtown Memphis while Nat and Tara stayed at Grizzly House with Brennan. He had finally been given the all-clear to leave the unit, but his virus kept him in isolation status and therefore quarantined from Target House. We are planning for Christmas in Memphis again. Despite our unconventional family environment, we realize we have been given the greatest of gifts. But I cannot look at this gift in terms of price. No gift, in my mind, is worth a cross borne by a child.

How many Christmas mornings have been dampened by the "Thank you . . . what's next?" perspective. How often do we truly say, with feeling, "Thank you, this is one of the most special treasures of my life"? I know that my answer includes significantly more of the former.

The children who suffer and inspire us should not factor into the equation; nonetheless, they are clearly part of it. Why is a wake-up call of this magnitude required? Why did man require the sacrifice of God's son to realize the basic tenets of love, giving, and gratitude that had been there all along?

I guess we truly are flawed, even to the extent of struggling to see the light that shines forth from our children and people who love us each and every day. That alone should be enough. Love should be the only thing necessary for gratitude. I certainly struggle to see the light through the often clouded veil of fear and doubt. But when it shines through, even for a moment, there is such a tremendous sense of peace. This is our gift this advent season and our wish for all others struggling to reconcile suffering and hardship with love.

Today Brennan's ANC dropped to 200. His platelets are consumed at a rate of close to 40,000 per day. Consequently, the BMT team has decided to do a bone marrow biopsy tomorrow. But he looks good. He is eating. He is happy. He is cheerful and funny and loving. He is the light of our focus. —NTS

'Tis the Season
Posted Dec 16, 2010 7:08pm

On Tuesday, Brennan woke up feeling surprisingly strong again. This was biopsy day, so I felt like these signs were pointing our way to a good start. I had stayed with him for the past two nights at his request. Had I not been with him, I would have been a nervous wreck.

Late that morning we received an unexpected call from Dr. Leung. Tara and I arrived to a family consultation room so full of doctors and other members of Brennan's treatment team that we moved to a conventional examination room. Standing adjacent to the wall battery of scopes and monitors, Dr. Leung leaned over the examination table to draw a chart on the protective paper roll.

"OK." He started drawing little boxes for notes. "The first and biggest concern, of course, was the leukemia," he noted with the large X in the center. "But the bone marrow actually shows signs that the donor cells are doing their job and that, indeed, the leukemia burden is less now than it was in November. It is still higher than it was when Brennan relapsed, but it is trending in the right direction."

He drew a bell curve on the white examination room paper, marking a Y where the leukemia was when we got here, another at the top of the bell indicating where it was a week or so after the ICU incident, and another one equal in degree to the initial one, indicating where we are now.

"With this data," he concluded, "Brennan's present condition is a result of aplastic anemia, not leukemia." Aplastic anemia is also a terminal disease. It falls within the same family of blood disorders as leukemia, and indeed was one of the assumed culprits when Brennan was first diagnosed almost two years ago. Dr. Leung continued to draw a circle adjacent to the bell, making lots of little markers inside indicating the nearly thirty medications Brennan takes every day. "The aplastic anemia could be a side effect of the medications," Dr. Leung continued. "What this means is that hopefully his body will work its way through this process and hopefully leave enough residual healthy T cells to start over yet again. It is my experience that this is the likely outcome, but it could take several weeks until we know for sure." He kept drawing in tighter and tighter circles until he had nearly colored in what had evolved into a confusing and frightfully meaningless graphic. "In the event this desired result is not reached, the only alternative is another bone marrow transplant." He looked seriously at both of us. "And I told both of you before we started this one that I do not believe we are capable of pulling off a fourth transplant."

I have been trying to think of the best analogy for what is happening and where Tara and I find ourselves emotionally and spiritually. The simplest way I can explain it is this: amid a frightening storm, our roof, which appeared to be giving way, is still creaking but holding together, despite a handful of leaks. But as the water drips from the rafter, an audible plop and cold splash reveal that the basement is now flooded, and the water is quickly rising from beneath. I honestly do not know what my reaction should be. All I can think is: *If it does not stop raining, we're doomed.*

Walking from the consult room, I was tangled up inside. Relieved from my worst fears earlier in the day, I was no longer preoccupied with another relapse and leukemia. But the thought of a second terminal disease was beyond my worst and most paranoid capability. Dr. Leung had said that in the majority of cases, this situation would work itself out on its own.

223

Tara and I have to hang our hat somewhere. Looks like this is the only hook available.

Back at the house, I was trying desperately to act like "fun dad." This is easier said than done when one finds oneself speechless. As I played with Nat and Christopher, Brennan woke up from a catnap, and Tara suggested that I take the Brothers with me to hunt down a couple of Christmas presents. Walking to the car, I must have appeared unsettled, doing my best to accept the assignment with alacrity but not really capable of doing so with even a remote air of sincerity.

On our way to the store, the backseat conversation transformed from good humor to a minor altercation about whether or not Nat was going to root against GA Tech vs. Air Force in the Independence Bowl later in the month. The argument digressed to the point that the boys started shouting at each other, at which time I suddenly switched on the radio and turned it up as loud as it would go.

"What are you doing, Daddy?" Christopher yelled from the backseat. After about thirty seconds of having jolted them into silence, I turned down the volume and shouted, "I am sick of listening to you guys!" My knee-jerk reaction succeeded. They became stone-cold silent, and I instantly felt terrible.

After a few awkward minutes, Christopher chimed in, "We're sorry, Daddy." Nat sat quietly with his head leaning against the rear window, looking out at the gray and wet evening between the car lights passing in the opposite lane. Tearfully, he said, "Me too, Daddy. We didn't mean to make you upset."

They clearly sensed a larger issue. Indeed, they had not made me upset. I was simply cracking.

Once at our destination, the Christmas retail atmosphere broke the ice a little bit and the boys lightened up. People were bustling about in search of gifts for their own reality. Tony Bennett's voice was overhead, singing his version of "I'll Be Home for Christmas." I thought, *I guess this is home now.*

For half an hour or so, we talked, joked, and held hands. To the rest of our little shopping community, we may have actually fit in. I bought Nat and Christopher each a pair of warm hunting boots for an early Christmas present. For Brennan, I bought a sturdy and warm camouflage coat, which I assumed would be more practical for him, considering the likelihood of him going hunting anytime in the near future was somewhere between zero and zero. But on the way home, I started to feel bad about his gift. I should have gotten him the boots. He's still part of the Band.

On the way back from lunch at the cafeteria today, I witnessed a father breaking down emotionally in public. He and his wife were walking together when his legs just gave out beneath him like a plastic toy assembled with elastic string. Confused and apparently frightened, he plopped into a chair, placed his hands in his lap and wept, right there in front of everyone. I felt compelled to sit down by him, but walked right on by, concerned but afraid to respond, like a gawker at a roadside car accident. I know how he feels.

We are approaching the dead of winter, yet it feels like the ice we are standing on is getting thinner by the day. At the same time, it's still holding, and we can still see the other side of the lake. Our minds struggle with so much, but our hearts are focused on solid ground.

Through it all, Brennan's light continues to shine. We are asking a lot of this little boy.   —NTS

'Tis the Season, After All
Posted Dec 25, 2010 4:35pm

It was the gift of a day. Brennan did not need a transfusion. Uncle Ward was in town for a holiday visit, and we were off to Frank's Main Street Deli for a fresh smoked-turkey sandwich, a delicacy that I am always eager to share with my out-of-town visitors.

I noticed a homeless man fixed on this particular corner and decided to drive around the block in order to avoid a panhandler "negotiation," particularly in front of Christopher. But despite my evasive parking plan, the man made his way across the street straight to us as we walked to the awning at Frank's. With our hands firmly in our pockets and shuffling our feet, we shivered in front of the store as he told his story. He was clean and articulate, and he started weeping, telling us how he'd moved here from Nashville, but that his new job in Memphis was eliminated after the first week. He and his two daughters were simply trying to raise enough money to stay at the Salvation Army through Christmas. Ward and I both gave him some money and wished him a Merry Christmas and good luck, but Christopher could not get this experience off of his mind.

Throughout the wait in the deli, it was all he could talk about. "Is it a real army? Do people have to live there? Do they have to live there during Christmas? Do the children get Christmas presents? Do they have other family and friends who help them out?" It was a lot for a little guy, and his thoughtful mind was racing.

Leaving the store, Christopher asked that we seek the man out again in order to give him some more money for Christmas presents. We drove around the block, and to my surprise, we found the man. He had made his way east into a fairly desolate area of demolished warehouses and rusted chain-link fences. He was on the curb talking to a guy with cameras around his neck. We honked our horn, first startling and then astonishing him. But when Christopher gave him the money (his own money, which he paid me back for, at his insistence), the man said, "Thank you", and gave us the sign of the cross through tears. He was still crying and waving as we drove away.

Inspired from his experience, Christopher rallied Brennan later that day and we all set off in search of the Salvation Army to donate our old coats. The Salvation Army had moved from downtown Memphis well out into the eastern suburbs (a planning decision I do not understand); so programming the address into my GPS, our computer-lady-guide took us on a circuitous route through the eclectic mix of businesses along Summer Ave.

For Brennan, the hour round-trip journey was the first real drive he had experienced in some time and triggered some wonderful conversations with the boys. Compared to the cold and gloom earlier in the day, it had become a sunny afternoon. Each time I looked in the rearview mirror, his face was pressed against the window glass, smiling in his anonymity at the outside world.

When we finally dropped the coats off at the amazingly modern Salvation Army campus, we were impressed and somewhat relieved that folks in need had such a facility to serve them. With the charity behind us, Christopher started to worry about his own Christmas list. "You know, Daddy, I only put four things on it before you mailed it off with the rest. Nat and Brennan had a lot more. I hope Santa just knows what I want."

"I am pretty sure he does," I said. "What is the biggest thing that did not make the list?"

Looking out the window as we emerged back into the tree-lined vicinity of Overton Park, he said, "I want Brennan's leukemia to go away."

"How about yours, Brennan?" I asked him.

"I agree with Nat," Brennan said, referring to a specific request Nat placed on his Christmas list to Santa several weeks back. "I want it to snow for Christmas."

Relying once again on the navigation lady who lives within my phone, we continued to drive and accidentally found ourselves passing the entrance of a beautiful military cemetery. Turning in, we walked through the uniform white tombstones for half an hour. There were POWs, men killed in action, retirees, and an astonishing number of Vietnam combat veterans who had died in their thirties and forties. Christopher was silent and pensive, often looking up to the awesome vastness of rows that extended seemingly to every degree of the compass, just as the souls of each person who now resided there.

"Do you think these people wanted to die and be buried here?" he asked.

"I doubt it," I told him. "I guess none of us knows where we want to die."

"But it is nice to see that they are among friends," he said.

"Yeah," I said as I turned to see him on his knees staring at the tombstone of an unknown Union soldier. He held my hand as we walked back to the car, with Brennan waiting warmly for us inside.

Tara was correct two weeks ago when she said that we had already received our Christmas present. Being with these three boys on Christmas Day, who are playing together and having fun despite the special needs of one, is enough. To be witness to all that is happening because of him is an overwhelming experience, but one that bears out in our minds and our hearts that we are all, without a doubt, a product of design, a design that is woven within the common fabric of love and the sublime awareness that one kid's destiny is enough to motivate everything we do. It is what guided the wisemen, uncertain and unknowing, to a child who would change the world.

As I sit writing my blog at the Christmas breakfast table, the little boys install batteries and organize their toys. Tara cleans up the mounds of wrapping paper. Nat walks around the tree, proudly donning his new Christmas outfit. This evening we will break bread, along with some smoked ham, mashed potatoes, green beans, and a killer salad. We are celebrating the very gift for which I had prayed numerous times. Brennan is happy and grateful, as are all of us whose Christmas wishes have been satisfied. Let us rejoice and be glad.

As for the wishes outstanding, let me just say that as we opened our presents this morning, it started to snow. They believed. Shouldn't we all?   —NTS

Trust . . . 2011
Posted Jan 3, 2011 8:16pm

We were still residing in our Christmas loaner house, courtesy of a new friend who was away for the holidays. I had a bad cold and was therefore alone in my bed one dark and wet afternoon, quarantined from Brennan and reading *Unbroken* by Laura Hillenbrand (the amazing and Brennanesque life story of Louis Zamperini, a WWII POW). Looking across the street, I saw a man roughly my age, presumably arriving home late from work.

It was raining. The man dashed from his door to the rear of the car where, hunched over, he struggled to procure all of the plastic grocery store bags from the back of his SUV in order to make a single dash to his front door. Once on his door stoop, he had to lay down a single armful of bags in order to open the door. As he bent over to pick them all back up, two little kids ran to the door to greet him and hug his leg as he struggled both to carry his groceries and embrace his children.

I saw lights come on inside and little heads darting to and fro. About ten minutes later, the door reopened, with both Mommy and Daddy taking the lead while the two little ones, all dressed up in their rain slickers, hats, and rubber boots, skipped to the car. Maybe they were going to the movies. Maybe to Grandma's house. Despite the rain, they were happy; and they drove off to wherever it was that made them feel the way they were feeling.

By this point it was almost dark outside. Going downstairs to make myself something to drink, I started rifling through the basket of Christmas cards that Tara had left on the kitchen island. I found myself looking at children of close friends. Many looked totally unfamiliar, not because I don't know these kids (half of them I've watched grow up since birth), but because they are growing up without us, and we're not there to see it. Two years have passed since this all started. The remnants of Christmas presents remained stacked around the house, in piles designated by and for each child. Each had begun to sort their piles of gifts, occupying their time with new toys and games. This is our best normal. It ain't what it used to be. I stopped lying around and moping that night and started reading *Unbroken* again. Thank God for that book at that time.

That evening, Brennan started feeling pretty lousy. Sometime during the night he started urinating blood. Tara woke me in the morning on their way out the door to bring me up to speed. In addition to the blood, Brennan was also experiencing an excruciating amount of pain, and plans to readmit him to the transplant unit were made that afternoon.

Nat, Christopher, and I immediately started packing stuff up at the borrowed Christmas house to begin the move back into our own living quarters. Packing Brennan's stuff, there were footballs, golf equipment, remote control boats, cars, helicopters, and box after box of toys and games yet to be experienced (ever to be experienced?). Pulling out of the driveway, I saw the happy little family from across the street heading into their front door.

I was forced to stop the car for a little while, as road crews were temporarily blocking the driveway while working on a water main. Watching the family walk into their home, I thought back to that late afternoon—feeling sorry for myself in the bed while I watched them enjoy their holiday. I thought to myself, *What if Brennan never had leukemia? Would our family be any better off? Would we truly be any happier? Would we be struggling from something else?*

I have no idea what this family may have experienced, survived, or conquered. As far as I know, this guy could be a walking Louis Zamperini right here in my front yard. They are on their own road through life with their own harrowing views and, God willing, their own good fortune. We have what we have. Most importantly, we have a family that loves each other very much. It makes no difference whether you love each other from a hospital bed or with an ocean view. You take it where you find it.

It's Brennan's part in it all that I can't get my arms around. Having been the recipient of so much unfavorable news over the past couple of years, I had prayed for God to just give us one more Christmas together. We got it. It was beautiful. Now I wanted more.

As a child, I remember an overwhelming sense of emptiness on the day after Christmas. With weeks of eager anticipation followed by the realization of such a vibrant environment of celebration and fellowship, the day after was more often than not marked by a significant void. In a way, I think I am so flabbergasted by what has just happened that I have yet to articulate goals for the next step. The year 2011 seemed unattainable, yet we made it. All I know is that we are still pushing up a long, hard stretch of the road that guides us through the ever-changing elements of life, death, grief, love, and happiness.

Unfortunately, the order in which those elements appear does not necessarily correspond with the order one assumes when the journey begins. Life's little brochure, at least in our part of the world, tends to highlight the "life, love, and happiness" part. Acknowledgment of the other parts is usually relegated to the fine print. Though it's a new year, everything seems oddly familiar. On the good side, the family is together. The boys are wonderful. Friendship and love abound. Looking back on 2010 and knowing that a year ago I would have given my right arm to be sitting here, writing and reflecting on a full year with my entire family still intact, it is clear that we all have much to be grateful for.

In other ways, though, it's too familiar. At this moment, sitting at Brennan's side in his hospital room at the Chili's Care Center, the same IV monitor beeps. The Great Pyramid of Memphis is still off to my left. There is the familiar cloudless sky of pure blue. The same cars pass by.

Once Brennan became inpatient Thursday afternoon, an ultrasound examination determined his bladder lining to be significantly inflamed. He was to have been discharged tonight. But earlier in the day, when it was uncertain what time he would get out, he unexpectedly said, "I want to stay here."

This place is comforting to him. The staff loves him, and he knows that he is well taken care of. I cannot imagine ever predicting my son to find comfort in a hospital room. But such is the life role he has been given.

That afternoon the doctor on call remained behind after his rounds and quietly watched Brennan work on his Legos. "You know, I have boys his age," he told Tara.

"How old are they?" Tara asked him as she gathered her things. "My Lego guy is nine," he replied, to which Tara responded, "Super, just like Brennan."

With that, Brennan stopped what he was doing, looked over at his mother, and asked, "I'm nine?"

"Well," Tara said with a grin, "you're almost nine; you have a birthday in less than a month."

He paused, raised his index finger to acknowledge understanding, and returned to his Legos. "Whew," he said. "For a second there I thought I had slept through my birthday."

As we enter 2011 with less than defined resolutions, Lord knows there are plenty of personal habits I can work on. The main one is to look back on 2010 as a miracle and believe that future miracles are possible. No regrets about what we missed out on or what we would have done if we were not a cancer family. We are the beneficiaries of an abundance of love and compassion that I cannot comprehend. But as I said earlier, for Brennan's sake, I want more.   —NTS

Patience . . . Still
Posted Jan 10, 2011 2:39pm

Good feelings are few and far between these days, so when they come, the relief is nostalgically refreshing. The first obligation that morning was not until 10 a.m., for school, which gave Brennan a rare but useful window for sleeping in a bit. We were off to a good start, and despite the pending afternoon conversation with the doctors, I had a feeling of confidence.

Brennan has been separated from his brothers since Wednesday, when we got a call from Christopher's school that he had a temperature and was not feeling well. Keeping the family apart, even for a few days, is tough, but it seems like this has more often been the case than not lately. But being Brennan's designated parent is a gift, and I was looking forward to my two nights alone with him.

The previous night, he had picked out a movie and started a new Lego set while I went through the hour-long pre-bedtime checklist (new NG feeds, IV fluids, meds, etc.). His Lego set is a pirate ship. With 1,664 pieces, it's a monster. But as I quietly tidied up around the little apartment, he patiently opened up each little bag of pieces, dumped them on the kitchen table, and started sorting each one by color and size. "This one may take a while, Daddy," he told me.

Waking early Friday, I took the time to read some devotionals and to focus on a positive day and a favorable conversation with the doctors, but also to be prepared for whatever it was they had to say. That morning, the message in my book was simple: Be patient and give thanks on all days, particularly on the ones filled with adversity.

Once in the medicine room for Brennan's daily platelet transfusions, I was truly feeling good when his counts came back to reveal a small yet material ANC of 100. His white blood count had increased also, giving us another positive sign. Tara was elated when I called her with the news. I was feeling good enough to take off for a little exercise of my own and thoroughly enjoyed my hour by myself, listening to my iPod, sweating a little, and worrying little.

Rushing back to the hospital for our "favorable" meeting, I was cutting it close. Unexpectedly, we were told to wait in the conference room, which by definition made me nervous.

Dr. Leung entered with his team. He first asked us for our impression of how Brennan felt about himself. Moments earlier, Dr. Leung had slipped into Brennan's medicine room to pry a little on his own, and after talking to us about it for a while, he came to the same conclusion we have: Despite virtually living at the hospital, Brennan does not feel that he has a problem. He is just waiting on word from us to tell him that he can go home and be a normal boy again.

"So what do you want to do?" Dr. Leung asked.

Tara and I looked at each other, puzzled and tongue-tied. "Well," I said, "given that we had used up the last of the DLI over the holidays, we were under the impression that we were here to get your opinion about what to do."

"The number-one problem right now remains the aplastic anemia, not the leukemia," he stated. "I am quite worried about the fact that he has not worked through the aplasia. It has been three weeks with little improvement."

He continued, describing Brennan as "a time bomb." The continual dependence upon platelet transfusions had created a physical dependency with diminishing returns. "Ultimately, most people in this situation either bleed to death from a simple cut, or they have a stroke or aneurism from sudden bleeding of the brain, or they are the victim of a viral or bacterial infection."

What he proposed was the introduction of an immune system stimulation drug for the purpose of jump-starting Brennan's immune system in order to wipe out the aplastic anemia. However, because this could simultaneously stimulate the leukemia cells, it would be administered concurrently with a drug that would trigger the appropriate protection and defense of Brennan's immune system.

He said, "I think we do this for three weeks." (The drugs would be administered by two shots in the arm three times per week, an activity with which Brennan would have serious objection.) "After that, if we do not have any success, the only option is the fourth transplant."

"But," he added, "we can also give him some more time to see if he turns the corner on his own. I am OK with this if this is what you want to do, but you need to understand the dangers associated with this as well." He reminded us that from a medical perspective, an ANC of 100 is no different than one of zero.

Tara and I replied that we had been under the impression that he was opposed to a fourth transplant. "I am," he replied, "but my team has faith that it is a viable option and faith that Brennan can handle it, so I am deferring to their opinion in this case."

Again, Tara and I just looked at each other with mouths agape. "There is no need to make the decision today, or even early next week," he said. "But we need for you to make the choice soon."

Breathing deep sighs all around, doctors included, we all shook hands and wished each other a good weekend. Tara departed quickly to pick up the boys, but not before a strong hug. We did not have to say anything to each other. We were on the same page.

I did not see her again until well past dark. Christopher had his first basketball practice with his new team that afternoon. It must have felt totally odd for her to change channels so quickly from that conversation to being an enthusiastic mom at a basketball practice in a new community. But she did it, and she did it well.

When the boys arrived at the rental house, all expecting another great dinner as the night before, I was preparing to whisk Brenny off to sleep at Target House. They were all talk and smiles. There was talk of snow the next day. There was also a lot of chatter about basketball, and lots of questions from Brennan.

"Hey, Daddy, remember that time I made that shot after the kid fouled me and knocked me to the floor? Can you believe the ref didn't blow the whistle?" Brennan said.

"Yeah," said Christopher. "You should have told that ref to get some glasses."

They were talking about something I could not recall, something about Brennan's days of playing basketball for St. Mary's Church, three seasons ago. To him, though, he was right there with his brothers, side by side, shot by shot. "Ain't no thing. I'll be back in the game soon."

This morning, Brennan's ANC is still 100. His white count, though, is dropping. Tara and I will talk with the doctors more today and tomorrow about the "choice." Are we simply investing in a new aplastic anemia weapon? Is the fourth transplant imminent regardless? Can he handle a fourth transplant?

We are getting further out on the limb than we want to be, but Brennan is patient. We are trying awfully hard to be like him.

Brennan is asleep now. His pirate ship lies on the table, partially assembled and waiting on a boy to finish it. Outside my window, the cross from the little chapel across the yard is covered in snow. The limbs of the trees behind it are heavy and weighted.   —NTS

Peace and Confidence
Posted Jan 16, 2011 5:06pm

There can be no greater weight than a decision affecting the fate of one's child. When no option appears stronger than another (or if, indeed, there are any others), there is not much more you can do but pray and believe that somehow, something will show you the way. God-fearing parent or not, if you find yourself in this place, you will pray. I can promise you that.

We have come full circle so many times with regard to Brennan's disease that we are physically dizzy. Fortunately, Brennan remains steadfast in his cheerful and positive demeanor and strength of spirit.

A week ago, he appeared strong and on an upswing. Sunday, his fevers dragged him back down, and with him, what hope remained of salvaging his third transplant. Since then, with every day of fever, with every test, and with every discussion, the list of options has become narrower and the urgency of our decision more acute.

Ever since our meeting with Dr. Leung last Friday, talk of a fourth transplant has dominated our minds and hearts. With the facts in front of us and the situation progressing, the bottom line was this: (1) wait and pray for the aplastic anemia to work its course and for transplant three to recover; (2) commit to transplant number four with Tara as the donor (apparently my stem cells have become tolerant of his leukemia). This is the only viable option to eliminate the immediate threat of the aplastic anemia while maintaining a reasonable anti-leukemia effect; or (3) Well . . .

To choose number 3 is to quit and go home. As our comrade-in-arms Stephen Chance said, "We did not come all this way to punt." As long as our player has his heart and mind in the game, and as long as there are plays in the book, we are going to support him with every ounce of energy in our bones. Nonetheless, the medical team here, and at any other institution, is obligated to discuss palliative care with all families in our shoes. In this respect, they have contacted the Augusta area hospice to determine whether they can perform blood transfusions at home, as he would require these more and more frequently, until finally they became unnecessary.

On Monday, Dr. Leung indicated that the fourth transplant was the recommended protocol by the majority of physicians on his team. He and his PA Lisa pulled us into the parent room adjacent to Brennan's. He spoke quickly and frankly. I sat in the desk chair and could see Brennan watching TV through the little room divider window. "It is not my choice," he stated. "Ideally, I want Brennan's body to resolve itself. But now I am afraid that we may have passed the point of no return, leaving this, currently, the only viable option for cure."

"Palliative care can be pursued as a means of preserving quality of life without the risks associated with transplant," he reminded us. "You guys have done more than almost any family I have worked with. But there are young men walking around today, miracles of fourth and even fifth transplants. The difference is that in all of these cases, they were older kids who refused to quit. You are in a situation of having a young child with whom this discussion is quite delicate. And no one has ever done all this within a period of eighteen months."

Walking from Brennan's room to the nutrition room located at either end of the transplant floor, I happened to see through the narrow slits of the venetian blinds that are in place to offer privacy to the floor office and conference room of the on-call doctors and nurses. Our PA Lisa, who had just finished speaking with us about our "choice," was sitting at her desk, head down, weeping. How do these people deal with this as a vocation?

But after this discussion, I do not think it requires much to describe the enveloping weight of what we were to consider. In our hearts, we knew Brennan would ultimately tell us what to do. First and foremost, with regard to quality of life, we believe we have plenty of that, regardless of where we live or what activities we are restricted to. Even in the transplant unit, Brennan is active, pursuing his own little challenges with Legos, doing schoolwork, joking with his brothers. We may not be home, but he is surrounded by love, here or anywhere. That is quality in our book.

It is impossible to describe the volley of fear, emotions, and issues we wrestled with during those few days. Suffice it to say that we prayed a great deal, we talked seriously and deliberately as a couple, and we confided in experts here at the hospital, as well as with our priest, Jerry Ragan, back in Augusta. We talked to other families who had wrestled with the same question: the Chances, the Clarks. It was time to commit, one way or the other, but there was no time for a panicked parent to survey the moral argument and make a decision on their own. Therein lies one of the thickest parts of the tangle: how to allow a child to express his honest input into a matter that has the potential of damaging his will to live.

The agony and heartache associated with indecision demarcate a wretched place. Nonetheless, it is a place one must navigate with conscious, spiritual intent. Easier said than done, I know; but one thing we've learned living in this world is that there is no other way.

An unavoidable march through a brutally dense and thorny patch, every step is deliberate and strenuous, offering no sense of progress until the other side reveals itself through the briars and leafless crags. Potential decisions appear as sharp and ragged as the place of indecision itself, asphyxiating the mind, puncturing the flesh, tugging the heart, and draining the spirit. All directional options are painful to consider and excruciating to pursue. With deep sighs and prayers, you trudge forward, grinding step by step, until light emerges. The path of refuge. And at the end of the path, there, with his peaceful, beautiful smile and his arms outstretched in receipt, is a little boy.

With the small burst of confidence brought on by the ANC, Tara found a way to begin discussing this matter with Brennan. This, to both of us, and indeed the entire medical team, was the most important and delicate part of the whole shebang. How do you do it properly without introducing fear or doubt into the discussion? Even the implication of "going home to die" could be enough to kill his will.

That night, Tara was staying at the hospital alone with Brennan, with me wide awake all night at the Bluff rental house with the Brothers. Brennan was in a pretty good mood and talkative, so she decided to talk to him.

"Brenny," she said, "how would you react if we told you that Daddy's transplant had been set back because of your virus, and you had to have another one?"

Eyes looking at the floor and lips pursed, he sat motionless for a moment, then shrugged his shoulders and said, "I think I'd go for it."

I do not know how many hours I spent praying for the strength to handle this properly, strength for the boys, and the capacity to make the right decision. But as we garnered the strength to move forward, the answers started to reveal themselves to us on their own.

Confirmation of Brennan's outlook on everything occurred the next day with me present. Dr. Pilai later came into his room to speak to Tara about a number of things relating to Brennan when Brennan stopped what he was doing and his ears perked up. "Are you still talking about me?" he asked.

Tara explained, "You remember last night, when I talked to you about a fourth transplant? And you remember how hard the third one was, how sick you got, going to ICU? We just want you to know absolutely everything if the doctors tell us that they think another one is necessary. What do you think about this?" she asked him again. He said, "I want to do it. I want to do whatever it takes."

He knows what is at stake. He's a smart boy and has been in this fight too long not to read through the cracks. At the same time, as long as his circumstances contain realistic hope, that hope must be the context in which every other thing is addressed or implied. Knowing that we can look him in the eye and deliver this, he has taken us by the hand and led us the rest of the way.

Friday was the day that pushed the issue over the top. That morning I did not awake to any alleluia phone calls from Tara telling me that Brenny had miraculously turned a corner. I just had a heavy feeling that this was going to be a heavy day.

The Brothers were lovely as I prepared them for school at Bluff House. Nat made lunch for himself and Christopher and even made up his bed. On the way to school, with a vocabulary test ahead of him, Nat gave me a very assertive lesson on the etymology of the word "civic," its derivations, and how we use it today, leading into a surprisingly interesting discussion about our duties to others as members of society. At a traffic light, a shivering man passed the front of our car wrapped in a box, shuffling down the sidewalk with his belongings dragging behind him. Christopher said, "It looks like these civic people forgot about him."

We turned from Riverside Drive up Adams Street to make a left on Front, my usual route to their school from Bluff house. The municipal building and a parking garage reside at the northeast and southeast corners of Adams and Front, respectively. These four corners are covered in murals. While I rounded this corner this morning with the boys, discussing Nat's vocabulary words, it dawned on me that this single physical location in Memphis, above all others, triggers a powerful sense of déjà vu for me. It was at this same corner last year that I cried in the car, worrying about whether Brennan's second transplant was failing. It is this corner that I see in my sleeping dreams of Memphis. In my dreams, the city is desolate. Buildings are empty, and I am alone with the exception of a sense of anticipation that I am there to meet someone. The murals loom overhead.

That morning, as the light changed and I turned toward the school, I became awash with a genuine feeling of cognizance that the day was to be significant. The feeling was not heavy, nor was it liberating in any way. It was just real, like a single unexpected drop of cold water across my forehead.

That revelation came one hour later in conference with Dr. Leung, when he delivered the last bit of information we needed to move forward. "I am not going to push you one way or the other, but we are past urgent." To prolong the decision any longer would create a point of no return.

Without ever having left the battlefield (his hospital bed), on his own Brennan picked up his gun and decided to keep fighting. This time, though, he seems to truly understand what he is fighting for, and it is incumbent upon us to demonstrate 100 percent confidence in his decision.

That night Tara and I had been in the parent room for a much longer period of time than usual. I could see him watching us through the Levolor blinds, trying to focus on his Legos while Tara and I talked about everything. Later that night, he began to cry.

"What's wrong, Brenny?" Tara and I asked as he turned his face to the pillow.

"I don't know," he said. "I don't know what is happening. It makes me feel like I might not survive."

"You can stop worrying about that, my little man," we said, looking him in the eye. "We are here with you every step of the way. Your Brothers are with you, your family and friends are with you, and the doctors have a good plan for you. You are in the game. So let's forget about all that."

With this little pep talk, he somehow managed to smile through his own march through the thorny woods. And three hours later, when we told him we were committed to number four, he seemed to have found refuge through his own personal struggle, through the crags of doubt. He has a game plan; we have a game plan. The doctors are more confident now than when they implied this thing a week ago.

After Tara and I signed the consent forms to pursue the protocol, I realized that Brennan was about to spend his third birthday in a row in the hospital (on the 21st). Mentioning this to the room in general as I signed and dated the documents, Dr. Leung said, "Then we will look forward to celebrating the next seventeen birthdays outside of the hospital."

Today we celebrate Christopher's birthday. We will bend the rules and all sing Happy Birthday to him in Brennan's room. And with Tara's birthday on the 31st, we have much to be grateful for every January. This month we reconfirm our family's commitment to one another. Today is a blessing. Tomorrow will be a blessing when it comes.

We press on and are trustful and confident in transplant number four. It's about time we give a girl a shot.   —NTS

The Perfect Storm
Posted Feb 13, 2011 11:47pm

Watching my son at the free throw line. Not much at stake other than Nat's pride. His team is down 23 to 15 with 35 seconds or so on the clock. He twirls the ball in his hands backward, composing himself before the shot, dribbling the ball as he focuses at the goal. I did a quick calculation in my mind.

"Nat has seven points so far," I said to Christopher. "He told me before the game that he was going to score eight today for Brennan. This means something."

It's funny how many dots the mind can connect on matters relating to chance, fate, destiny. With Brennan on my mind constantly and trying to direct every ounce of spare energy I have to him, the most ridiculous notions trigger thoughts about cause and effect. Somehow the prospect of making a traffic light teetering on yellow seems as if it might determine the entire shooting match. My capacity to do one more push-up; my one-in-four chance of picking the correct bottle of pills from my Dopp kit; whether or not I play a song on the guitar error free; a basketball flying through the air in a peewee basketball game that's already been decided. But for his suffering and pain, Brennan's life—like the rest of ours—teeters in the wind, with no more or no less certainty than I can muster after the ball rolls from Nat's palm, rotating silently toward its goal.

The silence of anticipation is shattered by an eruption of cheers as Nat's ball swooshes through the net. His uncanny ability to focus at his age, to place

241

pressure on himself for the purpose of honoring others, to truly believe that a little extra effort on his part can help someone else. He's just eleven, but if you ask me, he has the hard part figured out.

• • •

For twenty-one days, the Brothers and I were separated from Brennan and Tara. The virus Christopher picked up at school demonstrated its last signs of being symptomatic on January 16 (Christopher's birthday). We therefore entered the realm of quarantine in preparation for transplant on this day, and thus birthday celebration plans for the rest of the month toppled like dominoes. Brennan's and Tara's birthdays were both celebrated over the phone.

Likewise, the transplant itself (an event no less sacred than childbirth) on January 25 took place in room 9 on the transplant unit with only one parent to hold Brennan's hand; fortunately, it belonged to the one whose cells were giving him yet another chance at life. The extent of my participation was limited to Tara calling on the phone and allowing me to listen in as the deed was commenced. While we remained coupled through prayer and constant focus on Brennan, not being with Brennan was hard, very hard.

As presumed carriers of the virus, the boys and I became totally off limits to anyone coming to help out at the hospital. After Tara's cells were harvested and transplanted to Brennan over the 24th and 25th, our communication with Brennan diminished by the day. At first, and indeed for the first week, he was talkative and would even call me on the phone. But then the chemo started kicking in, and the conversation changed.

Twenty-one days goes by pretty quickly for most folks these days. But for someone accustomed to constant contact with his family, it's a long time. I had never been away from Tara for more than a handful of days and had certainly never been away from the boys for that long either (and certainly not Brennan). For the first two weeks, it was overwhelming to be alone during the day. Dropping the boys off at school, I would return to the house to assume my duties as hausfrau (laundry, dishes, shopping, etc.). I was basically alone at this time of the day. Midday Mass, the guitar, and the gym became important. Improved stillness. Focused patience. Attributes that have evaded me for most of my life now stare me coldly in the eye.

A week or so before the quarantine, I was walking out of Target House when Ms. Joe, the matronly front desk greeter at Target House, called me over to the front desk. "I need to talk to you," she said sternly. "Listen to me. You need to smile. Those boys need to see you smile. I know you are having a hard time of it, but you are losing it and need to pull it together."

It felt like a cold slap in the face. I accepted her handout with a "Thanks," and I sulked out to the car.

But as I turned the car on, I thought, "You know, she's right. You've been at this for two years and haven't learned a damn thing. Get with it."

In my case, I don't know if the audible nature of my emotions can be muted fully. But driving to pick the boys up at school that afternoon, my mind magically began to play second fiddle to a heart that had been screaming for center stage. I arrived smiling and grateful for my reprimand. For crying out loud, I was sitting here with the opportunity to be sole caregiver for these two fantastic boys for three weeks. Take advantage of it.

So, while desperately missing Brenny and Tara, the boys accepted our time as a window of freedom. From that moment, my appreciation for each of them grew: for their unique personalities, for their singular capacities to express themselves, for their own senses of humor, for their own fears. We've been mindlessly dragging them back and forth so many times over these past two years that it's easy to overlook them for who they are, irrespective of how well they are handling the whole cancer-family thing.

So, somewhere around Day Plus Four, or Five, my mom called and encouraged me to use our remaining quarantine time for an adventure. Maybe a train ride somewhere, which sounded like an ideal father/son jaunt; but then Nat asked, "Why don't we just go home?"

Sounded like a good idea to me. I was soon on the phone securing two big-time favors from two generous friends, who agreed to pick us up and return us immediately after. First, however, Nat wanted to make sure that he would not create any ill feelings with Brennan by going home when he could not. Nat made the call himself, and Brennan said it was okay.

Within twenty-four hours we were back home, which was almost instantaneously transformed into a location set for a *Lord of the Flies* remake.

As fate would have it, St. Mary's school had an open house, allowing the guys to visit with their teachers and peers without interrupting. Overnight, they felt at home.

Christopher even managed to work up the gumption to make his first reconciliation at church that Saturday. He wanted Ms. Hoffman and his grandmother Nonnie to see him slip behind the curtain, presumably as more credible witnesses than myself, but it was very sweet and wove yet another purposeful thread into the fabric of our journey. No one pushed him. He knew that his classmates back home had been prepared for theirs; but mostly, he told me, he was eager to eventually have Communion with his brothers . . . both of them.

Things were good. We had planned a game of golf the next afternoon, as Nat had been determined to post a great round for Brennan. He had been rehearsing how he was going to cheer up his brother with news about his "record score." The day was clear, crisp, and almost cold. With so much foul weather this winter, this little window of sunshine was yet another take-it-or-leave-it-type gift.

But when we arrived around 2 p.m., things got weird. Walking to the practice green, Christopher started acting peculiar. He suddenly became very teary, and I could not figure out what had happened. No one had said anything to him. Ten minutes earlier he was boasting to anyone within earshot; now he was breaking down for no apparent reason.

He began yelling at me. Two older men looked over to me, irritated, and I began to panic. Despite the blue sky, a cloud had settled over our little group. Christopher skipped the entire first hole, pouting in our respective cart seats as we watched Nat play by himself, pretending not to notice us.

The first change in spirit began as I waited for Nat to finish on the first green. Staring beyond the green through the shrubs and briars of a wooded area are the grounds of an African-American cemetery. In a sparse corner of that place, Molly Aaron is buried. Molly had worked as a nurse to me when I was a baby. She served as our housekeeper, our cook, and our chief ethics officer. She could be as stern as boiling water and as beautiful and kind as a child herself. She lived to be an estimated 105 years old and was a powerful force in my life, often times reprimanding me, like Ms. Joe had, for my childish behavior. I sat in my cart where I had been a hundred times before, but somehow I had never seen it from this perspective. Something was going on.

As I turned around from my trance, I noticed that Christopher was no longer next to me but was sprinting across the golf course. As I raced to collect him, I could hear Molly's voice, scolding, "You get yourself together, boy, and go get that child!"

I caught Christopher in my arms. He collapsed into my shoulder. "I am sorry, Daddy!" he wept, with his chest heaving into mine. Turning around, Nat was walking by himself to the second tee box. His head was low, and when we made it back to him, he too was crying.

"I really wish you guys would stop what you are doing and play with me," he said. "We came all this way, and I am trying to play for Brennan."

An honest wave of fresh warm air blew across our faces. Christopher looked at me and said, "OK."

Like the warm breeze that came from nowhere on this cold day, I still didn't know what was causing the wave of emotional turmoil. But the three of us began to play together, and as we walked up the expansive hill to the next green, a golf cart driven by someone official came straight up the hill toward us.

A young golf professional walked up to me holding a walkie-talkie. "Mr. Simkins, I hate to bother you, but your wife is trying to find you. She says it's an emergency."

My cell phone was in the car. In her effort to track me down, Tara had called the golf shop out of sheer luck. Waving the boys to get in the cart so we could leave, they all stopped and looked at me with worried, puzzled looks. Noticing my predicament, the pro said, "I have a phone if you need one."

Tara answered after one ring, and hearing the peeps and bells of heart monitors in the background, I knew where the conversation was headed and started welling up.

"Turner, I am sorry," she began, "but Brennan has had a difficult night and day breathing and needs help. We are at that point now. So I need you to tell him that you love him and that you will see him soon," she said, clearly trying to give me enough information to understand what was happening but not wanting to reveal so much that she upset Brennan.

As I stood on top of this hill with my boys staring up at me agape, I could barely hear Brennan saying, "I love you, Daddy," through what sounded like a wind tunnel. I envisioned an oxygen tent from the old days, but later learned that he was breathing through a full facial mask that was pumping high-pressure oxygen into his lungs.

As with the last ICU episode, his lung capacity filled with fluid in a short period of time, putting him into a very fast and dangerous tailspin. Tara told me later that between forced and panicked gasps for air as he was whisked to ICU, he'd managed to squeeze out the words, "Today is the hardest day of my life."

"Can I rush home to get my computer and tell him I love him on Skype?" I asked, knowing that I could be home in less than ten minutes.

"No, the doctors say we have to move now," she said.

With this, I waved the Brothers closer so that they could tell Brennan that they loved him. They could not hear him, telling me that all they could hear was "the wind."

I told Tara I loved her and handed the phone back to the kind man, fighting tears and wondering if the boys and I had just said our last goodbye to Brennan on a borrowed cell phone. The pro kindly apologized and left us there.

So there we were. Looking westward toward Memphis, large white clouds had crossed the horizon, heralding a storm that would take charge for the remainder of the week. But for the time being we stood on top of this quiet high place watching the heavenly white blanket envelop the warm blue with cold wind.

With disruption of our little universe now defined, we held each other. Before I knew it, we were kneeling on the ground praying together. We finished and stood up, as if to say, "What next?" It was all so surreal. Nat looked to me and said, "We can go home, but I think we should play golf and all make our best scores for Brennan." And that's what we did, quietly together.

I knew that if we were in a critical life-or-death phase, I would be summoned to Memphis. I tried to get that thought out of my head. Letting go and staying at the golf course proved to be the right thing. Brennan would not have wanted us to go home and cry. When Nat actually accomplished his record score, we got back to the house and immediately called Tara. She reinforced that the ventilator Brennan had been put on was "a bridge" to give his body a break. Most importantly, and surprisingly, Brennan's peripheral blood chimerism test showed that his immune system now consisted of 100 percent donor cells (i.e., 100 percent Tara, 0 percent Brennan, Nat, donor #2, or me. Go Mommy!). Talk about a mixed bag of news. One hundred percent donor cells, less than one week from transplant . . . Wow. But he was headed into a brutal fight.

Everything was driving my heart back to Memphis, walking through the house on Gardner St; looking at Brennan's things; watching movies we all used to watch together; finding some of his clothes still in the dryer; conversations with friends; visits to grandparents' homes. We could not leave for two days. Because of the quarantine we could not enter ICU anyway, and we were surrounded by family and friends. But things were dire with Brennan, and I could think of little else.

The night before our flight, I received a sudden call from Tara. "Please, get back as soon as you can," she said, not having any time to elaborate. She tried to sound confident, but clearly she was truly frightened.

Earlier that day, an old friend and acquaintance named Jim Weathers had arrived in Memphis to help Tara per our arrangement. I had met him at the Masters tournament several years ago where he was serving as the physical therapist for a number of tour players. Jim is an ex-Green Beret turned healer, having discovered his gift in Japan some thirty years ago. He returned the feeling to my right arm some two years after I broke seven vertebrae in a car accident. Having performed on me something barely short of a miracle, I learned that he was using his gift through Reiki energy work, reflexology, and massage to help people with many illnesses. The cowboy healer continues to do his work from long distance. Why not take a chance with Jim? When I called, he said there would be no charge; we just needed to get him there, and he would stay as long as we needed.

I called Tara back many times but had yet to have successful communication by the time we boarded the small plane the next morning. I was in the dark and very nervous. Suddenly my phone rang, but just as I answered, the pilot gunned the engines and I could hear nothing.

Trying desperately to plug one ear and listen while bent over double in the crash position, I missed the call. It would be three hours before I knew anything. I stared down over Augusta with my mind racing louder than the twin engines laboring through a major headwind. Looking down, we passed over Forest Hills Golf Course, where Brennan had won his first golf trophy three years ago. I saw the roof of Mimi and Pat Pat's house. I wondered if I would see them again with Brennan.

Christopher was in the copilot seat, wearing his headset. I asked him, "Christopher, would you like to play with my computer?"

"That's OK, Daddy. I'll just look out the window and enjoy the ride with you and Nat."

He grinned at me with his beautiful smile. In his little face, I let go of the whole thing and found peace. We were on the free throw line. The ball was on target and in the air, rotating slowly. It was past the point of my control. What else could I do but rely on my player's own confidence, rooting for him with my own grateful intentions? God's grace presented itself with a call from Tara as soon as we landed. "I am so glad you are home. Everything is amazing. Jim arrived late last night as Brennan was at his physical blood pressure limit with fluid retention. When we talked last night, his system was shutting down, but three hours after Jim started his energy work, the kidneys began to function and the pressure of so much fluid slowly subsided. Maybe it's the medicine and maybe it's Jim, but Brennan has turned a dangerous corner."

The Brothers and I drove straight to the ICU. We walked into Brennan's room for the first time in over three weeks. Tara, Aunt Martha, and Jim were all there. Tearful hugs all around, as Brennan lay motionless in what was unfortunately a familiar position, breathing on the ventilator. Later in the week, I counted thirteen different tubes either directing fluids into or out of his body. There had been five new IV placements in his veins, in addition to the central line. He was hugely puffy and swollen. But he was breathing. We had made it back to celebrate good news.

"You got some kind of fighter here," Jim told me, looking straight into my eyes.

"This is a remarkable kid. In every situation where I've tried to help someone in similar dire circumstances, their bodies have such a deficit of energy that everything I can give them is consumed," Jim said, referring to the time he had spent praying and working with Brennan's chakra, which is believed in the Hindu religion to be a center of activity that receives, assimilates, and expresses life force energy. "But Brennan was directing energy back to me. Almost as if he was saying that he was grateful for what I was giving him and he wanted to give something back. That never happens."

Dr. Pilai, who was the BMT physician on duty that week, was very interested in Jim and in our openness to more holistic and spiritual treatments. When she heard this story, she told me that as the intubation process was occurring, just prior to the anesthesia putting Brennan to sleep, he grabbed her arm, looked her in the eye, and said, "Tell my Daddy that I am all right."

Jim stayed through Wednesday morning, working with Brennan day and night, subsisting on two hours of sleep or less. When I asked what he was doing as he held Brennan's feet, he said, "I am praying with touch." I stayed with Brennan in his room from the moment I returned until Wednesday night, and the Brothers were here every day this week. For the first time since Christopher's birthday, they were able to tell their brother, although he was sleeping through induced paralysis, that they loved him. They touched him. And as with Jim, Brennan touched them back.

In the presence of such a strong source, the mind takes its rightful place in the rear. The heart takes the lead. In these conditions, peace prevails.

On Thursday night, the paralytic anesthesia was eliminated, and Brennan could open his eyes and move. Relatively quickly, he recognized the reason for his captivity and established his own means of communicating. At first, he slowly lifted his feeble little hand into the air, forcing his eyelids to stay open long enough to look us in the eye, then shuddering as they closed. He could not talk, but he was able to mouth words around the vent. "I love you." "Thank you." "Bathroom." "Ice chip."

By Friday, as the vent was turned to its lowest setting, he was in full yes-no-maybe communication, expressed by faint nods, head turns, and shrugs. A private language established for everything he needed in a matter of hours. He was on his way back.

At the end of the day, they were chalking it all up to a rapid engraftment syndrome. Effectively, every part of Brennan's body that had been impacted by infection or the leukemia generated a violent immune response to rid his system of toxins and restore him to health—a dangerous but ultimately lifesaving response. His little body was in such dire straits that we were in no other position than to pull out all the guns.

Friday afternoon Dr. Leung walked into the room with as close to a beaming smile as I had ever seen. By this point we were scheduled for the extubation Saturday morning and things were going well. Tara was off with the Brothers. I was appreciating my overdue time at Brennan's bedside, holding his foot, when Dr. Leung walked in.

"He had ice chips today," I said.

"What do you mean? That can't be," he responded. "I have never heard of anyone on a ventilator eating ice chips. It is a physical impossibility."

"You know," I said, "he doesn't think about it. Nobody told him he couldn't. Just like with everything else, he just believes in himself and does it."

"Well, we all certainly believe in him," he said with a fist pump as we walked out to talk in the hallway.

"It looks like everyone followed their heart this time and just trusted Brennan. I could not be happier with everything. The fourth transplant was the one that made the difference. I believe this one is here to stay," he said with as much confidence as I have ever witnessed (which is saying a lot coming from the most confident man I have ever met).

Today, the guns are quiet, but the smoldering consequences of their role in all of this are evident in our little boy, who is down to one IV pole and off of the ventilator. Yesterday morning, they pulled the tube. Prepared for all of the potential problems associated with post-intubation, the ICU team literally high-fived when Brennan looked up and said in a crackly but sweet little voice, "Can I have some more ice chips?" He now raspily talks as if nothing ever happened.

When the tube was removed, Dr. Brandon Triplett, who had been on staff all week, sweating through all of the kidney, liver, and edema issues, told Tara, "I am going to have a T-shirt made for this kid. It's going to read, 'I am why St. Jude's does four.'"

Brennan is still very feeble. With the fluid all gone, he looks like a concentration camp victim. Watching his emaciated little hands shake short, uncontrollable spasms as he struggles to play solitaire on his iPad, fears and doubts sprout from the mind. He's so skinny; he needs to get stronger; will he actually make it home? Will he get strong enough to enjoy the things he used to like?

Despite the uncertainty and fears about the long road ahead, though, right now I feel like we finally won the Battle of the Bulge.

I grab his hand, close my eyes, and cry through the most profound prayer of gratitude my heart can conjure. As the passage says, "Behold, the kingdom of God is within you. God is love." Not trying to oversimplify the whole deal, but if we truly love with our heart, then does God not reside within us? Is there anything more all-powerful than that? Does there need to be anything more than that? I say this because I am witness to it, and therefore am obliged to. Maybe it's just Brennan rubbing off on me. But right now, it seems like that's all there is to it.   —NTS

Press On, Indeed
Posted Feb 26, 2011 12:19am

Walking into the clinic, Tara and I entered the BMT floor to see Brennan's PA, Lisa, looking like the Cheshire Cat.

"Has Dr. Wendt spoken to you yet?" she asked, referring to the Fellow assigned to Brennan's case for the week. She sounded very much elated, revealing only that Dr. Wendt had some news we would be very interested in. But although held to an apparent pact of secrecy, perhaps it was Lisa's own recollection of our previously awful conversation about hospice that made her exclaim, "To heck with it—Brennan's MRD showed zero percent leukemia."

We had a feeling all day, but to hear those words . . . There is no means of describing the response other than to say that we were all grinning and crying just like Lisa.

Ever since Brennan made it out of ICU two weeks ago, everyone who has been even remotely associated with Brennan and his care has been glowing in his presence. Regardless of any previous doubts about this transplant, everyone here has conducted themselves with nothing but the highest level of respect for our decision and commitment to Brennan's full recovery, representing to me and Tara the most genuine testimony of true patient and family care.

Indeed, at its root, it is love. It is their love for him, manifest in their determination to return him home to his family and friends, healthy and happy. And it is his love for us all at the root of his determination to beat the odds yet again. If you were ever to write up a recipe for a miracle, this might be a good start.

It is a very real possibility that Brennan could be in Augusta and playing with his dog, Lucky, by Day Plus One Hundred. A lot of pieces have to come together in the meantime, however. He has to start eating and gaining weight (a lot of it). He has to start walking. His blood pressure must be managed. He has a demanding rehabilitation in front of him. Dr. Leung tells us that "at all costs he is to avoid exposure to viruses of any kind," meaning that for some time now, he will effectively live life as "The Boy in the Plastic Bubble," without the bubble.

He is as fragile as fragile can be, but he is alive. I don't think that this gift horse will mind if I look him in the mouth when I ask the inspiration of today to carry over for others. We are further inspired by news that our fellow warrior Patrick Chance came home today. We celebrate!   —NTS

Baby Steps
Posted Mar 11, 2011 3:27pm

On discharge day, for the third time in less than a year, the BMT floor nurses threw yet another confetti party, congratulating their BMT patients while singing the words to the discharge song (a variation of the Oscar Meyer Weiner jingle): "Pick up your things, walk out the door, and don't come back no more."

He didn't walk out this time. The hospital provided him a kid-sized wheelchair. So around 6 p.m. that Sunday afternoon, we wheeled him outside, a fragile little living, breathing miracle. There was a tremendously bright sunset over the Pyramid as we walked west toward the car. It was the first time Brennan had experienced the out-of-doors in sixty-three days.

"How's it feel, Brennan?" Tara and I asked him almost in unison. "Good," he said nonchalantly. But looking at his eyes barely above his protective respiration mask, you could see them shining as brightly as the sun in front of him.

Arriving at our Memphis house for the first time since January 8, I gently lifted him out of the car so that he could walk in the door himself. On my shoulder was the ubiquitous backpack containing both IV and G-tube feeds. With the two pumps, bags of fluids, and miscellaneous accessories that go along with it, the weight of his pack is a bit more than his little frame can handle. I held his hand, helping him leverage his way up the two back steps. His brothers and grandparents were waiting inside.

Christopher and Nat had taken it upon themselves to decorate his room with St. Patrick's Day frills (green crepe paper streamers, strings of shamrocks across his bed and a huge "Fat Head" photo of him and the Brothers bursting through the line as they led the Aquinas Fighting Irish onto the field last fall). It is a profound and jubilant "welcome home" celebration.

His hands are shriveled. Holding his little bottom as he steps up the first stair, there is nothing but bone sheathed in chapped skin. "I got it," he says as he takes the second, determined to show that he is just fine. But as he

253

crosses the threshold, his knee buckles and he collapses, fortunately close enough for me to catch him and avert disaster. He never acknowledged the need for assistance.

That was a week ago, Sunday. Yesterday, he was sitting up talking about what we are going to do today. Watching him flush his central line after I disconnect the morning TPN feeds, he takes his eyes off of the TV, looks up at me, and says, "Can you hand me the Heparin, Daddy? I can do this part." He carefully cleans the IV lead with alcohol and flushes his own line. He is doing more than his part.

He is now outpatient, which still means full days in the hospital. It is more than a full-time job, underscoring for me the extraordinary appreciation I have developed for single parents facing pediatric cancer. In addition to the meds and other scheduled daily needs, he is still fighting diarrhea and nausea with unpredictable timing. Several times a night and regularly through the day, he is provided no warning for immediate bathroom demands. Also, the feeling of nausea persists almost constantly (ad nauseum).

Each day this week has represented another baby step of small improvement. His counts continue to remain strong. There are now small excursions out and about. The improbable deliverance of freedom encouraged him to request that his new putter from Christmas be cut down to his size. And there was "I want to fly a kite, Daddy." We hope to fly this weekend.

In the car for one of our afternoon drives, he asked me, "Daddy, what does remission mean?"

"Remember the MRD being negative?" I said. "That means that you don't have any more leukemia in your blood, so you're in remission."

"Hmmm," he said, looking at the putter in his hand. "That's pretty cool. I guess now I need to get rid of those bad GVH cells that are still in my body."

We pulled to a peaceful stopping place in Overton Park. "Brennan," I said, hugging him and lifting him from the car to his little wheelchair. "You've got the best attitude I can possibly imagine. I cannot tell you how proud we are of you." He reached around my neck, hugged me back, and smiled knowingly.

That night at Bluff House, just the two of us, Brennan and I finally finished watching *Raiders of the Lost Ark*, having paused it at least three times throughout the week. As the credits rolled, he asked me to turn off the TV and turn out the light as he closed his eyes.

"Would you like for me to say our prayers?" I asked him. He rolled over, looked me in the eye, and said, "Daddy, I think that's a good idea."

"Now I lay me down to sleep . . ." Lying there in my own thoughts, I think about the things I pray for that, for whatever reason, I leave out of the spoken bedtime prayers with the boys.   —NTS

Storm Stations
Posted May 7, 2011 7:13pm

This entry began as a prelude to Easter, but the anticipation of colorful linen outfits, pastel eggs, fresh spring flowers, and the celebration of the most improbable of family gatherings had been replaced by tornado sirens and minor evacuations of Target House. As I sat in the stairwell with Christopher and his friend Evan from school, half-laughing at their callous antics and half-concerned about the noise outside, my thoughts were with Brennan and the irony of ending everything by the ill-fated placement of a storm. Tornados outside or not, the presence of patients, parents, siblings, and friends huddled in the hallway reminds me of how many tough lessons can live under one roof.

Still in isolation, Brennan missed out on this experience with his brothers, as he does most. Despite their average one-hour visit every day, the two Brothers rarely share any of their daily rituals or special events with Brennan. Two weeks ago was the first exception: All he could talk about was getting on the putting green and driving range. One day he even tagged along with the Brothers in the cart for a few holes until we were told by the BMT team that golf on real turf was strictly off limits.

His intermittent signs of vibrancy have been sufficient for all of us to hold a stronger sense that the storm inside Brennan may be subsiding, and that despite the too-often devastating news of what is happening around us, we will come home someday. We made our plans to return to Augusta on Easter weekend, of all times. The next morning, Christopher and I left our abode du jour to meet Mimi, Pat Pat, Nat, and Nat's friend Max for a Good Friday ceremony, leaving Tara behind with Brennan for his "final" clinic visit. The observance we were to attend was for the Stations of the Cross at St. Patrick's Church, entitled "A Walking Meditation." Members and friends of the parish would march in unison through the streets of downtown Memphis's south side, stopping at places of historical significance. Each stop was intended to commemorate the conviction, execution, and burial of Jesus Christ.

As both a nouveaux Catholic as well as a newcomer to "the Stations," I didn't really know what to expect. It was going to be a very nontraditional Easter celebration for Tara's parents (and certainly for Max, who gave up a day of basketball at the Jewish Community Center to be there). But strongly familiar with the inner city blight surrounding this church (represented primarily by careless "urban renewal" style demolition and a multitude of vacant lots littered with trash and relics of buildings long since victim to the wrecking ball), I could not quite piece together how the Memphis Southside would overlap with ancient Jerusalem.

But as our band of worshipers and followers-along congregated outside the rear of the church, a wave of guitar music and passionate singing from around the corner traced a faint outline of what we were to experience. This was an image I could comprehend. An older visiting priest revealed himself as the guitarist, maestro, and leader. Ahead of him on the street corner was an older gentleman wearing a floppy sun hat, khakis, and tennis shoes, leaning into the arm of a life-sized cross that he toted with some degree of effort. He was the focal point keeping everyone walking in the right direction.

This was just a few blocks from the place where Christopher was inspired to track down the homeless father just prior to Christmas. But today was warm, and Christopher was hopeful. Daffodils adorned the stoop of an absent demolished home, somehow surviving the destruction of their host. At this strangely beautiful site we gathered to honor the day.

The wonderful mixture of celebrants, represented by people of all ages, races, and even disabilities, walked in unison down the street. We stopped for the reading of the first Station, and then, to the tune of "Amazing Grace" we all marched to the Clayborn Temple. The shell of this beautiful building is the remainder of what was the heart of the sanitation strike that brought Dr. Martin Luther King, Jr. to Memphis. Now it sits boarded up without a congregation and often without a second look, but nonetheless, it is a relic of a very real and poignant local history. It was a perfect Station.

On like this it went. Block to block, station to station, hymn to hymn, we marched through the streets reliving this most meaningful day, but in a way that forced us to acknowledge the many crosses we bear as both a community and as individuals.

We walked to the Lorraine Hotel where King was shot, turning an extraordinary number of heads who, as pilgrims to this site on Good Friday, were interested and curious about this mass of mostly white troubadours.

We walked past vacant lots where children had recently been shot by drive-by killers. We acknowledged the offices of people who had dedicated themselves to the common good. Every station represented someone willing to wipe the face of others in need, others willing to bear the weight of another's cross after falling. (We even made a station at the Elvis statue, representing Jesus being nailed to the cross, and referencing humankind's predisposition to praise people for their gifts and talents while averting our eyes from addiction and death, lest we interfere with our amusement.)

It was at the Elvis statue that Pat Pat offered to take the cross from our floppy-hatted leader. Having felt its weight for numerous city blocks, the man agreed. As the reading concluded and the guitar music started again, Pat put his shoulder to the yoke and carried the cross across the park and into the center of Beale Street. Our group began to sing "We Shall Overcome," and our singing got louder as we started to compete with the cacophony of blues bands emanating from bar to bar. For heaven's sake, we were in the middle of the most crowded and festive of places in all of Memphis (on a holiday!), with my father-in-law leading the marchers with his gigantic cross across his shoulder.

Awkwardly interrupting the hopeful anonymity of the beer drinkers, we marched on back to St. Patrick's, watching the folks on the sidelines peering over their plastic mugs and gnawing mindlessly on ribs.

Somehow, the entire weight of Brennan's journey, with all of its stumbles and with all of the people looking on—the point of it all for that moment appeared clear as the day, not heavy, but wonderful. We have been carrying this cross for a long time, but we've never been alone.

Not long ago, I would have been way too embarrassed to have participated in such a spectacle. But having been stripped naked and shivering in front of God for the past two years, I felt on that walk as if the magnitude of what had happened to Brennan gave me the right to sing out loud and let it all go.

Memphis, Tennessee, is part of our lives forever. As our first oncology nurse practitioner advised me and Tara about life with pediatric cancer, we have a "new normal." Our new normal includes stations that must be revisited for the sake of all who have suffered and sacrificed and for the sake of suffering itself. It cannot be dominated by fear as we struggle for spiritual balance. Fear is there, but rather as the waves against which we brace our keels for safe travel.

The storm may have passed, but the water rises. And if this year's storm pattern continues as it has, there are certainly more looming in the distance. Fortunately, we have a lot of smart and loving people doing everything they can. So we sit once again in the shelter of this amazing place, praying that the dark hand once again passes us by, but armed with the confidence that we have weathered worse.

At each station along the way we lift our crosses and walk among the ghosts of those who responded to the circumstances of their lives with trust in God. I have to believe that Brennan will do as he says, growing up to help others, and that this is just another reason to huddle together in the stairwell. It's just a station along the way. Nothing has really changed. I hope we make it home next weekend.   —NTS

The Water Rises
Posted May 11, 2011 6:23pm

For the past two years, I have participated in a 5k run along the banks of the Mississippi on Mud Island for the boys' Montessori school. This year's race was held about a week before the flood waters rose enough to cover the entire course. On race day, the waters were already rising at an alarming pace. I recall making the turn to run downstream. It was allergy season, and I was wheezing. Had it been an ordinary run, I would have stopped to walk, but Brennan and the boys were counting on me to have a good finish. I looked over my right shoulder in search of a "pace log" in the river. I discovered plenty, but with the river rising, there was no way for me to keep up. I had no choice but to focus on the horizon in the distance.

Arriving in the hospital this past Friday represented the night that the floodwaters started to pour over the banks. When the Mississippi was near its crest, Brennan's fevers began to spill into the danger zone. All three boys were in Grizzly House with me because Tara was away on a trip to California. Brennan woke up screaming and doubled over in pain. When he was admitted, finally his temperature was normal. But by 9 p.m., he was near 105, prompting immediate blood cultures and the ultimate determination that a highly antibiotic-resistant bacterial infection had entered his blood system.

In a way, he was lucky. We could have been on the road to Augusta, or at someone's house when the fevers started. But we were in the hospital, where it was detected immediately. With this specific infection in the bloodstream, an hour can make all the difference. It is deadly.

Brennan was delirious most of Saturday, and even with the cooling blankets, his temperature never dipped below 101.5. Fortunately, however, without any antibiotics on hand to tackle this unusual situation, a relatively new drug was found in Seattle and flown in just for Brennan. By Sunday he had dropped down into the 99 range.

Dr. Leung ventured into the room to comment on the fever break. "You know he is quite lucky. This is a very serious situation. Just a few years ago, these new antibiotics did not exist. It used to be that once this infection made it to the bloodstream, that was it." Indeed, when Brennan was diagnosed two years ago, we were told that this very infection in the bloodstream was not survivable.

The previous day I had been a wreck, doing everything possible to fight off the negative thoughts. For crying out loud, we had just received the positive

MRD results. I felt like Brennan could see the goal just over the horizon; but all of the positive touchstones were leaving me wheezing and dragging.

Tara was still on her trip and couldn't get to St. Jude until the next day. At the exact moment Brennan was being admitted, vomiting with high fevers, a teacher called and informed me that Nat had broken his arm. I laughed and called a friend to rush Nat to Baptist hospital for his own emergency surgery. Two boys in two hospitals and another being shuffled from house to house—the whole scene was nuts.

With Tara finally here, Sunday night was much easier on the nerves. I was focused more on the rising water outside and wondering if the Brothers were going to be allowed access to their school on Mud Island, which had been closed to everyone but residents. We slept, and the river still rose.

On Monday, I could feel the water lapping at the door. The fevers were increasing, and the doctors started switching meds again. I showered and packed my gear for the hospital. But before I left, my meditation chair in the corner of our Target House apartment called my name. This is the place where I often sit and focus on the little chapel steeple next door. From autumn to frozen winter skies to spring flowers and now almost to summer, it has been there for me every season. New leaves from a maple tree have matured to the point of almost blocking my view; but the wind that day was strong, billowing the newly green limbs like fans.

The skies were clear blue. It was impossible to conceive of a flooded countryside just a mile away. I don't know exactly how long I sat there. But I watched my focal point appear and reappear between waves of leaves, forcing my heart to center, uncovering the belief that we would finish this race. Forget the rushing water surrounding us.

I then made the drive down Parkway to St. Jude for the umpteenth time.

Brennan's doctors arrived soon after me. The flood outside had indeed reached its peak. The waters were expected to maintain their current level for several days before dropping. In the meantime, the surgical team had been hovering about Brennan's room, gathering more and more data and conferring with our doctors to try and establish the best strategy for the removal of the infection source: a nonfunctioning, bloated gallbladder.

I had a hugely optimistic goal during all this: to arrange transportation plans back to Augusta for me, Nat, and Christopher in time for Christopher's First Communion rehearsal on Saturday. As it stands now though, things are very tense. We will stay in Memphis until we are certain that Brennan's surgery is successful and that this hurdle has been cleared. Brennan wants his brothers at his side as he is taken into surgery. They have to be.

It feels like the waters are subsiding. The finish line may be submerged temporarily, but it is still where it has always been, close, waiting for us. And with a little help, the youngest of the Simkins boys will make it home Saturday to share in the Communion that binds these Brothers so closely.   —NTS

The Last Patrol
Posted May 13, 2011 1:32am

Last night Brenny started complaining of substantial pain in his shoulder, in addition to the always prevalent pain in the lower right portion of his belly. His bowel movements also increased from zero in many days to many in just a few hours. They also all demonstrated the look and substance of the GVHD poop post-transplant.

The early morning consult with his surgeons started as an innocuous and run-of-the-mill pre-surgery meeting, but then Brennan's appearance started changing right there in front of them. Eyebrows were rising. The general indication was that they were moving things up as quickly as possible. When Dr. Leung came by the room, he took less than a minute to explain very seriously to Tara and his attendants: "This infection is not under control and needs to be handled now!"

Unfortunately, the fellow on duty in the surgery center did not agree with Dr. Leung. Not being a conventional twenty-four-hour pediatric hospital with a surgery program organized for unscheduled procedures, she was maintaining course with her team's game plan from earlier in the week to wait it out. On the surface, this was a simple gallbladder excision. She was clearly not up to speed about Brennan's history and the collateral consequences associated with delay.

We picked up the phone and had started dialing in our concerns to higher-ups when the chief attending surgeon showed up. He could not have been more gracious, understanding, and apologetic, and he told us that within no more than two hours they would be ready.

GVHD and the healing process work contrary to one another in terms of treatment. GVHD requires immune suppression. Infections and open wounds require a healthy immune system to get better. This balance represents the art of a true bone marrow transplant team. Given the two sides to this pretty serious coin toss, they had determined to once again put Brennan on a ventilator post-surgery until the doctors could determine which issue was more urgent. Besides, ICU is the place to be when you need constant attention. But ICU and ventilators had been at the center of our last two brushes with "the end." This was not what we wanted to hear.

We were over-the-top lucky to have a friend, Ashlee Palmer, in town for a conference, who dropped everything and agreed to sit with the brothers during Brennan's surgery. As Brennan's nurses commenced the silent-but-hurried preparation for surgery, Tara, the Brothers, and I walked across the parking lot to Grizzly House in order to pick up a few essentials for Christopher's hopeful First Communion. The boys, oblivious to the looming situation, skipped across the parking lot like ordinary little kids on a hot afternoon. The newness of the summertime humidity delivered relief from the cold, dry hospital rooms.

Walking past the automatic doors of the Grizzly House lobby, we sat them on a bench to explain that Brennan may once again be in ICU and if that were the case, I would not be able to accompany them home for Christopher's First Communion. The conversation involved a feeble explanation of how I would do the same for anyone in our family. It did not work, and Christopher blew his lid right there in front of everyone in the lobby; and rightly so, considering how excited he had been about this important rite for which he had been so diligently working here in Memphis. Once again, his dreams had been arrested and dragged into the cellar of pediatric cancer.

We sat silently, looking across the Grizzly House common areas at other children, some in wheelchairs, some sunken on couches with their bald heads nestled in the crook of a parent's arm. One boy, clearly sick from chemotherapy or radiation, blindly stared up at the depressing white noise of TV news. A sibling stroked his bald head and tried to help him hold a video game. Christopher saw this too and cooled down just as Ashlee arrived to look after them.

Tara and I rushed back to Brennan's room to find the morphine doing its job, as he was sitting up laughing at the TV, whereas when we left him he had been writhing in pain. "Daddy, did you hear that? These game shows are nuts." As we wheeled him to the OR, I took this as a sign of encouragement.

It was nighttime by now. The hospital seemed conspicuously empty, but the emergency surgery team was here, many having been recalled from home or from their weekend plans. Almost immediately, they wheeled him away. Brennan suddenly became terrified and cried out for both of us. We stopped. "Brenny, it's OK," we said with as much gentle confidence as we could muster. "It's just the way we used to do it at the CMC in Augusta, remember? It will all be over soon and you will be feeling a lot better."

"OK, Daddy," he said as he wiped his tears and sucked it up. But man, was it a hard goodbye.

As the secure doors closed behind him, Tara and I broke out of the surgery area barely in time to get the remnants from the cafeteria dinner buffet. For an hour or so, we sat next to each other in a small pocket garden outside of the dining room. Sitting head to shoulder, saying nothing, we both surrendered to the sweet fragrance of a magnolia that bloomed in the courtyard. We held hands, numb to what was happening upstairs.

Back in the waiting room, we were told that the gallbladder was out but that the laparoscopic plan had to be scrapped for the old-fashioned cut-and-suture. According to the three or four people who visited us in the waiting room, the organ was grossly infected and truly nasty. Once he'd seen it, the chief surgeon confessed that he was grateful that the decision was made to expedite the surgery. Another day, he said, "could have been disastrous."

We were told that Brennan would remain in ICU on the vent until they determined whether his lungs were strong enough. We asked the doctor how long; his answer was a cautious, "I just don't know. Hopefully by the end of the weekend. It all depends upon him."

But then the anesthesiologist popped his head in. "This kid is amazing. Given his history and the severity of the surgery, I was afraid that he would have shown some more signs of pulmonary distress or some significant variances in blood pressure, but he just sailed right on through the operation. I am telling you, there is something special about this kid."

We both got impatient and decided to walk into Brennan's ICU room prior to being invited by the nurses. There we found a small army of people around his bed. The new BMT fellow caught our eye and shooed us away with his hand. Peeking outside the door, he said, "Give us another ten minutes."

In no more than five, he found us. "Sorry to turn you away like that, but he was starting to breathe on his own, so we decided to extubate him. The kid is strong." He was already off the vent.

He is going to be in a lot of pain, given the size of the incision made from the surgery. Tomorrow morning, we will see how he feels. If he is not burning up with fever or in major pain, I will accompany Christopher to his First Communion. Otherwise, Tara and I need to remain here. But after what just happened, how can you not have faith in this boy?

Walking out to give the boys the good news, we found the husband of Brennan's adored PA, Susan, in the waiting room by himself, just sitting there. He had heard of the situation and left his family in the middle of the night to pray for this kid whom he hardly knows. Like so many others, Brennan had affected his life.

Looking back at the day, the number of people who came through to do what was appropriate for this one kid is astounding. Tonight I hold Brennan's hand as he sleeps and pray for Christopher's communion.   —NTS

Amen!
Posted May 13, 2011 2:39pm

I woke up at seven-thirty in the dark, windowless parent room just outside of the ICU. Draped in my blanket, not having had the chance to fall asleep with pajamas, I felt my way to the doorknob, empowered totally by the eagerness to see that Brennan was truly still breathing well on his own. Emerging into the lighted hallway, I bumped into the attending ICU physician, who was preparing to turn off the propofol keeping Brennan asleep.

"Your boy is a real pro," he told me in his beautiful West African accent while fiddling with various dials on Brennan's anesthesia support. "He seems to be doing everything right."

As I absorbed this glorious information, the BMT team of physicians and nurses entered the room. Every one of them grinned from ear to ear, shaking their heads with the same sense of joy and relief. Dr. Srinivasan, undoubtedly the most reserved and quiet of the entire team, clapped his hands with a loud crack. "Yes!"

Everything for which we are grateful for this day must be acknowledged as a product of love. The love of Brennan's medical team for this boy, and the commitment of St. Jude never to quit. The love of so many people in Brennan's court, praying and sending positive vibes our way. And the love within a little boy who has proven to me that the notion of "the kingdom of God" is not a transcendental concept, but something that simply exists within each and every person who breathes the air.

The bread that feeds Brennan is life itself. Because of his love of life, tomorrow his little brother will get to look Father Jerry in the eye, mindfully accept the bread of life, and say, "Amen!"   —NTS

Love In
Posted May 24, 2011 7:23pm

"At this time, I would like to ask you all if there are any milestones or special days of recognition that you may like to share with the congregation?" The priest poses this question every week before the Sunday recessional hymn at St. Patrick's church in downtown Memphis. Our entire family was gathered in church for the first time since September.

St. Patrick's was the source of our unforgettable Good Friday Stations march, and while physically dwarfed by the Fedex Forum across the street and sitting in the shadow of the defunct yet beautiful African-American church next door, St. Patrick's rises above the otherwise derelict, emaciated city blocks, ruins of a more prosperous time. An entire city block behind the church is empty, with the exception of a single brick building. A single shade tree delineates the stoop of a houseless front yard. In winter, area residents hold gatherings that are defined by the fire of barrel drums. But the combined magnanimity of this place and the community within it combines to create a welcome refuge from so many devastating personal experiences.

By the Wednesday after Brennan's gallbladder removal, the little plastic drain tube that had been installed just outside of the surgical incision was removed (as a matter of fact, Brennan removed it himself). And the underlying infection and GVHD seem to be headed on the right track. Tara and I were both happily shocked when Dr. Leung told us that with the completion of the antibiotic regimen and the GVHD under control, Brennan should be back on track to head home after the third week of June. "There is no reason that you shouldn't be able to get home within a couple of weeks of your original plan," he proclaimed. This was amazing news, considering Tara and I had been discussing how best to explain to the Brothers that we might be spending the summer in Memphis.

Like the tree outside that attempts to flourish in damaged soil, there are and will remain concerns for some time. There is still plenty of wasteland to navigate. The most pronounced, of course, is the resurgence of his GVHD and the long-term management issues related thereto. GVHD remains what keeps his disease in check and his biggest threat. As his immune system also attacks his organs, his gut suffers the most. And of course there is nutrition, that pesky little inconvenience that gets in the way of those who remain shackled to the food chain. Brennan still has not eaten a speck of food in months that he has not vomited back up.

But something grows and flourishes among the ruins. It is now our responsibility to nurture and cultivate what we can from the gifts we have received.

During the above-referenced Sunday Mass, Brennan and I arrived about ten minutes before Tara and the Brothers. (Still living separate lives to a large degree, the boys will most likely maintain separate living quarters and lifestyles until we officially hit the road.) The sanctuary's vast white ceiling was brilliantly lit by the setting sun through the stained glass. Being the only two in our pew, Brennan nudged up close to me and placed his head on my shoulder where I could run my hands through his velvety new head of hair. The light shifted, prompting Brennan to turn his head toward me and shield his right eye with his little hand. The window responsible for the light depicted Jesus and Lazarus.

As we drove to the church earlier, Brennan had told me that because of his nausea, he did not want to take Communion. I assured him this would be just fine. But with the liturgical part of everything coming to a close, we were about to stand to share in this first familial rite when Brennan whispered, "Daddy, I want to take the bread." We walked to the altar. He took it confidently, his first real food.   —NTS

A Homecoming Miracle
Posted Jun 26, 2011 2:26pm

Wednesday night in Grizzly Hous, Brenny was all wrapped up in his "snuggly" Georgia Tech blanket with his little body enveloped by the mound of pillows behind him, sipping red Gatorade and visibly smiling through an hour of TV. (Needless to say, we are still in Memphis, having reshuffled the deck more than once with hospitalizations but still focused on home.) Before going to bed, I got a text from Tara. Jeni Clark was on campus with her daughter Cassidy in preparation for Cassidy's bone marrow aspiration the next day. They wanted to stop in to say hi to Brennan.

This was how Tara and I learned that Cassidy's graft from her third transplant was failing and that her treatment options were on less than thin ice.

On arrival, Cassidy stood in our doorway with her mom. Her hair was growing back beautifully thick, curly, and black, like most of these kids' seem to do after so much chemo. But for the telltale sky-blue respirator mask, she would never have been taken for a transplant/leukemia kid. And her mom's vivacious "Wake up, boys!" let us know that they were there to visit, not to mope.

As she meekly walked into our room, I realized that almost every previous visit with Cassidy had been filtered through the perspective of the transplant unit. In the midst of fighting, you see everything through a gray veil. Nothing can disguise the gaunt pallor of a child dragged to the brink and back again. But outside, when life's light shines again, oh, what a difference. I had no idea what was on Cassidy's mind that evening, but she looked alive.

Brennan looked over from his movie, almost too bashful to say hi. But he smiled, waved his hand, and managed to get the word out.

Standing still as a soldier at attention, with her elbow pressed firmly to her side, Cassidy waved. "Hello," she said, and she shyly closed her eyes, turning her head behind her mom's back.

These two kids have been in battle literally side by side for so many months. One and a half years ago, Cassidy took the initiative to paint an army helicopter for "the boy down the hall" from the same hometown with the same disease. "To Brennan, from Cassidy," it read. On this night, she took the initiative to come see her buddy, who she has hardly had time to visit despite the odd commonality of the ground they share. Despite the looming inevitability of Cassidy's bone marrow aspiration, I cannot adequately express what this visit meant to me; and I will never forget how, giving Cassidy a hug goodnight and holding her soft new head of hair, she squeezed me back. Her cancer may have been mushrooming inside, but her love flourished.

The world has turned a million times since that night. Cassidy is home now, graciously and stoically preparing for a reunion with her first mom, who passed away just prior to Cassidy's initial diagnosis. In speaking with her father, Chad, at length the other day, we shared a refreshing conversation about how they are all managing life with a death sentence. He told me how he now believes that the death of his first wife (Cassidy's "first mom"), which seemed too painful and wrong at the time, was revealing its purpose. He now sees that as a link in the chain of miracles, connecting him to everything. He explained that Cassidy's strength in the face of it all has been fed and shaped, in part, by this event that four years ago felt so purposeless.

We've certainly been affected by the loss of fellow soldiers along the way; but this is very different. As such, our homecoming will be bittersweet. Sweet for the obvious reasons. Bitter for obvious reasons. Brennan will soon say goodbye to another fellow soldier.

I know there have been too many false alarms, but we are confident that in less than a week, he will be home. Yet leaving on immune suppressants is not an ideal scenario. Tara and I explained to him that he would not be able to do most of the things he is accustomed to doing at home. Lucky (his dog) can move back in with us, but we are to keep his guest visits limited as much as possible. We explain all this to him as carefully and caringly as we can. Every time, he says, "I understand. Its fine, Daddy. I just want to be home."

Were I writing this part of the script, it would have turned out a lot differently. First and foremost, Cassidy would greet Brennan at home in full remission and paving the way for another fifty-plus years together, pressing on as old veterans. But she will be lucky to survive the summer. This is a reality.

I am not ashamed to say that I have blatantly asked for a miracle. I have pleaded for Brennan's life to be spared, all the while knowing other kids around us who were not making it and who have not made it. But what is the miracle? Is it the cure? Is it the sudden turn of events when the ICU docs are down to their "bag of tricks" and the kid suddenly turns the other direction, free of cancer? Is it the science? Is it a record fourth bone marrow transplant in less than eighteen months? Or is the miracle the experience itself, the people who have changed our lives and the love that we have received and, hopefully, pay forward to the next person? Is the miracle not our capacity to find meaning in the wake of something so awful?

As we return home, we celebrate the opportunity for our family to live together again, but also to greet and touch this beautiful little spirit that has taught us that a miracle is not necessarily an unbelievable event, but rather how we respond to what is placed before us every day.

The miracle is ongoing. Whether we are here to experience it for another week or for generations, the miracle is rooted in forgiveness and flourishes through love. It is always there. What a homecoming.   —NTS

7

REENTRY

2011

At the end of *Band of Brothers*, all of the major surviving characters play a carefree game of baseball in a grassy field of the Austrian Alps. Captain Spiers arrives and calls everyone to attention. Placing their bats down and holding their gloves, they all quietly receive the news that the war is over. The Japanese have surrendered. They are going home.

The scene pans to each individual survivor and delivers a brief profile of the rest of their lives. Some live to old age. Some barely make it a few years. Some find success. Some disappear. Some just fade away quietly, as far away as they can hide from the reminders of war. Yet each of them, even if for this final parting moment, shared a unique and wholly unfair experience that would guide them through the remainder of their lives, regardless of those lives' brevity.

Though Brennan was certainly grateful for this most unexpected of homecomings, there was no defining moment of conclusion. Indeed, his reentry this time around was drawn out, at times to the extent of not truly leaving Memphis and St. Jude for almost two years. Graft-versus-host disease, that double-edged by-product of bone marrow transplantation, tackled his leukemia but took its toll and remained very much in play through the summer of 2013. We made it home, but returned to St. Jude frequently. Brennan's case is a true record. It has, and will continue to have, a valuable impact on the treatment of pediatric AML and bone marrow transplantation. Brennan will remain a case study for the remainder of his hopefully long and prosperous life.

Like many members of the *Band of Brothers*, his status as a hero has affected countless others, from families we personally know in addressing their own decisions with regard to cancer treatment; to couples who decide to reconcile with their families; to individuals who make the decision to return to the Church; to athletes who determine that they can push harder and achieve more; to people who decide they can run a marathon for the first time; to philanthropists who decide they can make a difference in a child's life; to researchers who are inspired to create less toxic treatments than this little boy had to endure; to the little girl who made bracelets to cure neuroblastoma; to the stepmom who decided to press on with the loss of a daughter and have a new baby; to a sister who decided she could become, and became, a songwriter; to brothers who grew up faster than they should, but who understand why; to working moms who develop the confidence to be happy and "make a change"; to dads who decide they can write a book; to casualties of pediatric cancer who die with dignity . . . Brennan and those who know of him and love him have made a difference in making this world better. And to think: they did it because of a war.

But like most members of the Band of Brothers, to live in the world after the war was to reconcile a mishmash of perspectives. There are the recollections of life before, and then there are the recollections of the war itself, its relentless indiscrimination and heartlessness. And there is the present, clouded by the hazy coldness of experience, yet ripe with hopefulness. One must assume that the individuals who lived on and prospered somehow held firm to their beginnings, despite what they witnessed. To live in the present is to experience and share the enduring love that links us to the past.

As a participant in this unique war, and having been one who was obliged to make decisions that affected the life of another, I experience my own version of post-traumatic stress. My perspective on life, and my little cocoon of a universe, has been altered forever by what I saw and what I learned about childhood cancer and the formidable path forward if we are to ever claim victory over it. Winston Churchill stated that the history of mankind is a history of war. In our detached Western culture, the suffering around the world is mostly limited to television bytes, which can be turned off. I do not care where or how one lives in this nation, but we each are fortunate. And as the privileged, we tend to prefer the delusionary comfort of our insulated communities and, if we are lucky, our indulgent possessions. We would be crazy not to.

To me, while these privileges remain available—much more so than to most—I now find that to shut off my recollections of the war is easier said than done. Thus far, it has been impossible.

Fortunately for me, this last reentry was more gradual than sudden. Brennan's GVHD symptoms after returning home worsened to a frightening degree, even requiring admission to ICU here in Augusta and an airlift to Memphis in the fall of 2012. And even as things began to taper off, the deadly threat of GVHD often required bimonthly visits to Memphis until just this past year. In Memphis, as strange as it may sound, I find my new cocoon among the corridors of the hospital where I once paced in fanatical prayer, among the parents and children who are still in the fight.

I had become adapted to St. Jude, but to my life at home—my career, my social circles—I had become estranged. Work outside of my house was drudgery, and to respond to a phone call requesting my opinion or to answer an unsolicited email was to react to an affront of an almost personal nature. The motivations of my creativity, which had previously allowed me the privilege of several professional and civic accomplishments, had changed, and my passion (dream, to be more accurate) to excel as a musician and songwriter had faded to a faint pulse.

Returning home felt like going into a grandmother's house just after everyone had left from her funeral. The ambience of previous days had faded, and the light that I thought of in that place now seemed different and somehow wrong.

Physically, I began to slip. A long-postponed surgery related to a chronic ankle injury eclipsed my capacity to do the many active things I enjoyed (golf, hiking, sports with my kids). And while I have been fortunate to avoid the convenient solace of alcoholism, my injury and subsequent surgeries triggered almost a year of dependence on regular pain medications, first to keep me on my feet, second to get me through the day. You can always remember your old sins, and you can always regret them just as you did the first time.

Sleep became a calming warm pool that I sought whenever possible. Immersing myself beneath my covers in my dark room, I avoided the sharpness of the air above where everyone else dwelled. Yet my obligations to the things I love didn't hide. Sustained deception is exhausting. Pretending to be engaged, charading through the day with the mask of someone happy and eager to get back to work and move on, I often fake my way through the days, minute by ticking minute. How do criminals make it day in and day out? Have they simply practiced their vice for so long that something fundamental becomes broken? But when I lie there, eyes wide open, I pray to the true casualties: to Patrick, to Carissa, to Cassidy, to Andre, to Cameron and Carleton. Each of them whispers back with silent forgiveness, reminding me of Brennan's grace, of Christopher's smile, of Nat's eagerness to make us proud. I think of them as they had been, as they are now, outside of my fears. I leave the pillow and find my shoes.

There is another powerful scene at the end of *Band of Brothers*. Major Dick Winters recalls a conversation with his grandson, who asks him if he was a hero in the war. "No," he answers. "But I have served in a company of heroes." For them, he persevered. All of the surviving Easy Company guys interviewed in the film made reference to this one common thread, crediting those with whom they served for their capacity to cope.

Yet almost simultaneously with Brennan's fourth remission, kids started dying—specifically, those to whom we had grown the closest.

We had a lot of last visits over those many months, and looking into those kids' eyes for the last time tested my composure as I feigned strength. Yet when I said goodbye to them, I looked in Brennan's face and saw theirs. Despite—or perhaps because of—my weakness, their sincere faces lifted me up. May we all one day be graced with such looks.

In the war of pediatric cancer, there are no inspiring battlefields where one can point to the ground that hosted the great campaigns or where the valiant infantryman fought, sacrificing himself up front for his brothers clamoring on the hill behind. There are no great memorial cemeteries of the fallen to inspire the next generation of soldiers and the next generation of peacemakers. But the places where they continue the fight, and which offer their only hope, are there. Their stories are many. This is one story of a miracle. I must, therefore, regroup, press on, and tell it.

With God's grace and a patient and understanding circle of colleagues, I now have a fresh new business, and my feet are capable of finding the morning's floor much easier. I am playing music again. And although my injured leg is still a question, I have three boys who see no defects and who love being with me. They are in school. They are playing sports. They love each other. They are a Band of Brothers.

In their company, and that of my wife, Tara, I have served with gratification and pride. For their company I accept the new perspectives our experience gave me as an arduous yet indispensable gift. They have taught me to pray. They have allowed me to see miracles as the stuff of reality. Because of them I have, even if for a moment, let it all go and touched the cool safety of the eternal. To feel it again, must death reside so close? But then again, does it ever not?

Independence
Posted Jul 23, 2011

The waning hours of Independence Day, 2011. All three of our boys were upstairs watching *Evan Almighty*. Sitting downstairs for a late-night movie of our own, Tara and I could hear thumps, giggles, and the staccato rapid-fire of Brennan's new Nerf gun. We glanced at each other with like smiles as we heard the sound, which we'd never once experienced in our little apartment in Memphis.

We were watching, of all things, *Band of Brothers*, which I had uncovered as we sorted through the myriad boxes to be unpacked. We were absorbed by the emotional testimonials of the aged surviving members of Easy

Company. They talked of their amazing capacity to endure discomfort, pain, and hardship. They recalled fear and the fleetingness of hope. More than anything, they recalled their dependence upon each other.

An hour before, I had sat on the rear steps, listening to the sputtering of celebratory fireworks in the distance. The local baseball team had won a game. It was sticky, hot, and dark. A bouquet of Mylar balloons lay prostrate in the yard, encumbered by the humidity, and there was a large yellow ribbon around "the big tree," tied with care and stealth by one of the friends who had left "Welcome Home" banners for Brennan's arrival.

But returning home has not been all champagne and trumpets. Having lived away for as long as we have, and having established bonds with people and a place, the first couple of nights were met with a bit of homesickness. Nat was almost glum, missing his Memphis buddies, and Christopher cried the first night, telling me and Tara, "I feel like we left some of our family back there."

For the most part, folks here have been extremely respectful of Brennan's condition of isolation. As long as he remains on the immune suppressant medications and steroids to manage the GVHD, which has demonstrated serious symptoms, he is stripped of any effective means of managing infection.

So, as much as we may have been tempted to let things slide a bit like we were two years ago, we do our best to avoid even slight temptation. The stakes are too high, and we are well aware that there may be no more treatment cards in the deck. But he's back in his own room. He's rediscovering his own toys and enjoying the familiar afternoon visits of grandparents. Lucky greeted us with the excitement of a long-lost twin. It is uncanny how she totally knew Brennan after all these months. She ran straight for him, twisting her thin, sinewy body in uncontrolled emotion.

We do have some exceptions. The first is church. We do our best to pick one of the less well-attended services and seek a corner away from the crowd. I think this is working out fine, although there is always the awkward participation in the "sign of peace," when everyone is supposed to shake hands with their fellow churchgoers. Of course, everyone wants to shake hands with Brennan, and even if they don't know him, they are inclined to seek out the boy in the mask and leg braces who is so clearly special. We tell people to bow, Japanese style, but it never really works. We do our best.

Brennan is scheduled for monthly visits to St. Jude. We are planning/hoping for a year's worth of "well visits." Since beginning this journey, we have never made it past the fourth week before another bomb would drop, but this time I feel different. Indeed, everything feels different. Perhaps it is the fact that we have basically been living underwater for two and a half years. We meet babies who are now playing tee-ball. We observe grown young men and ladies who just a few years ago were still in elementary school. I feel a bit like Rip van Winkle.

While we all do our best to find the value of this experience, it is easy to find the mind wandering toward the childhood and family experiences that have been forfeited in exchange for a miracle. Or maybe the difference is that I have more than a mild case of post-traumatic stress. To be quite honest, right now I have no desire to assimilate or reintegrate with much of anything. If I could wave a wand, I would take off with my little family for parts unknown and do a little living for a change. But with Brennan's fragile nature and ongoing medical needs, not to mention the fiscal practicality of it all, that's clearly not going to happen.

How do you saddle back up to the real world without taking your eye off the true ball? I wish I had the answer. All I know is that sitting in the neighbor's pool at dusk with Brennan, throwing a tennis ball back and forth across the water for an hour or so, I feel alive and complete. Working, I feel lost.

There was a time when we were able to just live. Not beating oneself up over life's circumstances is easier said than done. But my collective experience over the past many, many months at least has me trained to let go when the pull of inconsequential matters graze the palm of life's hand—a hand that, if allowed, will always protect the heart and push the spirit toward what is right.

Nat is slowly getting back into his Augusta groove, loving golf once again now that his arm has healed. Immersing himself into projects requiring intense amounts of focus is how he keeps it between the lines. It is how he did it at Maria Montessori, and it is how he is doing it as he tentatively prepares for the new school year. One on one, he expresses how many real friends he has in Memphis and how much he misses them. "I don't know what to do, Daddy," he will say. But as with the prior moves, he will clearly do fine. He is a great kid and knows that, above all, being with his brothers is the only real choice he has to make.

Christopher is something else altogether. Always smiling. Always trying to get a laugh out of the crowd. He also may be handling all of this inside harder than anyone. Here, as Brennan is confined to the indoors pretty much twenty-three hours a day, Christopher is once again the wingman. His friends are at the pool or at the beach. His cousins are all at the family reunion. And as he has been since day one, Christopher is right here, next to Brennan and missing out on a lot. He is very sensitive to even constructive criticism, primarily due to the fact that he still does not really know what to make of this crazy childhood. The notion of friends dying is something he asks about when we say our prayers. If I am upstairs alone with him and walk down for a minute or two for whatever reason, I will hear the sudden pounding of little feet thumping down the stairs once he realizes he has been left alone.

Tara's motherly instinct and perceptive intuition continue to manage the ties that bind us all together. For the past few weeks, she has been up to her eyebrows in boxes and organizational projects as we do our best to restore our home. But throughout it all, she is the one who monitors the heartbeat of all who dwell under this roof.

From my perspective, I think she is the Holy Spirit manifest as my wife. As I struggle with emotions and decisions of every type (from things to address in blog entries to work matters to how I am responding to a child's emotions), she is a fountain of remedial counsel. I do not know if she can just feel what I am struggling with inside, but the more I focus and pray for solace with regard to my struggles, the more she always seems to hold the key.

As for Brenny, needless to say that he remains appointed to a role that, while seemingly unfair, has served to strengthen our faith and our love for one another.

With night swimming being basically his only allowed outside activity these days, every evening around seven o'clock he emerges downstairs in his baggy swim trunks with his swim shirt hanging loosely around his bony shoulders. Off we plod across the street to the quiet, shady pool of a generous neighbor.

"Jump in, Daddy," he smiles, coming up for air. I dive in sailor style, glide to the bottom, and back up slowly. As I make the turn for the surface, I look to see him suspended in the water, weightless. He is smiling. His beautiful gray-green eyes penetrate the water straight to my soul. He embraces me, and together we float, suspended from the world.

Like his friend Cassidy, who faces the worst consequences of cancer, fear is not a part of him. In his words, "When I felt like my life was being pulled from me, I focused through it." He has never felt separate from his origin. This uncommonly precious attitude is what keeps me going.   —NTS

Broken Alleluia
Posted Oct 13, 2011

The boys and I made our drive to school mostly in silence. It was a beautiful cool fall morning, as it had been every morning since the previous Saturday, when our dear friend Cassidy died in the arms of her dad.

Just a month before, we'd learned that another dear friend from St. Jude, Carissa, had died. All five us had arranged ourselves either on the bed or the settee at its foot to watch a late-night movie. Brennan was holding his mom's iPhone when he suddenly looked up to me with eyes wide open. His expression was sunken. "Daddy, look at this," he said calmly. It was a text from Carissa's mom; *Carissa received her angel wings tonight.*

He lifted his arms and hugged me, longer than usual. "Are you OK?" I whispered. Brennan released me from my hug and stared me in the eye. "I am OK, Daddy," he said.

"Are *you* OK is the question?" Tara asked me.

I decided to take a shower. Blankly staring at the floor, the streaming water kept me calm.

The next day, our house was far from relaxed. Brennan and I fought over the subject of GVHD when I caught him shooting baskets in the full sun. He retreated into a dark shell to himself, and I fumed, knowing how fragile his gift is to us.

Now, a month later, with three elementary-school-aged boys in the backseat, the quiet was occasionally broken by predictable questions about Cassidy. "Why?" "Why her?" "What do you think she thought about on her last birthday?" (She had turned nine just under a month earlier.) "Do you think I will be as brave as she was, Daddy?" "Do you think she will look the same in heaven?"

It was both my day with Brennan and the afternoon of Cassidy's visitation, to which Tara planned to escort the Brothers after school. While Brennan has been getting stronger by the day, we decided that while it was important for our family to be at the service, it was too public of a setting for Brennan to attend safely. Therefore, as we waved goodbye to Nat and Christopher, we left carpool knowing that just he and I had a full day together.

On this day, his homeschool teacher was not scheduled; consequently, it was my job to keep him occupied. Also, given that the whole Cassidy situation was hitting us all rather hard, I was very intent in keeping our dialogue open and honest. I wanted to gauge the degree to which it had affected Brennan's spirit. It was all certainly affecting mine.

Brennan and I arrived from carpool to find the sweep of a new fall breeze gently nudging the swing in our yard. It was not quite sunny enough to worry about Brennan being outside. Under the shade of the broad hackberry tree, I sat back and gazed at my little man with wondrous gratitude as he swayed to and fro, quietly singing a private song barely perceptible above the rustling, falling leaves.

"Brennan, what do you think about going to Mass with me at twelve-fifteen?" I asked him later. "Since we cannot attend the visitation today, it may give us an opportunity to pray together and to focus on her in our own special way. What do you say?" I was prepared for the Heisman push; instead, he looked straight at me, smiled in his way, and said, "I think that would be a good thing to do, Daddy."

Walking into the beautiful Church of the Most Holy Trinity where Tara and I were married eighteen years ago, I held Brennan's hand. We sat in the back of a mostly empty noonday congregation, staring up at the beautifully illuminated stained-glass windows. Multicolored beams of light were cast on his face and hair, and it was cool and quiet.

Although a few words here or there sunk in, the readings and the homily all dribbled off of me that day like light rain from an umbrella. I focused not just on Cassidy, but everything that had been stirring my soul. As I squeezed Brennan's hand, a cacophony of anxieties came streaming at me. Brennan, Patrick, the kids we were losing, the kids we'd lost, kids on the brink, work, finances, my ratty old car, the boxes still in our living room unpacked from Memphis, the boys and Tara—was I behaving around them as I should? Was I truly grateful of the miracle sitting next to me? Did I have trust, truly?

But a peacefulness began to wash over me when we both knelt for the Liturgy of the Eucharist. Brennan's head does not even reach the top of my shoulder, which he used as a brace for his new crown of curly black hair. It felt good to feel him next to me. I began to breathe, listen, and relax.

Down the aisle we approached the altar for Communion in slow, deliberate formation, walking stride by stride with the row adjacent to us, one foot in front of the other. Brenny walked in front. I tried my best to walk in lockstep with him as we eased our way toward this special source of nourishment. The floor was made from the same Alabama marble that lined the aisles of the little Dominican chapel in Memphis over which I'd marched almost every day at this time throughout the last fall and winter, praying for a miracle. Same color, same pattern, different path, same destination.

These particular floors are well over 150 years old and, of course, the marble itself represents millions of years of slow yet violent compression. Each fracture, each faint gray shadow, every beautiful discoloration and crack has collectively manifested itself as a treasured material, rendering structure for ancient temples, inspiration to Michelangelo, and on this day, a beautiful path for me and my son to receive the promise of God.

The flaws and imperfections embedded in this material are its nature. The cracks and disfigurements are its essence, not defects to the eye. They are evidence of ordeals long past, creating a beautiful portage for innumerable souls trying to believe, yearning for reconciliation.

Side by side, Brennan and I said a prayer for Cassidy and for all the kids along the way and yet to come. He then looked up to me and asked me to carry him to the car. I held him like I would a younger child, his arms firmly around my neck with his soft hair in my face.

The next day, we all attended the funeral. Needless to say, it was a hard one in many respects, but it was more of a celebration than not. Everyone who stood in the pulpit or who talked to us afterward said that Cassidy was ready to be reunited with her mother and not afraid.

There were many emotionally poignant parts to this service, particularly the eulogy rendered by Cassidy's father, Chad, but Cassidy's newly adopted mom Jeni's solo vocal performance of the song "Broken Hallelujah" truly drove it home for me. The moment, the message, and the profoundly appropriate words to this song.

Seeking to regain one's balance in life is a paradox. Life is broken, fractured over and again, oftentimes with seemingly unbelievable harshness and power. The inexplicable cruelty of it all may initiate fissures and cracks that change who we feel like we are; but at the end of the day, together, they function to create what we become. Everyone who leaves us, through cancer or otherwise, leaves a mark, often a substantial one.

I have been digging hard, trying to find the reason to "pop the bubbly" since Brennan has been home. That's what we should do, right? Celebrate? I too sing, overwhelmed with gratitude. But I am also tired, and the chinks in the armor seem to reverberate a bit louder than they used to.

Holding Brennan as I carry him up the stairs to bed; laughing with Christopher whose endless source of joy and laughter literally dries my tears at times; feeling the warmth of Nat's compassion for others as he quietly seeks out a pink bracelet to wear in honor of his friend who has just passed away; the embrace of my wife, who patiently guides me through the brambles of doubts, holding me firm, siphoning the demons from my mind with each rhythmic breath and stroke of my hair . . . each moment becomes a block from which I establish a place of balance inside, a place from which

I can feel the tender memories of those who have gone before continuing to inspire through the void.

These are the mortar of the splintered path behind me. Every tile, either pure of composition or grossly flawed, is necessary to guide us toward the course ahead. My navigation system can't tell me if the path ahead is rugged and long or unreasonably short. But I know where I've been. And I know that I could never have made it this far without the divine complement of grace expressed both through hard lessons and through the love of others . . . the cost of living. For that I must sing, "Alleluia!" After all, an alleluia is an alleluia, broken or not.   —NTS

Friendship
Posted Dec 18, 2011 9:24pm

Brennan and I spent virtually all of Monday, December 5, at the hospital clinic. Our third tour of duty in Memphis delivered our third Thanksgiving here, yet this year's celebration was quite different, marking the first in three years that all five of us were seated around the table together. Brennan even ate his meal (through his mouth, not a tube), and I am delighted to report that he is still eating.

Brennan is here because of chronic graft-versus-host disease. This whole mess was all triggered by a common cold, which he caught along with the rest of Augusta in mid-October.

His immature immune system responded to the cold virus by going a little haywire, and while everything is stable now, when we arrived in Memphis via medical airlift, the situation was more than frightening.

Brennan is active, impatient, and ready to go home again. Going for rides in the car has become our primary form of outside recreation, giving him a change of scenery from the hospital and the house. He and the Brothers are constantly jabbing each other in the backseat, playing "punch buggy."

He is being weaned from the new immune suppressant drugs slowly but surely. Time will tell, but the walls of his bubble are as thick as they have ever been. With stage 4 GVHD, we have become even more vigilant about what he can and cannot do. While most of our friends recognize his fragile nature, and hence the gravity of infections, we often find ourselves having to justify our nonparticipation in certain social and recreational functions.

His system is so hyper-suppressed right now that his clinic visits will remain at least weekly for the foreseeable future. And, despite the encouraging signs, he is simply too medicine- and hospital-dependent, and too fragile, for us to return home for good. The stakes are just too high. So here we are, and here we will stay until we are comfortable doing otherwise.

Our family has been apprehensive with regard to our friend Patrick's scans. As the first kid we had ever known with cancer and as a close family friend from home, Patrick has always served as our benchmark. His cancer has metastasized to his liver, and there are no more treatment options.

I had arrived in Atlanta from Memphis on business and was in a meeting when his dad, Stephen, called to tell me the news. Sounding as strong he could under the grip of such suffocating emotion, he triggered my own recollection of how a father feels when he is told there is nothing more to do for their child. The feeling is worse than you can imagine. I floundered my way through the rest of the day's meetings with single-minded intent to just get my work done, return to Memphis quickly, and hug my family.

Boarding the Marta train on Atlanta's far north side for the airport, we meandered our way through the entire length of the city. Neighborhoods and commercial centers flickered by as we made our way to the airport. A passing train stopped at the platform across from ours at Five Points. The darkness of the underground station was broken by the lighted windows of the adjacent train. It was filled with school children Brennan and Patrick's age, dressed in their blue chino pants and skirts with matching white shirts. One of the girls spoke, and the rest simultaneously leaned forward with delight and laughter. Behind them, one of the boys pushed another down into a seat, and a friend intervened, defending his buddy. Then our train lurched forward and departed the station.

It was a scene I could taste from my own childhood, but from which I could not have felt more detached on that day. What have our children missed because of their disease? What do these children miss, or misunderstand, by virtue of their presumed immunity?

We will celebrate Patrick's family this Christmas. And, with a little help from above, and a lot of friends, we hope to receive the gift of Christmas this year under our own roof. They honor and humble us with the gift of their love, therefore binding us for all time to the love of God. Things change. This does not.   —NTS

Homecoming
Posted Jan 18, 2012 9:56pm

This was our family's first Christmas at home since 2008. It was also the first in three years that we were not almost convinced would be Brennan's last. His doctors had found him fit enough to come home for two weeks, and here he sat under the tree, a smiling, curly-haired boy and his brothers, exuding delight in every breath. It was more than an adequate reason to celebrate.

At the same time, it was difficult for our hearts and minds not to wander across the state to our extended family in the Chances, a household that too was joyous, and hopeful to the extent that the meaning of this season—the gift of hope, defined by the life of a single innocent boy—could not have been more intensely relevant.

Despite the fragility of Patrick's physical condition this past holiday season, we all know that his perseverance through two relapses of an incurable childhood cancer demonstrated to the world that there is more to life than longevity. This kid truly milked more out of a minute than I have of an entire day. I am convinced that through his stamina, his joyous charisma, and his innocent yet bona fide perspective, he could do anything, and he paved the way for our family's determination to press on in search of a cure, despite the experts.

Two short parallel lives, so intertwined over the past three-plus years, ebbing and flowing with the baffling consistency of Old Faithful. Remission, relapse, remission, relapse, remission, relapse. The primary difference for us was that we have been consistently living away from home for such long periods of time. We were home for our first Christmas in seemingly forever. He was home for his last.

Passing through Atlanta to visit our friends while traveling to and from Memphis had become something of a small tradition for our little gang. For one, Patrick's extraordinary Lego collection has always been a thing of awe for Brennan, giving him new ideas and, I am sure, inspiring him to tackle more challenging projects as he fought the boredom and pain of almost constant hospitalization. The kids would dart away to their own private hiding place after shooting water balloons over the hedges at passing cars, hearts pounding with giddiness and fear of being caught; shooting baskets; hitting golf balls across the yard (and the street). There has always been playing army and, of course, music.

Previously, we had packed up our Christmas stuff from Augusta and were headed back for what was slated to be a long winter in Memphis. On the way, we all stopped by the Chances'. It was January 3, less than a week before Patrick's ninth birthday. We were there for the kids to spend time together. We had no intention of changing the energy with talks about "last visits" and such, but simply wanted to share whatever residual Christmas joy we had with this family, particularly Patrick. (Our kids still had no idea.)

Stephen and Erin asked me how I was feeling. I told them I was "tired." Patrick peeked out from under his blanket while curled up in his mother's lap and told me, "You should do some Legos. That'll help."

Albeit sweet, the stopover was quick. Loading our gang back into the overstuffed SUV, a hollowness lingered with me and Tara as we continued on for Memphis. We drove mostly in silence, listening to music. I will always remember Patrick's last words to me: "I love you too," he told me as I left.

The boys were great all the way back, even starting school the next day. Adjusted to the prospect of another winter in Memphis, you could feel the groove struggle to find its place. Nat settled back into the Montessori school like an old pair of slippers. Christopher squeezed into his shoes that morning with painful scorn, proclaiming that he had been betrayed about spending yet another winter away from home. But by the end of the day, he was brilliantly covered in mud, having played with his classmates near the riverbank looking for driftwood. Glancing at Brennan's lab results on the first day's clinic visit, our PA Richard's face appeared almost giddy. "Brennan looks great, and his labs and chemistries are as good as they have ever been. He really only needs to be here every two weeks. You guys can go home."

Of course, I was ecstatic, but actually felt a bit confused and undone. While Brennan napped, I just sat there, quiet in the dark room. I thought about whether or not we should actually leave Memphis. Tara and I talked about it later that night. Like me, she was simultaneously delighted and uncertain. The boys were already in Memphis mode; our stuff was here; we were managing to work long distance; and Brennan was close in the event something went wrong. And every two weeks is still a lot from 400 miles away. But in the end, we knew what we had to do.

We will head back for Memphis every two weeks. The first anniversary of Brennan's fourth transplant is January 25. In February, he will undergo an extremely comprehensive battery of tests. We hope that from that point forward, and assuming that we avoid any more bugs, the checkups will become less frequent.

The rest of the week was, as my friend Ben Hale described, a "joyful pain in the ass." Not only had we just unpacked, we had collected three months' worth of clutter, toys, etc. Thanksgiving, two birthdays, Christmas, and general disorder can lay a foundation for quite the organizational trial. Before hitting the road, we made our round of usual goodbyes. Having visited the Lackie family who had become such a close part of our extended family, I turned left onto Poplar Ave. and noticed a middle-aged man and woman raking a vacant lot on the corner. Surrounding the piles of leaves was the bright green of fresh ryegrass as the sun filtered through the limbs above.

Sometime during Brennan's second transplant, I recalled making this same turn and noticing this same yard. At that time, it was raining, and a fire engine and ambulance were out front. At the center of the lot was a white brick house with the roof totally burned away. The smell of wet singed wood was overwhelming, and it stayed in the car for a while that day. Later, I learned that the elderly couple in the house had died in the fire early that morning two years ago.

At a time when I was so prone to self-pity and fear, it was one of life's snapshots that forced my attention in the right direction. What memories from that place had evaporated with the couple who perished? But now, today, the ashes were gone. Life was once again flourishing in the ground as the new couple worked with intent and purpose.

The next day Brennan, Christopher, and I headed for home. We made it to Atlanta, stopping for the night with Uncle Rob and Aunt Susie. (Tara had stayed behind with Nat to finish a school project and would meet us in a few days.) It was a cold night, and the children were playing inside by the fire when I received a text from Stephen. Patrick was "unresponsive and would be checking into the hospital for the last time."

Needless to say, without Tara there, the next days were heavy back home. I kept Christopher out of school that Monday so that he could play with Brennan while I did my best to unpack and get things organized around the house . . . again. I would unpack a box, quietly venture into their room, and just watch them, praising the innocent integrity of it all and waiting to hear from Stephen.

The next day, I got the text about Patrick at 2:10 p.m.—on his ninth birthday. Arriving to pick up Brennan at his grandmother's, I made the conscious decision that I needed to stop and tell him right then. Otherwise, we would have been riding in silence with my mind racing. Two days after receiving the early heads-up from Stephen, I had told both boys that Patrick was going into the hospital and that he was very sick, but I hadn't talked about death. After all, he wasn't the first kid they knew who was dying. Just the closest.

Before putting the car into drive in the driveway, I stopped and turned to Brennan. "Hey Brenny, I have some tough news." He was fiddling with his iTouch and looked up at me. "Patrick died today at two o'clock."

For a kid who had stoically listened to so much difficult news, he truly looked distraught. His eyes widened, and the corners of his little mouth tightened like he was going to cry. He looked at me seriously and asked, "Did you know he was going to die?"

"Brennan," I said, "I always pray for miracles and try not to give up hope, ever, but we knew that he was not in remission and that his cancer could not get under control. Are you OK?"

"I'm OK," he said. "I just saw him. Is he going to have a funeral? If he does, I think I need to go."

For the rest of the day, the kids played like they always do. Brennan promised me that he wouldn't say anything to the Brothers before I could talk to them. He maintained his promised silence until then.

As we got ready for bed that night, Brennan was asleep early, as he always is these days. While getting Christopher's camo pajamas on, he said, "You know, Daddy, I know more kids who have died than grown-ups." Then he looked up at me and asked, "Was he scared?"

"No," I told him. "It's all part of the miracle of life."

"So you mean dying is a miracle, just like being born?" he asked, looking up at me again as I sat on the edge of his bed. I hugged him for answering the hard part of the question in a way that made my description appear much more insightful than I had ever intended or considered.

The funeral this past weekend, which I had dreaded for so many weeks, was truly a celebration. Patrick's sisters, Madison and Anna, were bright and steadfast, and they served, in my humble opinion, as the benchmark for how we were all to behave.

Madison sang at the funeral with the brilliance and fluent effort of the most innocent and beautiful songbird. And whether rehearsing at the church or interacting with the other kids at the house among all of the adults, they played, as children do.

"You know, Mom," she told Erin Friday night before the funeral. "Kids handle things better than grown-ups."   —NTS

Full Circle
February 2012

Gasping up the steps leading from the Mississippi to our home away from home atop the bluff in Memphis, the remaining warmth from the setting sun cascaded around the gigantic steel girders of the railroad bridge in front of me. It was blinding, and for a few seconds, the bridge's silhouette was burned into my eyes after I closed them and covered my face with my hands. It dawned on me that I may have just finished my last run along these banks. I thought back to the countless times I made this same walk home, exhausted, each time experiencing a different point along the full spectrum of human emotion, from sublime fear to tearful gratitude.

This time, I strolled among the latter part of the scale. Closing my eyes again, I could see the entire stark black-and-orange image of the bridge: a traverse across one of nature's mightiest forces, made by man and overcoming what was once impassable.

As the picture faded, I lowered my eyes to a mound of scattered daffodils and azaleas in bloom. Then I made my way back to the little house that provided such a comfortable haven for us for the past three years. It is still winter yet everyone I pass is in short sleeves. A swirl of fall leaves mingled with the flowers, revealing a tender and naive season that does not yet know its place. It was beautiful, and I am grateful.

We started our journey to Memphis for Brennan's first annual physical, the first anniversary of the fourth bone marrow transplant. A milestone in its own right, as one year ago, while we fervently prayed to reach this day, there were times when it certainly looked like we'd made the wrong bet. Fortunately, the common thread holding our faith together has been consistently woven by the little boy in our house who happens to represent the best that life has to offer, emanating love and courage at all times.

It was for Brennan that we felt it a good idea to accept our friend's invitation to stop at their family home in North Georgia on our way to Tennessee. It was one of those newfangled teacher-conference weekends, and we found ourselves with four days of no school. Tara and I saw it as an opportunity to complete a circle that had been left painfully unsecured since our last visit to Nacoochee over two years ago. Our last trip there had been with the same friends, but at the time they had invited us to help relieve our minds of the seemingly hopeless verdict the doctors had given: that there were no viable treatment options for Brennan and nothing left to do but let time and life take its course.

This trip, there was no weight, just the opportunity to return to a spot that had once been unfairly painted in doubt and foreboding and to seek amends at the creek of broken rocks. On our arrival, the boys all took off together exploring the forests, playing army in the woods, talking about bears, and making plans for extravagant trips to the candy store in the neighboring village. The next day, we all toured the Easy Company 101st Airborne museum in the town of Toccoa and all made the trip to the top of Mt. Currahee, "three miles up and three miles down."

The men we came to honor and study had been etched into our minds permanently due to Brennan's fascination with the courage of these WWII soldiers who had been forced, over and over again, to lead the way through seemingly hopeless circumstances. Currahee is Cherokee for "stands alone." As the men of the Airborne ran up and down the steep three miles of that mountain over and over as a brutal, fixed component of their weekly training regimen, "Currahee!" became their motto. And on this particular Saturday afternoon, the boys stood atop Mt. Currahee, proud and happy, almost as much as their parents who could not have been more emotional in feeling the significance of them all standing there together.

Once in Memphis, though, a long week lay ahead. Brennan was booked solidly every day with tests for every conceivable body and organ function, in addition to the standard tests for residual disease, GVHD, etc. Although he continued to experience severe digestive issues, these remained the only conspicuous issue that he was facing. By the time we left that Friday, everything evaluated (leukemia, GVHD, and post-transplant organ function) revealed a patient who was once again pushing the envelope of miracles.

"So, Brennan," Dr. Leung said when we all met with him. He spoke to Brennan as a mentor to a prize student moving on to bigger and greater things. "How would you like to go back to school and be with your friends? Does that sound like a good plan for you?"

Brennan beamed, with a look revealing almost as much astonishment as Tara and I felt inside. "Go back to school? I want to do that more than anything," he said.

"You know, most kids are trying to find ways not to go to school, and you're telling me that you're excited to go back," he said.

"Yes, sir," said Brennan with a smile.

"Well, then, I think you should go home, and assuming that we can wean you off of these medications over the next thirty days without any surprises, that should be your plan. It is time for you to be with your friends and to start showing your buddies how good of a golfer you plan to become. By spring break, I see no reason for you to have to wear that blue mask over your handsome face wherever you go."

The terms of the deal were pretty simple: wean him from the nasty steroids and most of the dangerous immune suppressant medications over the next month. With no symptoms of GVHD, he would be free to eliminate the mask, eat normally, and begin reassimilating himself into life as a normal (guardedly normal) kid back home.

Tara, Brennan, and I walked out of the hospital in quiet astonishment. We could not wait to break the news to the Brothers.

It was Ash Wednesday, and after a gloriously carefree afternoon of children playing at our old Montessori school, the suggestion that we make the five-thirty service was accepted by all three boys with unusual affirmation. For me and Tara, it was yet another noncoincidental coincidence.

The astonishment and gratitude surrounding our feelings about this day were blessed with a certain degree of clarity as we all quietly sat through this service that marked the official commencement of a new season of preparation and reflection. With such pronounced fear and uncertainty surrounding our lives one year ago (or even this past month), we, like the cycles of life and the seasons, had clearly come full circle. Such intense experiences are not easily mitigated by time, particularly with everything still so tangibly real about what we had just learned, where we were, and what we were now focusing on. The liturgical season of contemplation, where one is asked to assess what has happened in one's life and how one's intentions can be directed toward yet another opportunity for rebirth, had fallen directly on our heads and in our hearts. We were reminded that the season is not about sacrifice, but about the lessons taken from life's changes.

Brennan told me the morning after we arrived home, "You know, Daddy, I am glad that I get to go fishing again, but I really want to be back in school more than anything. I love our days together, but I really want to be with my friends."

I love our days together too. For me (and Tara), splitting our time between work and days with Brennan at home has been one of the most wonderful gifts. One way or another, though, these days too will change, and Brennan will be free to share his life and his spirit with his friends he has known and the children he is yet to know. Full circle. It's been a powerful lesson. — NTS

Looking Forward
Spring 2012

Attending church by myself, particularly ones to which I do not belong, is not something I grew up doing; and not that long ago, I would have creeped myself out by having done so. Things change, though. What would at one time have been a straight shot into the bowels of discomposure has become an amazingly accurate channel for insight. I am not saying this necessarily with regard to the sermon du jour or the Scripture readings (although they often do serve as tools), but more from the quiet focus of being alone amid the vastness of everything. The poignancy of luminous icons, the surrounding images in stained glass, the architecture itself, and every living (and formerly living) soul around me on that particular day. All are seeking something, whether for themselves or someone else; everything is there for a reason. It has become a ritual of comfort.

Sitting by myself in the pew on a Monday, with about a dozen or so other folks all quietly sitting alone, I looked up to see the painting of a baby boy, held by his mother but sitting upright, his arm extended as if, even at that unworldly age, he was teaching and she was listening. I smiled, knowing that the message I had been seeking was already delivered.

The past month-plus has been a blur. While we have primarily been living at home, we continue to move back and forth between Memphis and Augusta, dealing with the residual effects of war and reconciling our standing in the eternal crap shoot.

Let's face it: Brennan has experienced, in the doctor's exact words, "more than a lethal dose of chemotherapy and radiation." His physiological future, therefore, is more uncertain than those who have avoided such a beating.

The issues with the digestive system are dramatically improving, but he will continue to take oral chemotherapy twice per day indefinitely in order to keep his immune system in check. For now, he seems to tolerate it like a champ. The high iron content in his blood will require monthly bleedings. His orthopedic baseline is fragile at best, suffering from osteopenia that leaves him brittle and more susceptible to injury than most kids. Neurologically, there has been permanent damage to the hippocampus that affects his short-term memory. Indeed, his neurologist states he is as much a neurological miracle as a cancer miracle. As he grows and finds his way through the educational system, it will be necessary for him to compensate, much in the same way that dyslexics must discover their own system for recognizing and processing information. There are potential developmental issues. There is the not-unlikely possibility of secondary cancer (AML being chief among these).

But the only difference between Brennan and the rest of us is that he has had his road map defined earlier. We are all driving into a vast, empty highway. His road, while clearly full of potholes and sharp curves, has at least been illustrated.

With each day of improvement, his focus becomes more and more fixed on the homefront. Tara and I both remain quietly prepared for battle at any notice, making us resemble more the veteran who jumps at the sound of the car backfiring, maintaining one foot in one world and one in the other. Brennan is ready to move on, though, so for Brennan's sake, we are unlacing the combat boots for less durable gear.

Assured that his medical schedule was loosening (to once a month, and maybe every other by next year), we woke up feeling a bit stronger. Perhaps it was being home for Easter Sunday, on a beautiful sunny morning. Perhaps it was the uniqueness of actually celebrating this day with all of the family and a number of friends, old and new, in the green and quiet secret corner of a garden; or perhaps it was the fact that while still in pain, Brennan started looking better that day. He has begun eating more, his color is coming back, and he is once again among us.

On the night of Easter Sunday, a late thunderstorm passed through, and the evening air was cool and enlivening. We returned home truly feeling like we had emerged into a new world. Darkness cloaked a week that had commenced with uncertainty, and the weight of another humid and turbulent day gave way to the fresh coolness of a new day to come. As soon as we walked into the house for the night, Brennan swiftly left for his room. Tara followed him upstairs to find him alone in his bedroom, crying. "What's wrong?" she asked. "Nothing, Mommy," he said. "I'm not sad. I'm actually happy."

He then looked up to her with a seriousness and told her, "Mommy, I have so much to look forward to, don't I? I am so glad I didn't quit."

I hate to think back to the crossroads in our past where "quitting" was presented to us—on at least three occasions—as inevitable. But somehow, this little boy was able to focus through it all for something that he felt he must hold onto.

There are so many kids we've met, each with his or her own story of grace and human endurance, telling us that there is strength within each one of us to defy what the broader culture may assume. How many times are children and people who should be instilled with hope being told to turn their backs on life, or at least on a chance to live, to love, and to cherish the day? There should be no sense of defiance in looking forward.

Our lives have been forever changed by cancer, Brennan's certainly. Today, back in school with his peers, there is no reason to look at him and not feel confident that he will be a creative and energetic adult, father, and mentor some day. He may be a nurse on the transplant floor at St. Jude (which he says he wants to do). He may be a PGA Tour player. He may be a quiet and loving advisor for others. Cancer has changed his life. It has limited his capacity for realizing what most people hope to realize. But it never affected his capacity to dream, to hope, and to look forward.

Cancer is itself analogous to our dreams. It is powerful and creative, transforming itself in ways that defy treatment. As Siddhartha Mukherjee says, "In a cancer cell, the circuits that regulate cell division and cell death have been broken, unleashing a cell that cannot stop growing. Cancer cells grow faster, adapt better. They are more perfect versions of ourselves."

But the same source that instills the cancer cell's sense of formidability can also unleash—within our own hearts, within our souls—the capacity to awaken, to seek and truly experience life. Like a rose snipped from its stem, the promise of something new, something sharp and dangerous but beautiful, is revealed from the place once occupied.

To look cancer in the eye is to see it as a normal, albeit beastly, part of our own physiology. It is analogous to our capacity for living each day with gratitude, regardless of its consequences. Darkness and fear disguise the beast as something that we believe should not be part of ourselves, but part of ourselves it is. Like war, it is part of life.

The visible bumps in the road define the uncertainty in Brennan's future, and therefore the future of our family . . . the Band of Brothers. But is there not always uncertainty? We have no choice but to look forward. Brennan demanded it of himself. He changed himself from a condemned soul to a living one. Through his will, the very spirit of the cancer was harnessed for the purpose of living for another day. Medical science suggested that he reconcile himself to a limited and potentially incomplete quality of life. This he has eluded. Brennan has taught us that there is grace and beauty and fullness of love in even the most helpless being. And within that fullness is the true power of living.

Look around. The pictures we see every day on the news are not exactly those of wine and roses. Even the pictures looming above us in virtually every traditional Christian church, while brimming in beautiful color and light, depict scenes of torture, wretchedness, humiliation, and defiance. Yet they are beautiful. And from the light that streams through each pane, through each colored cell of each story, the message is there; Live with a purpose. Love, believe in the possibilities, and press on.   —NTS

8

ALL QUIET ON THE WESTERN FRONT

(AFTERWORD)

"Christopher!" I shouted up the stairs, wiping sticky sweat from my forehead for the umpteenth time. "You told me that you had plenty of long underwear! The only stuff I see would barely fit you when you were five!"

It was departure day for summer camp. The "little boys," Brennan and Christopher, were off to their second annual summer in the western Rockies. They would live in tents for two solid weeks as they backpacked their way up into the heart of Wind River Range, Wyoming, to climb, raft, fish, and live in one of the world's most beautiful, and challenging, environments. To think of Brennan living in the woods, much less mountain climbing, would have felt both foolish and inadvisable in recent years. But, last summer the two brothers thrived in a similar Northern California program and it was once again time to see them off.

Packing has never been my strong suit—particularly when I am under the gun to do so in an efficient manner involving detailed lists. My wife, Tara, and I had been checking our lists twice, scrambling to find the half dozen or so items that we "swore" we had catalogued away from the summer before, not to mention make it to the car in time to catch their flight. The fact that it was 100 degrees, and 200 percent humidity, was the perfect ingredient to keep my aggravation and stress factors firmly peaked.

"I have it, Daddy!" Christopher called back to me as he came downstairs. "Why are you yelling at me?"

"Turner, you are not helping." I felt Tara slip behind me and rest a soft cool hand on my shoulder. "We are doing everything we can."

Admittedly, I was frustrated with myself, as much as anything. I knew I should have gone through all of this stuff a month before to ensure things like long underwear and gloves were handy. And I could have sworn that I had efficiently stored all of these items so that we could simply pick up and go. But I also should have had enough sense not to stash all of the cool camping-related things too temptingly close to the boy's playthings and sports equipment, hence their migration to Lord knows where.

I turned to give Tara a contrite kiss. "Thank you."

Eventually, enough of the lost gear was tracked down to get the bags loaded in the car. Suddenly, the stress and aggravation gave way to an oddly sweet taste of melancholy. Brennan and Christopher were about to leave for two weeks, and while I was so happy and excited for them, I began to get terribly sad about missing them.

I ran through the house one more time to make sure no one had left anything, then headed out to Tara's car for last-minute hugs. I was somewhat surprised that Brennan was not standing out by the car to say goodbye and offer some last minute advice about how to work on my short game while he was away. I opened the passenger door to find him strapped in the backseat by himself with his head turned down.

"Hey, Brenny," I said, hoping for a smile. His head remained locked downward, refusing to look up at me. "What's up, buddy? You okay?" I gently reached out to raise his chin and saw that tears were pouring from his eyes. His cherubic little face still reminds me of the sweet little seven-year-old who so bravely walked into transplant four times.

"I am going to miss you, Daddy," he managed, his voice strained. "Why can't you go on the plane with me?"

I reached down to wipe his face and then pulled him into my arms. I could feel his little chest start to heave against mine. Fighting back my own tears, I murmured, "You know what, Brennan? I remember when I left for camp when I was your age and how terribly sad I was to leave Nonnie and Pop's. I think I sat on the floor of the car and cried the entire way to North Carolina. But as soon as I got there, I saw how beautiful and cool it was up in the mountains. You have to admit it is not exactly mountain weather here in Augusta." I gave his tummy a soft, playful punch, and he looked up into my face, trying to smile. I told him, "Just a few minutes after Nonnie left I was happy again and not even tearful when I told her goodbye. And you have to remember that you had a great time last summer."

"I know, Daddy," he said. "But I am really going to miss you. I just wish you could come with Mommy to drop me off."

At that moment, Tara looked back at us, her eyebrows raised as if to say, "We are ready to go." Brennan gave me a reluctant smile as I gently closed the door and walked around to the front seat where Christopher was sitting. He too was fighting tears, but he grabbed my hand and said, "We're going to look after each other. Don't worry, Daddy." I squeezed him hard, then stepped back to wave as Tara backed out of the driveway.

When the car disappeared, I returned to the house, empty but for Brennan's dog, Lucky, who greeted me with enthusiastic wags. Then a wave of loss swept over me, and all I could do was sink onto the couch and literally weep. I wasn't weeping about the boys being gone for a measly two weeks, but about what they mean to me. I had gotten to a point where I could hardly do anything without them.

Ever since the pediatric cancer war started in January of 2009 and we moved across the river to South Carolina, my world has come to revolve almost entirely around the boys. Sure, Tara and I still enjoyed doing things with our old friends, who had been at our side throughout the entire ordeal. And we had been blessed with an amazing list of new friends—both from the new neighborhood and from the amazing families we met throughout Brennan's fight. But instead of eating out with co-workers and colleagues at lunchtimes like I used to do, I more often walk home from my office to spend time with Tara and talk about the boys, our cancer research efforts, the book tour schedule or just quietly be together. And the weekend hours I used to spend with my running buddies are now spent doing things with the boys: school projects, playing golf, fishing, or just messing about town. I love being with them. As much as I thought I was living a fulfilled life before, the greenhouse of my world consisted largely of cunningly attractive yet blatantly artificial silk flowers. But I had been tending it mostly alone, with more of a focus on appearance than authenticity. It required the hands of my family tending the soil together for genuine roots and blossoms to emerge.

It was comforting, at least, to know that Brennan had Christopher, his wingman, with him for the two weeks in Wyoming. I could not imagine a greater gift in his life than Christopher, who has one of the most cheerful and dynamic personalities I have ever met. Having played second and even third fiddle to Brennan, who has gotten four lifetimes of attention because of his miraculous story, and to his brother Nat, who gets the lion's share of accolades about his world-class golf game (even though Christopher is showing signs of perhaps being just as talented in that regard), Christopher has finally come into his own. He has stoically continued to play his role of wingman, supporting his brothers, attending all of their events, participating in all of the news stories, and getting almost none of the spotlight. But with Brennan now having reached the all-important five-year benchmark for remission, he is gradually becoming just another kid in the class, and Christopher is thriving. With his own personal brand of style, he has preened his way through the eighth grade and is participating in so many sports and activities that one would think he is playing catch-up. Sometimes a report card suggests that he may be having a little more fun than studying; but given his quick wit and humor, we have often joked that we are all probably going to be working for him someday. He finally has the opportunity to shine, whether it be competing to have a better golf score than Nat, to be the best shot in the family, or simply to have his own friends over for the weekend, and not have to succumb to the boring and subordinate role of lowest common denominator.

It was still a stretch to wrap my mind around the fact that Brennan was about to enter his first year of high school. After being forced to drop out of first grade, and then suddenly finding himself back in sixth, he had somehow kept up with his peer group. We had thought he would be so woefully behind that he would have to repeat at least one grade. But the same unyielding determination that got him through his fight with cancer had gotten him through middle school. Thanks to the toll of the cancer treatments, he is still quite small for his age. But where I had been self-conscious about being the scarecrow-like, skinny one in the class, Brennan would walk into his first day of high school with all the pride and swagger of a varsity football star.

Along with reading, practicing the piano, and fishing, Brennan remains committed to golf. Just this spring, he walked his first eighteen holes (ever) carrying his own bag. His size certainly affects how far he hits the ball, but he is very accurate. We almost had to coerce him into playing in a junior event this summer, because he was embarrassed that the bigger kids his age could hit it so much farther. But he demonstrated to his competitors, and to himself, that there is more to the game than distance, and secured third place all to himself.

Nat, our oldest, could not be there to see the boys off because he was caddying for a friend playing in the City Amateur. A perfect student (4.3 GPA as a sophomore), Nat is bound and determined to play Division I college golf. Even more impressive, he is simply a true little gentleman. His gracious manners and mannerisms reflect the thoughtful young boy who moved to Memphis in 2009, terrified that his brother was going to die.

Perhaps the only benefit of young children dealing with cancer is the fact that their naïveté is such that they don't know enough to be afraid. That is exactly why Tara and I spent so much time forcing our game faces whenever we walked into Brennan's hospital room or talked about treatment options, even when it looked as if there were none. Of course, it was pretty much impossible to keep that particular cat in the bag once our friends started dying, but for the first year or so, this was a crucial psychological weapon for both Brennan and Christopher. Nat was just old enough to get it, however. He had lost a beloved art teacher to cancer when he was in third grade, so when it all started, he understood the grim consequences. Even at that young age, he was conscious of what Tara and I were wrestling with and he stoically went about his business, studying hard, helping about the house, and doing literally everything he could to make sure that he was not a burden to us and that he was a supportive big brother for Brennan.

Just this spring, Nat reinforced his strong and stoic nature by insisting that all of us make the cross-country trip for the funeral of our dear friend Markell Gregoire. Markell was probably the most inspirational kid we ever met at St. Jude. Talk about swagger…even with his leg amputated from osteosarcoma, Markell would seek us out at Brennan's annual St. Jude checkup appointments. Even on crutches, he walked into the room with so much confidence and poise that it almost made you feel jealous. Markell was Nat's age, and they corresponded via social media all the way up to a week or so before he died. Nat wanted to honor his friend by making the trip. And he made sure that we all did.

I got up from the couch at last, wondering how to make myself useful before Tara returned. There was a time when saying goodbye to my boys, even just for a couple of weeks, felt like I had just been given a hall pass to play more golf and do my thing for a while. Not anymore. I cannot shift my gaze from Brennan's eyes to my own world without a profound realization that everything I hold dear is fragile and fleeting. Instead of spending this time apart on myself, I decided I would spend every day pursuing things that honor them and give meaning to their experiences and my own.

• • •

For the past twelve months, Tara and I have been blessed with the opportunity to leave our cocoons and travel the countryside telling our story to everyone, from the committed yet dwindling assembly at a Lions Club across town, to a packed house of familiar prayer warriors, to the newly recruited fans of the book gathered at an archetypal bookstore along the Gulf Coast. On our travels, Tara and I have been able to share many windshield hours together, talking about literally everything—everything that has happened, everything that has changed, everything that is miraculously intact, and mostly, everything that makes us committed to telling the story of Brennan and all the good things that are happening because of his brief but entirely consequential and decent life.

Because of Brennan, kids are living and still fighting, owing to the experimental protocol that St. Jude initially created for him. Indeed, St. Jude is now having as much success with half-match (parental donor) transplants as with perfect matches, meaning that children with severe AML and other cancers can avoid much of the toxicity that he had to endure. And multi-millions of dollars have been invested in St. Jude Children's Research Hospital, both in Brennan's name and through the Press On Fund, which was created in Brennan's honor, Patrick Chance's memory and, more recently, in honor of a little girl named Hallie Crawford, representing the third face of the Press On Fund. In just a few short years, the Press On Fund has generated over $7 million in research grants in pediatric cancer research facilities in New York, Pennsylvania, Georgia, Tennessee, Missouri, and California. There are new grants in queue at other institutions, and Press On is progressively becoming recognized as a national brand and a forceful resource in the fight for a cure.

Because of Brennan's story, two bright New York entrepreneurs decided that no cancer patient should ever be told that "no treatment options exist," and subsequently have launched Flatiron Health, an oncology-based data cloud that connects research institutions and community oncologists with real-time data, which will eventually include all cancers and virtually all patients so that doctors and patients can make informed decisions and find new treatment options.

Country music star Darius Rucker has recorded a song, "Possibilities," co-written by me and three friends, offering a hopeful perspective on cancer through music and benefitting St. Jude through sales on iTunes. Kids across the country are having bake sales, setting up lemonade stands, and starting leadership groups to raise awareness of and money for research. People are being challenged to pursue their passions (music, sports, work) to raise awareness and money for research through an exciting campaign called "Play It Forward." But, maybe even more meaningfully and importantly, parents who are still being told "there is nothing we can do for your child" are encouraged and empowered to press on and find new options because of Brennan's story. New legislation is being considered to ensure that federal funding for cancer research *must* include dollars for childhood cancer. And, on and on.

As proud as I am of the story's impact in changing the pediatric cancer research landscape, I have been overwhelmed by the opportunity to meet countless others who have experienced loss or who have been encouraged to stay in the fight. To have a stranger tearfully embrace you and say "thanks" is enough for me to say that, as hard as it's been, the rewards have fully eclipsed the difficult parts. I press on for them, and for all of the kids we've met along the way who are not here anymore. Their lives will continue to have meaning. The pure and innocent hearts of those who have fought the good fight have taught me that the scale of life is not measured linearly, but in caliber. I can say confidently that the courage and dignity I have witnessed in the trenches of childhood cancer are as relevant and consequential as that of any brave soldier who has triumphed over fear in the face of fiery defeat.

All throughout our recent road tour, Tara and I felt like we were looking at the world like loyal American soldiers must have felt in the aftermath of the Revolutionary War. They knew there was no way they could ever win, and there must have been days they felt sure would be their last. There were probably times when they questioned why they were putting themselves and their families through all of this. Yet, the day came when the stunning victory was achieved. The guns fell silent, and they were handed the promise of a new life among the ruins of a previously unfair, yet stable and predictable way of life. I imagine they must have looked towards heaven with a new understanding that there is no means by which one can measure the capacity of human determination.

• • •

Despite our emotional farewell, the boys' two weeks at camp passed swiftly and without incident. Though we didn't get to speak to them directly, their counselors sent occasional emails whenever the troupe passed through the sparse civilization in northern Wyoming with updates and messages from the kids. Brennan's message was, "Mom and Dad, you were right. I am having a wonderful time and doing things I never dreamed I could do."

We finally made contact with them by phone when they checked in at the airport for their return trip. Christopher actually called us several times to protest his umbilical attachment to a Delta Airlines representative, presumably having envisioned a day wandering airports freely with Brennan.

"We have to stay in this room until our next flight! We are prisoners!" he protested. When prodded a bit further about the confined conditions to which they were subjected after experiencing the sublime openness of the Rockies, he confessed that they were in a lounge full of soft drinks, candy, pizza, sandwiches, and a library of movies to watch.

Later that evening, big brother Nat volunteered to drive me and Tara to pick them up at the airport. He wanted to be the first to meet his "Band of Brothers," and, once the backpacks and boys were loaded in the car, Nat directed the conversation for our drive home, probing them for details of their adventure.

The two boys' tales spun well into the next couple of days, as we drove up the North Carolina Mountains for our last family hurrah before school. Nat eagerly gave the brothers updates on the golf tournaments he'd succeeded in while they were away, talking confidently about his college golf dreams. Brennan and Christopher bragged about scaling a 12,000-foot peak in Wyoming and serving as group leaders during their two weeks living in tents, cooking their own food, and making new friends from around the country. For me and Tara, this trip was especially meaningful because we were celebrating the fact that Brennan was actually starting high school soon.

For a week, the five of us lived in a borrowed and remote Blue Ridge homestead, trooping up mountains, hiking in streams, eating dinner by the lake every night, and quietly reading during the predictable afternoon thunderstorms. Late afternoons, Tara and I would lie side by side in bed under the staccato of heavy rain on the tin roof—me reading, her writing, and the faint sounds of the boys trickling in from the room next to us. One afternoon, we heard Nat helping Christopher appreciate the outmoded Victorian dialogue of *The Hound of the Baskervilles,* the report for which was due in less than a week. Brennan joined in trying to dissuade his little brother of the "unfairness" of summer reading, telling him, "I had to read that, Christopher." He then launched into an overview of the book he is reading about Elie Wiesel's *Night,* which soon sparked a competition over who knew the most about WWII.

As I listened in on their conversation, I was reminded again that this little Band of Brothers, unknowingly, are wise beyond their years. Having endured the war on cancer together, and having more comrades who were casualties to the fight than those who survived, they are inherently well-equipped to face this new chapter of life that will, before we know it, lead to independence.

Even Nat, who always focuses more on sports stories than on tales of war, can hold his own in a discussion about WWII. It's not every big brother who can say that he had an opportunity to tour the battlefields of Normandy with his eleven- and ten-year-old little brothers leading the way; but when this was made possible because of Brennan's Make-A-Wish request three years ago, Nat experienced the enormity of it all with his little warrior brother, Brennan.

Brennan clearly developed a strong spiritual connection with the men who fought in WWII. After transplant number 2, he told me, "Daddy, these men fought hard every day not knowing they would ever live to see another." I have never watched a war movie with an adult who expressed it this way. But the veterans we happened upon during our tour of the American cemetery in Colleville-sur-Mer recognized this in his spirit. There to participate in the lowering of the flag at sunset, a disabled American veteran stepped out of line from the honor guard and asked us if Brennan would take his place. I do not think I have to describe the emotion from that scene, as I watched this little man stand among these heroes while the flag slowly lowered to "Taps." But seeing the expressions of tearful awe in the face of Nat and Christopher, I cannot adequately describe the tenderness of pride conveyed by each one of them.

Is it necessary to have survived a war to appreciate the essence of brotherhood? Is it necessary to look at your kids with tearful awe and fulfillment without staring over the precipice of an unsurvivable cancer diagnosis? Prior to Brennan's diagnosis in 2009, I enjoyed countless great times, laughs, and memories with my wife and kids. But, now on the other side, I can only admit that human beings often require awe-inspiring experiences to shake our senses from self-absorption and take notice of the everyday gifts before us. Our family's brush with the eternal unknown allows me to check myself more often and feel the meaning of these special moments. I am now more capable of receiving the love that is before me every day, whether it be the presence of my children, the kindness of my wife, or the generosity of so many others who give of their time to let me know that we have been in their prayers. I am overwhelmed by what has transpired in me and what is transpiring in the world through Brennan and all those other kids.

Major Dick Winters, Brennan's hero and the face of the real-life Band of Brothers stated, "The experience of war is unreal, and returning we earnestly hoped that it would never happen again, but we came back as better men and women as a result of being in combat, and most would do it again if called upon."

Knowing all the child casualties often creates somewhat of a sense of guilt when I look at my three boys every morning. But I am comforted in knowing that this Band of Brothers deeply understands the words of Major Winters. They are proud to have served in the company of those kids, and I am proud to serve in theirs.   —NTS

ACKNOWLEDGMENTS

Who to thank and acknowledge with regard to *Possibilities*. In a way, the book itself serves as an expression of gratitude for an extraordinary list of people, which of course begins with my son Brennan and his Band of Brothers, Nat and Christopher. Throughout our experience, we have learned that many families are torn apart by their experience with pediatric cancer. We represent a fortunate exception, and for that I need to express my enduring gratitude for the patience and wisdom of my wife, Tara.

Our families were and remain instrumental in our experience, and in the creation of this book, serving as nurses, supporters, proofreaders . . . you name it. Our parents, Sarah and Roy Simkins and Pat and Susan Rice, lead this pack, but we must offer special recognition to Aunt Martha and Aunt Susie, for their selfless devotion to our family, at the expense of their own, while we fought this war.

Every doctor and nurse throughout this experience represents a rung in the ladder toward the realization of Brennan's miraculous fourth remission. From Dr. Colleen McDonough at the CMC in Augusta, who helped guide us from the initial verdict through the awful decisions and post-treatment care, to Dr. Aplenc at CHOP, who, while never treating Brennan, gave us hope that a second transplant was indeed possible. But no one who has heard, or will read, our story will misconstrue the fact that St. Jude Children's Research Hospital plays the role of knight in shining armor. Bill Evans, Wing Leung and Jeff Rubnitz—you are heroes. Brennan's PAs, Lisa and

Susan, truly treated Brennan as they would their own child, in both care and prayer, as did all the nurses in Chili's Care Center. It has been amazing, and almost shocking, to witness both professional and public opinions about the culture and capabilities of this institution that are so far from accurate. We are living testimony to the greatness of St. Jude and are committed, for life, to their mission, and to the many St. Jude families we have met and will meet along this journey. And I would be insane not to recognize Brennan's only non-related donor, Jacob Wright-Piekarski, for hanging in there for a second transplant and for reaching out to us when he could.

Many thanks go to all the kids who did not make it, and to those who are still struggling, those we knew or know—you have affected our hearts forever. Those in this book—Carissa, Carleton, Cassidy, and Markell—have clearly left their mark on us. But we must offer special gratitude for Patrick Chance, his parents, Stephen and Erin, and his sisters, Madison and Anna, who remain part of our lifelong commitment to each other and to the Press On Fund.

I must thank my business partners, Jeremy Mace and Susie Adamson (Aunt Susie), for toting the water and carrying my load in starting Newfire Media while I was off the grid for three years. To Leyland Alliance and the Hull Firm, for keeping us on staff for as long as you could. To Travis Gamble, who inspired me to believe in my entrepreneurial spirit when all of this started. And to everyone who helped keep our house in order. But Rhonda Fry was the one behind the scenes, making sure our bills got paid and that we did not fall apart. To the boys' uncles, Will and Morris, thanks for your time, help, and friendship.

There are literally hundreds of people in the Augusta and North Augusta area who did everything from feeding us to decorating for Christmas, moving, airplane travel, automobile delivery, my gosh . . . we have so many dear friends, I don't know where to start. Many are mentioned and are part of this story, but so many names mentioned in our blog simply had to be omitted for the sake of printing costs. But thank you all.

Within these hundreds are the students and faculty of the schools that supported both Brennan and the Brothers throughout, particularly St. Mary on the Hill and the beautiful little Maria Montessori School, probably the coolest school in the country. Ellen Hoffman from St. Mary's has established herself in cue for sainthood, and the school itself has lived up to its namesake by allowing God's love to shine through its own sacrifice by making an extra effort for one little boy.

And this includes our new extended family and group of friends in Memphis. The Smithwick family opened their home to us on day one, as did all of my many W&L SAE brothers who live in or near Memphis. We thank the Wilson family for being the first to greet us, and to Kem himself for helping me in finding direction with this book. But we must also recognize John T and your beautiful family, the Muscaris, but mostly Margie and Jimmy Lackie for taking in a family of strangers and for the role that you now play in the lives of each and every one of us.

Jim Higgason, who is in Houston, I thank you for being my conduit to Hampton Sides, who has influenced me through his amazingly beautiful writing and many wonderful books, but who encouraged me to write this. Also within my Memphis writing family, Marshal Boswell and Rebecca Finalyson, two of the most talented writers I could ever hope to call friends, and who encouraged me and helped me create the framework for this book. Rebecca, I think you are the first real writer to call me and say, "You know, Turner, you are a talented writer." That was a big deal. Since then, I have heard the same from Hampton and Dan Brown, and I thank you both for your encouragement and help in sending me on the right path. My confidence in myself as a writer must also be attributed to dear friends Jimmy Boatwright, John Hagan, and Randy Pope. And we must attribute our gratitude for the gifts we received from this experience to St. Therese of Lisieux and her loving parents, Louis and Zelie Martin. Last, but certainly not least, in referencing my inspiration in the family of writers and learned people, my dear and long-time friend Ben Hale. To steal your phrase, this book has been a "joyful pain in the ass," but I would never have written my first blog post without you as my friend.

Amy Stephens, and your insanely enthusiastic brother Ed Meyercord, thanks for your invaluable redlining and feedback. Kevin Sharpe, I thank you for truly giving me an understanding for both the cold hard reality involved with constructing a book and teaching me how to define a framework. On the publishing end of things, many thanks to Janice Goldklang, the first book publisher to tell me that I had something here. And, of course, I will always be grateful for the wonderful folks at Greenleaf Publishing, who believed in my manuscript, were so tremendously helpful with my final editing, and who allowed the initial book to become a reality. I have always felt that this book had the potential to affect a lot of people in a positive way; and what better opportunity could one ask than for the world's largest bookseller, Walmart, to believe in it? Thank you, Christy Jenkins.

I have been blessed with amazing support for this story through the good folks at iHeart Radio, CSPAN, the TODAY Show, FOX and Friends, the Augusta Chronicle, Brian Roberts, and Michael Bamberger. And much thanks to the Dickey Brothers, who are helping me spread the word of this story in the mainstream media.

Finally, I would never have been given the opportunity to thank the wonderfully innovative and thoughtful people at NewType Publishing but for Dan Polk. Dan read the Greenleaf edition and has been my best friend and biggest believer ever since. It is because of Dan that I am able to thank Ryan Sprenger, Lexi Banales, Yvonne Parks and the brilliantly innovative people at NewType who have proved to me that the big-boy publishing world can be good, thoughtful and loyal.

And many thanks to you, who is now reading this. You are the reason that this book is in print. Press On.

ABOUT THE AUTHOR

Turner Simkins began his writing career as a staff writer at the Augusta Herald in Augusta, Georgia, after his senior year in high school, and developed his writing style studying English and majoring in philosophy at Washington and Lee University. He began a professional career as a copywriter and marketing manager for a national real estate development firm, from which he pursued a career in developing traditional communities in Georgia and South Carolina. There he is president of Blue-Beech, LLC, an entrepreneurial real estate development firm, and NewFire Media, a digital advertising agency. He, his wife, Tara, and partners Stephen and Erin Chance, lead the Press On Fund, investing in less toxic therapies and cures for childhood cancer.

He resides in North Augusta, South Carolina, with Tara and his three sons, Nat, Brennan and Christopher.